BELLA BELLA

BELLA BELLA
A SEASON OF HEILTSUK ART

MARTHA BLACK

ROYAL ONTARIO MUSEUM
TORONTO

DOUGLAS & McINTYRE
VANCOUVER / TORONTO

UNIVERSITY OF WASHINGTON PRESS
SEATTLE

First published in 1997 by:

Royal Ontario Museum
100 Queen's Park, Toronto, Ontario, Canada M5S 2C6

Douglas & McIntyre
1615 Venables Street, Vancouver, British Columbia, Canada V5L 2H1

University of Washington Press
P.O. Box 50096, Seattle, Washington 98145-5096, U.S.A.

Canadian Cataloguing-in-Publication Data

Black, Martha
    Bella Bella: a season of Heiltsuk art
Includes bibliographical references.
Co-published by: Royal Ontario Museum.
ISBN 1-55054-556-6

1. Heiltsuk art. 2. Indian art—British Columbia—Pacific Coast.
3. Royal Ontario Museum. I. Royal Ontario Museum. II. Title.
E99.H45B52 1997   704'.03979   C96-910838-9

Library of Congress Cataloging-in-Publication Data

Black, Martha
    Bella Bella: a season of Heiltsuk art/Martha Black
        p.   cm.
Includes bibliographical references.
ISBN 0-295-97608-X

1. Heiltsuk art. 2. Heiltsuk Indians—Material culture.
3. Heiltsuk Indians—Antiquities. 4. Large, Richard Whitfield—
Ethnological collections. I. Title.
E99.H45B53 1997   704.03'979—dc 21   96-52048 CIP

This book has been published with the help of a grant from the Canadian Federation for the Humanities, using funds provided by the Social Sciences and Humanities Research Council of Canada.

Front cover illustration: Ceremonial box (No. 48)
Back cover illustrations: *bottom left,* Eagle brooch (No. 88); house post (Bear-mother) (No. 18)

Design: Virginia Morin
Photography: Brian Boyle
Maps: John Beaudry

Printed and bound in Canada by Friesen Printers

CONTENTS

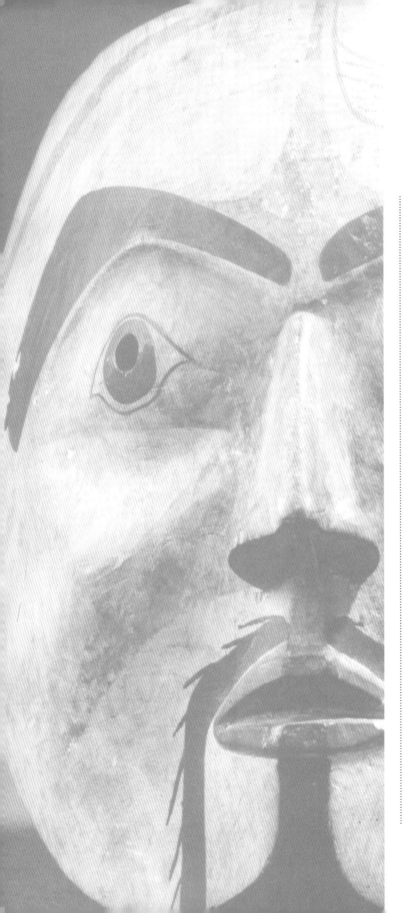

TEXT ILLUSTRATIONS

ABBREVIATIONS

AMNH	American Museum of Natural History, New York
BM	Brooklyn Museum, Brooklyn
BCPM	British Columbia Provincial Museum, Victoria (now RBCM)
CMC	Canadian Museum of Civilization, Hull
CPN	Collections Photograph Number, RBCM
DAM	Denver Art Museum, Denver
FMNH	Field Museum of Natural History, Chicago
HCEC	Heiltsuk Cultural Education Centre, Waglisla
MAI	Museum of the American Indian, Heye Foundation, New York (now NMAI)
McM	McMichael Canadian Art Collection, Kleinburg
MfV	Museum für Völkerkunde, Berlin
MH	Musée de l'Homme, Paris
NMAI	National Museum of the American Indian, Washington, D.C.
NMC	National Museums of Canada, Ottawa-Hull
NMNH	National Museum of Natural History (Smithsonian Institution), Washington, D.C.
NS	Toronto Normal School/Ontario Provincial Museum (collections now in ROM)
OPM	Ontario Provincial Museum (collections now in ROM)
PABC	Provincial Archives of British Columbia, Victoria
PAM	Portland Art Museum, Portland
PH	Peabody Museum, Harvard University
PS	Peabody Museum, Salem
PN	Photograph Number, RBCM
RBCM	Royal British Columbia Museum, Victoria
ROM	Royal Ontario Museum, Toronto
ROM Ethnology	Ethnology collections, Department of Anthropology, Royal Ontario Museum
SAM	Seattle Art Museum, Seattle
SI	Smithsonian Institution, Washington, D.C.
UBCMOA	University of British Columbia Museum of Anthropology, Vancouver

FOREWORD

From the Heiltsuk Nation's Perspective

The events described in Martha Black's work took place nearly a century ago. Because of this I was surprised that I was so completely swept into the book, and that my response to it was so intensely emotional. I was moved to anger, and tears, and joy.

The circumstances of our people at that time were not unique; similar situations were encountered by other First Nations on the coast. It was a shared experience. Perhaps ultimately it reinforced our sense of our own identity.

I was struck by the cultural ties we have with our ancestors, and by the resilience and strength of the Heiltsuk people. The cultural assimilation attitudes of the early twentieth century are shocking to us today. Indeed the after effects of those attitudes cause pain for us even now. But I know in my heart that because of our strength of character as a people our culture will survive.

This is a book about Heiltsuk art, an expression of our identity. But it goes beyond artifacts to reveal the lives of those who made the art, people who laughed and wept.

Our ancestors leave us a great legacy, and a great responsibility. We honour them. In particular, I honour my late grandmother, Louisa Humchitt, who was such an inspiration for me. Such people never let us forget who we are.

We continue to move forward to meet the challenges of the future, knowing that our heritage will never be lost.

> Arlene Wilson, Heiltsuk,
> Descendant of the 'Uyalitx̌v tribe
> Head, Heiltsuk Tribal Council

PREFACE

Culture has been defined as the total means by which a people
provide for their material, emotional, and intellectual needs.
It is a complex system which includes language, arts, customs,
and beliefs. Our ancestors believed that culture was a gift of the
Creator, given to them as the first born of this land, and
inextricably linked to the natural environment and resources of
traditional territories. Over thousands of years, our culture has
continued to evolve through an ancient and continuing dialogue
between our people, the Creator, and this environment.

—Heiltsuk Cultural Education Centre: Program Areas, Goals, Objectives, 1990

The Heiltsuk-speaking peoples count as their territory over 6000 square miles of
islands, inlets, lakes, mainland, and outer coasts of what is now referred to as the
central coast of British Columbia. In this geographically diverse area the Heiltsuk
developed a rich and complex culture, based on a detailed knowledge of their environment and sophisticated systems of social organization and resource management. The
Heiltsuk have always lived in this area and archaeological evidence corroborates over
9000 years of continuous habitation and cultural development. At the time of contact
with Europeans, the Heiltsuk were widely respected for their cultural achievements, for
their skill as craftpersons, artists, fearless navigators, traders, and for their productivity
in harvesting resources. They maintained extensive trading and family ties up and down
the coast as well as inland. The word "Heiltsuk" or "Hailh zaqv" means literally "to
speak or act correctly."

The 19th and 20th centuries, with their succession of fur traders, missionaries,
developers, law enforcers, Indian agents, and epidemics, came close to obliterating
Heiltsuk culture. Today there are 1200 Heiltsuk, most of whom reside at the village site
of Waglisla, known also as Bella Bella. In 1975 the Band's determination to ensure the
preservation and revitalization of Heiltsuk culture resulted in the establishment of the

Heiltsuk Cultural Education Centre. A non-profit organization, the Centre is responsible for a wide range of research and educational activities relating to Heiltsuk history, language, and culture. With a small group of paid and unpaid staff, the Centre operates under the guidance of the Hilistis society (our elders' group) and under the ultimate authority of the Heiltsuk Tribal Council. The Centre maintains its core operation and conducts specific projects through contributions from private and government sources.

Our people believe that knowledge of Heiltsuk history, language, and traditions, as well as an understanding of the changes that have occurred since contact with Europeans, are fundamental to our survival as a people. These will serve as a source of ideas and inspiration for further development of Heiltsuk culture and economy. Since its inception the Centre has participated in a number of significant contributions to the ultimate goals of recording and revitalizing Heiltsuk culture. These have included the compilation of a *Practical Heiltsuk-English Dictionary* and a practical alphabet; the establishment of the largest single archival collection about Heiltsuk history, language, culture, and environment; the establishment of research and reference services, including an active oral history program; and the implementation of a human resources development program.

Bella Bella: A Season of Heiltsuk Art explores an episode in Heiltsuk history and examines a collection of Heiltsuk art that arose from it. The Centre welcomes opportunities to promote understanding of the history and accomplishments of the Heiltsuk people and has been pleased to assist the book's author, Martha Black, and the Royal Ontario Museum, which holds the collection. We acknowledge their dedication and contribution in compiling and bringing this information before the public, and join them in celebrating this quest for insight into the Heiltsuk spirit.

Jennifer Carpenter
Director
Heiltsuk Cultural Education Centre

NOTE ON LANGUAGE

Heiltsuk, a rich and complex language with both conversational and ceremonial forms, is spoken at Bella Bella (Waglisla) and Klemtu. Like Oowekyala (a closely related language spoken by the Oweekeno of Rivers Inlet), Haisla (the language of the people of Kitamaat), and Kwaḵwala (spoken by the Kwakwaka'wakw to the south), it is a North Wakashan language.

Through the initiative of the Heiltsuk Tribal Council and the Heiltsuk Cultural Education Centre, the Heiltsuk Language Studies Program was begun in 1972. John C. Rath, a linguist who arrived at Waglisla in 1973, has spent twenty years studying the language with the help of Heiltsuk elders. The Heiltsuk orthography he formulated and used in his *Practical Heiltsuk-English Dictionary* (1981) is followed as much as possible in this book. The more than fifty sounds of Heiltsuk are rendered as shown on the accompanying chart.

Rath's practical orthography is widely accepted and gives some consistency to the Heiltsuk used here. It should be noted, however, that there are several orthographic variations extant, and that a revised Heiltsuk orthography will be used in the computerized "talking" dictionary that is a current project of the HCEC and Heiltsuk language teachers at Bella Bella. For example, the names of the five original Heiltsuk-speaking groups have been written in many ways. Three modern versions are tabled below.

VARIATIONS OF HEILTSUK ORTHOGRAPHY

Rath 1981	Revised Heiltsuk Orthography	Hilton 1990
ʾQvúqvaẏaítx̌v	ʾQvúqvaẏaítx̌v	ʾqʷúqʷaẏaítx̣ʷ
Uẁíhitx̌v	ʾWuríitx̌v	ʾuẁríitx̣ʷ
ʾÚyalitx̌v	ʾWúyalitx̌v	ʔúyalitx̣ʷ; Uyalit
ʾIsdaítx̌v	ʾYísdáitx̌v	ʔísdaítx̣ʷ
ˇX̌íx̌ís	X̌íx̌ís	x̣íx̣ís; Haihais

Early observers such as William Fraser Tolmie and John Dunn, who in the 1830s visited the Hudson's Bay Company's fort that had been established in Heiltsuk territory, had other ways of spelling these and other Heiltsuk names and terms. Ethnographers, including Franz Boas, Ronald L. Olson, Philip Drucker, and others, came later and transcribed Heiltsuk words differently again. The various versions used by ethnographers and other writers appear in quotations from and references to their texts. An informal glossary of some of the Heiltsuk words encountered in the text can be found in Appendix I.

HEILTSUK SOUNDS

CONSONANTS I) OBSTRUENTS				
		PLOSIVES		FRICATIVES
	plain	aspirated	glottalized	
labial	b	p	ṗ	-
alveolar	d	t	ṫ	-
affricate-alveolar	z	c	ċ	s
affricate-lateral	dh	th	ṫh	lh
palato-velar	g	k	k̓	x
velar (with liprounding)	gv	kv	k̓v	xv
uvular (with liprounding)	ǧv	qv	q̓v	x̌v
uvular (plain)	ǧ	q	q̓	x̌

CONSONANTS II) RESONANTS		
	plain	glottalized
labial	m	ṁ
alveolar	n	ṅ
affricate-alveolar	-	-
affricate-lateral	l	l̓
palato-velar	y	ẏ
velar (with liprounding)	w	ẇ
uvular (with liprounding)	-	-
uvular (plain)	-	-
laryngeal	h	'
		'ă

VOWELS		
	PLAIN	GLOTTALIZED
high tone	low tone	always low tone
ém	em	emṁ
én	en	enṅ
él	el	ell̓
í	i	iẏ
ú	u	uẇ
á	a	-

Note: Heiltsuk has tonal vowels. High tones are indicated by an accent (´). Accents are placed to the left of, instead of above, capital letters.

ACKNOWLEDGEMENTS

Although the remarkable objects discussed in this book are now geographically and contextually far from their origins, we recognize that they continue to be part of the rich cultural heritage of the Heiltsuk Nation.

The people of Waglisla offered me their wisdom and hospitality when I was researching the R. W. Large Collection. I thank the members of the Heiltsuk Tribal Council for their courtesy and all those in Waglisla who have lent their support and shared their knowledge. I am grateful to those who graciously took time out to answer my questions: David Bell, Ena Bell, Beatrice Brown, Rena Brown, Cyril Carpenter, Shirl and Robert Hall, Joann Hopkins, Mr. and Mrs. Johnny Humchitt, Mary Hunt, Tillie Hunt, Clarence Martin, Cecil Reid, Gordon Reid, Sr., David White, Bertha Wilson, Liz and Don Wilson, Nancy Wilson, Evelyn Windsor, and Maggie Windsor. Linguist John Rath helped me with vocabulary and with the Heiltsuk orthography that he developed in response to the Tribal Council's language-retention initiative. I am particularly indebted to Jennifer Carpenter, anthropologist and Director of the Heiltsuk Cultural Education Centre, who has been generous with time, resources, and knowledge. She made my visits to Waglisla very pleasant and her thoughtful scholarship continues to inform my work.

Anthropologist Suzanne Hilton helped me in the early stages of my search for information about Waglisla and its poorly documented history. Bill Holm, Professor Emeritus, University of Washington, kindly commented on some of the objects in the Large Collection. Douglas Cole (Simon Fraser University), Stanley A. Freed (American Museum of Natural History), Ira Jacknis (Phoebe Hearst Museum of Anthropology), Michael Harkin (University of Wyoming), and Audrey Shane (University of British Columbia Museum of Anthropology) also responded to inquiries. Dan Savard of the Royal British Columbia Museum, Leslie Tepper and Judy Thompson of the Canadian Museum of Civilization, and Bill McLennan and Pam Brown of the University of British Columbia Museum of Anthropology gave me valuable assistance with photographs and information for this project.

Others who have helped with my on-going research on Heiltsuk art in museum collections include Beth Carter (Glenbow Museum), Nicole Chamberland (Canadian Museum of Civilization), Sandy Cook (McMichael Canadian Art Collection), Alison

Jeffrey (National Museum of the American Indian), Grant Keddie (Royal British Columbia Museum), Janice Klein (Field Museum), Andrea LaForet (Canadian Museum of Civilization), Mary Jane Lenz (National Museum of the American Indian), Moira McCaffery (Musée McCord d'Histoire Canadienne), Lynn Maranda (Vancouver Museum), Felicia Pickering (National Museum of Natural History, Smithsonian Institution), Shelley Reid (Royal British Columbia Museum), Teri Sowell (Brooklyn Museum), Anne Stevenson (University of British Columbia Museum of Anthropology), John Veillette (Royal British Columbia Museum), Laila Williamson (American Museum of Natural History), and Robin Wright (Thomas Burke Memorial Washington State Museum). Alan Hoover of the Royal British Columbia Museum has been particularly generous in sharing the results of his research on Heiltsuk art.

I thank Aldona Jonaitis of the University of Alaska at Fairbanks, Victoria Wyatt of the University of Victoria, Peter Macnair of the Royal British Columbia Museum, and Richard Inglis of the Nisga'a Negotiating Team, Province of British Columbia Ministry of Aboriginal Affairs, for specific comments on the manuscript and also for intellectual stimulation and friendship.

The Department of Anthropology of the Royal Ontario Museum made the R. W. Large Collection accessible to me, and I am especially indebted to Arni Brownstone who facilitated my research in the Museum. I am grateful for the expertise, efficiency, enthusiasm, and good humour of Sandra Shaul and Glen Ellis of the Royal Ontario Museum's Publications Department, and for Virginia Morin's sensitive design. There can be no better editor than Andrea Gallagher Ellis. I have learned a great deal from her elegant and meticulous work.

I would also like to thank Darla Rhyne and Elizabeth Black for their helpful suggestions over the more than ten years between this study's inception and its publication, and my dear friend and husband, Paul Hutner, for everything.

This book developed out of a Master's thesis for York University's Interdisciplinary Studies Program. The project was made enjoyable by the instruction, encouragement, and friendship of the members of my committee: Ramsay Cook, John Price, and Zdenka Volavka.

INTRODUCTION

The Royal Ontario Museum holds a major but little-known collection of Northwest Coast native art and artifacts acquired by the Reverend Dr. Richard Whitfield Large at Bella Bella, British Columbia, between 1899 and 1906. Although the R. W. Large Collection is one of the most important Heiltsuk collections in existence because of its unique documentation, there has never been a comprehensive study of it.

The Heiltsuk Nation lies at the centre of the Northwest Coast (Fig. 1). The descendants of the original Heiltsuk tribes live at Bella Bella (Waglisla), a community of about 1500 people on the east side of Campbell Island on Lama Passage, and at Klemtu, a Heiltsuk/Tsimshian village on Swindle Island. The original Heiltsuk-speaking tribes inhabited the outer islands, protected inland waterways, and mainland fiords of the central coast between Rivers Inlet and Milbanke Sound (Figs. 2–3). Heiltsuk ancestral territory stretches from the southern tip of Calvert Island to Klekane Inlet on Graham Reach and encompasses Burke and Dean Channels. Haisla, Oweekeno, Coast Tsimshian, Haida, Bella Coola (Nuxalk), and Kwakiutl (Kwakwaka'wakw) peoples are all Heiltsuk neighbours (Fig. 4). This geographic centrality is mirrored by a cultural one. Heiltsuk ceremonialists, canoe makers, and artists were widely known and greatly influential on the coast. The spread of the tánís, or hámáċa, ceremony is just one example of Heiltsuk cultural influence. Now better known in its Kwakwaka'wakw manifestation as the hamaísa ritual, it may have been obtained from Heiltsuk chiefs in the nineteenth century (Boas 1897:427).

Despite the central position and significance of the Heiltsuk, their art and culture are not well known to non-native Canadians. Books and exhibitions about Northwest Coast art, culture, society, and history have dealt with the Heiltsuk minimally, if at all. This unwarranted marginalization can be explained in part by scholarly concerns about cultural authenticity and tradition. Heiltsuk territory became central to non-native as well as First Nations culture in the nineteenth century. The Hudson's Bay Company established Fort McLoughlin (1833–1843) on Campbell Island and a Heiltsuk village grew around the fort. After the devastating smallpox epidemic of the 1860s, the remnants of the Heiltsuk tribes gradually amalgamated at that community on McLoughlin Bay. It was known, in English, as Bella Bella.

In 1880 the Methodist Church made Bella Bella its base for mission work on the central coast. The community came to resemble (outwardly, not culturally) a European-style town. The non-traditional appearance of the village was one of the reasons for its ethnological marginalization. Such observers as Franz Boas of the American Museum of Natural History spent little time at Bella Bella because of the Methodist presence. Heiltsuk culture was, quite wrongly, perceived as no longer "authentic." To add to the misunderstanding, because Heiltsuk is a Wakashan language, the Heiltsuk were often referred to as "Northern Wakashan" and "Northern Kwakiutl." The former is too general to be meaningful; the latter is wrong—the Heiltsuk are not Kwakiutl (Kwakw<u>a</u>ka'wakw). Most of the nineteenth- and early twentieth-century art and artifacts from Bella Bella in museum collections are therefore minimally and confusingly documented.

The Reverend Dr. R. W. Large, a Methodist missionary, arrived at Bella Bella in 1898, just as the people were relocating to a site, Waglisla (Wáglísla), about 3 km to the north. The new village (which continued to be known as Bella Bella) was a prosperous community with large European-style homes, a wide boardwalk, street lights, native-owned businesses, a church, a school, and a hospital. Large sent 284 artifacts from Bella Bella to the Ontario Provincial Museum in 1901 and 1906. The 1901 collection is particularly significant because it is relatively well documented.

The objects collected by Large are authentic and traditional even though many were produced in the new and changing context of the "progressive" community of Bella Bella, a village that was promoted by the Methodist Church and the Canadian government as a model for native modernization and assimilation. Despite outward change, Heiltsuk culture did not stop. Bella Bella people absorbed, adapted, and appropriated selected aspects of Euro-Canadian culture to their own changing needs. This is not to say that cultural domination and repression were not powerful factors. Indeed, the role and voice of the turn-of-the-century missionary is controversial because the aims of the mission were in direct opposition to the traditional systems of belief and the social structure of the native population. Although Large believed he understood the Heiltsuk people and was helping them, his statements betray nineteenth-century attitudes of Euro-Canadian cultural superiority. His ideas, demands, and strategies seem arrogant and unreasonable today. But Heiltsuk culture was creative, rather than reactive, in response to such pressures. In fact, at the turn of the century the Heiltsuk appear to have been very much in control of the process of change. Today, the vital contemporary community of Bella Bella (Waglisla) is evidence of the Heiltsuk ability to creatively maintain indigenous cultural traditions in a modern context.

One of the noteworthy aspects of Large's documentation is the record of the people who contributed to his collection, including five artists at Bella Bella. The Large Collection, therefore, is an exceptional record of a specific time and place and of a specific people. It is a window on Heiltsuk society and one of the rare historical collections that does not present native art as the unchanging production of unknown craftsmen.

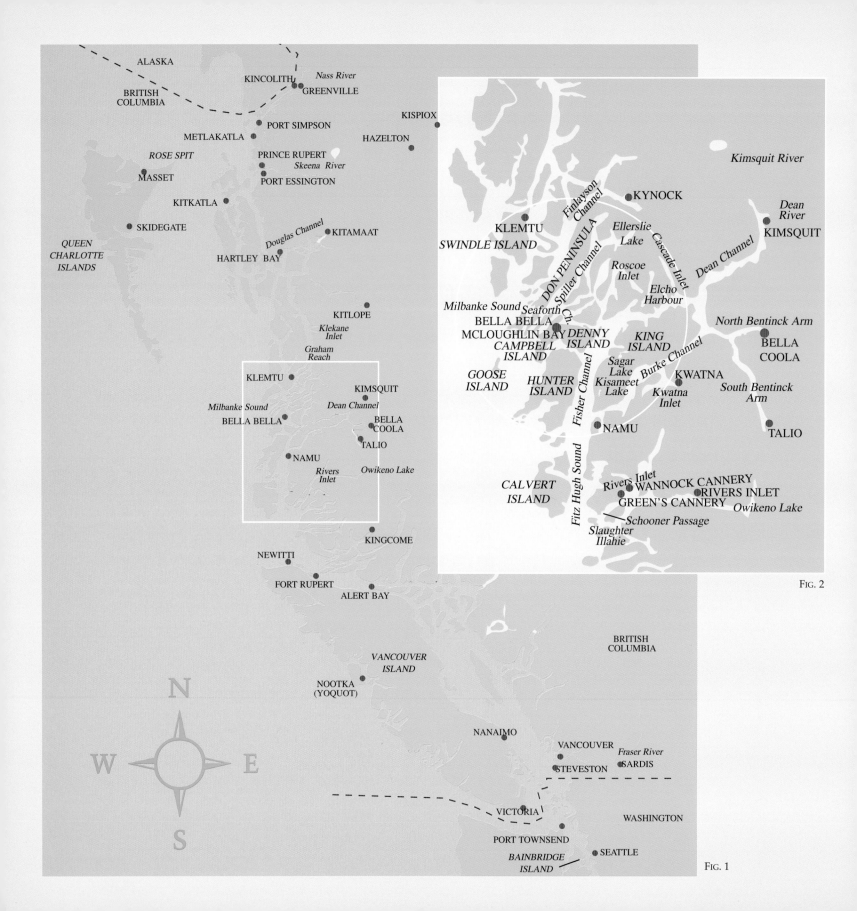

ALASKA

BRITISH
COLUMBIA

KINCOLITH
Nass River
GREENVILLE

KISPIOX

PORT SIMPSON

METLAKATLA
HAZELTON

ROSE SPIT
PRINCE RUPERT
Skeena River
MASSET
PORT ESSINGTON

KITKATLA

SKIDEGATE

*QUEEN
CHARLOTTE
ISLANDS*
Douglas Channel
KITAMAAT

HARTLEY BAY

KITLOPE

*Klekane
Inlet*

*Graham
Reach*

KLEMTU
KIMSQUIT

Milbanke Sound
Dean Channel
BELLA BELLA
BELLA
COOLA

TALIO

NAMU

*Rivers
Inlet*
Owikeno Lake

KINGCOME

NEWITTI

FORT RUPERT
ALERT BAY

*VANCOUVER
ISLAND*

NOOTKA
(YOQUOT)

BRITISH
COLUMBIA

NANAIMO

VANCOUVER
Fraser River
STEVESTON
SARDIS

VICTORIA

WASHINGTON

PORT TOWNSEND

*BAINBRIDGE
ISLAND*
SEATTLE

N
W   E
S

Fig. 1

Kimsquit River

KYNOCK
Finlayson Channel
*Ellerslie
Lake*
*Dean
River*
KLEMTU
KIMSQUIT

SWINDLE ISLAND
DON PENINSULA
*Roscoe
Inlet*
Cascade Inlet
Dean Channel

Spiller Channel
*Elcho
Harbour*

Milbanke Sound
Seaforth Ch.
North Bentinck Arm
BELLA BELLA
MCLOUGHLIN BAY
DENNY
ISLAND
*KING
ISLAND*
BELLA
COOLA
*CAMPBELL
ISLAND*
Burke Channel

*GOOSE
ISLAND*
*HUNTER
ISLAND*
*Sagar
Lake*
KWATNA
*South Bentinck
Arm*
*Kisameet
Lake*
*Kwatna
Inlet*

Fisher Channel
NAMU
TALIO

*CALVERT
ISLAND*
Fitz Hugh Sound
Rivers Inlet
WANNOCK CANNERY
RIVERS INLET
GREEN'S CANNERY
Owikeno Lake
Schooner Passage
*Slaughter
Illahie*

Fig. 2

FIG. 3

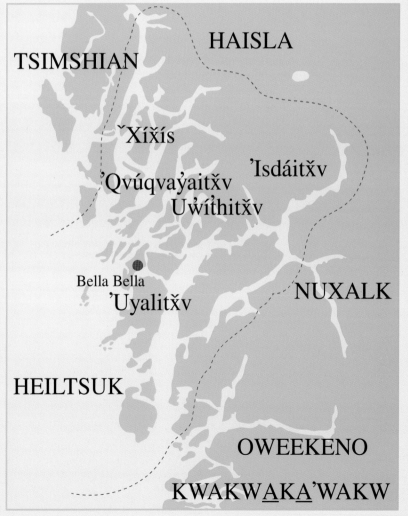

Fig. 1. *Bella Bella is at the geographical centre of the Northwest Coast.*

Fig. 2. *Milbanke Sound region.*

Fig. 3. *Bella Bella and vicinity.*

Fig. 4. *Approximate ancestral territories of the Heiltsuk groups.*

FIG. 4

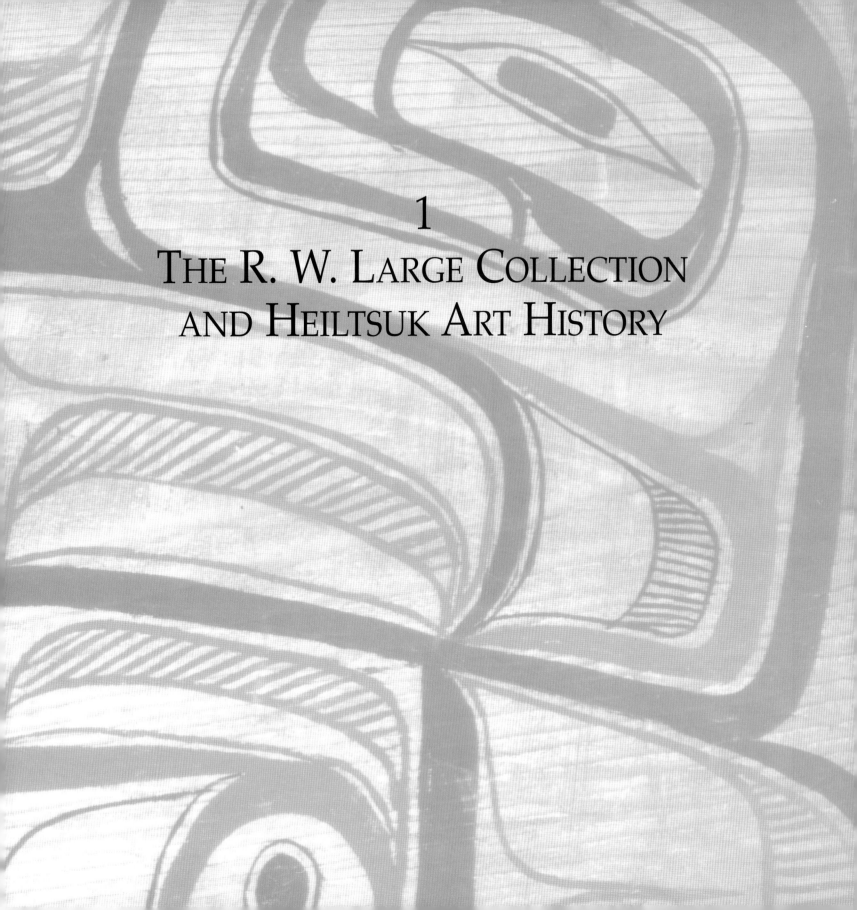

1
THE R. W. LARGE COLLECTION
AND HEILTSUK ART HISTORY

The "great period of museum anthropology" began about 1890. By the late nineteenth century anthropologists had concluded, wrongly, that the indigenous North American peoples were on the verge of total assimilation, if not extinction, and museums all over the continent scrambled to collect artifacts of the native cultures before they disappeared altogether (see Cole 1985). Missionaries serving among the First Nations communities at this time were approached by museum agents to assist in the acquisition of artifacts. This is the story of a collection made by a missionary in one Northwest Coast community.

Bella Bella, British Columbia, is the principal village of the Heiltsuk Nation. The Reverend Dr. Richard Whitfield Large (Fig. 5) was the Methodist missionary there from December 1898 until December 1910. Perhaps in direct response to solicitations from David Boyle, the Provincial Archaeologist of Ontario, he sent two collections of artifacts from his home at Bella Bella to the Ontario Provincial Museum (OPM) in Toronto.[1] In all there were 284 objects. Many were archaeological specimens and some were sold or traded to other museums (see Appendix H). The remaining 139 objects, plus four related objects, comprise the R. W. Large Collection now in the Ethnology collections of the Department of Anthropology, Royal Ontario Museum (ROM). Together with Large's notes from the 1901 collection, his published letters, the writings of ethnologists, and archival sources, these objects document the art and society of Bella Bella at a critical stage in its history, when the village was moving to a new site and the people were adopting a new way of life. They illustrate the continuity of Heiltsuk traditions despite the rapid modernization of the community, and they constitute a chapter in the history of an important native nation whose culture and art have until recently not figured prominently in Northwest Coast studies.

The history of the Heiltsuk Nation is not widely known. The confusing and often erroneous terminology adopted by early observers has obscured the distinct identity and cultural importance of this people.[2] The name Bella Bella—derived, perhaps, from a local place name, Pélbála—has been applied to the Heiltsuk-speaking people who moved to Campbell Island over a sixty-year period that began in 1833 with the establishment of Fort McLoughlin. Bella Bella is also the name for the principal Heiltsuk reserve, which was allotted in 1882 (see Fig. 2).[3] In December of 1898 Large arrived at the village on McLoughlin Bay called Bella Bella ('Qélc in Heiltsuk; Fig. 6).[4] He soon moved to the new village at Waglisla (Wáglísla), also referred to as New Bella Bella, about 3 km to the north.[5] Waglisla had been surveyed in 1897 and the relocation of the community was a gradual one. For the period under discussion it is difficult to distinguish between the two sites in the literature. As both the old village and the new one were known as Bella Bella, it seems reasonable to continue to use this name for the main Heiltsuk community. For the period before 1897 the name Bella Bella refers only to 'Qélc, or Old Bella Bella (Old Town), at McLoughlin Bay.

Heiltsuk, the language spoken by the people of Bella Bella, is one of four North Wakashan languages. The others are Haisla, spoken by the people of Kitamaat on Douglas Channel; Oowekyala, spoken by the Oweekeno of Rivers Inlet; and Kwak̓wala, spoken by the Kwakw̲aka̓wakw people (Lincoln and Rath 1980:3; see Fig. 4). Because of this linguistic relationship, the Heiltsuk, Haisla, and Oweekeno have in the past been referred to as the "Northern Kwakiutl," another misleading—and absolutely incorrect— term. The amalgamated Heiltsuk-speaking groups that settled at Bella Bella are properly called the Heiltsuk.

This study vividly illustrates the response of one First Nations community, Bella Bella, to a particular historical situation; it also examines issues that pertain to the study of native art history in general. The Large Collection is especially appropriate for this analysis because of its unusual documentation. Because Large lived at Bella Bella and was involved with the community as both missionary and doctor, he was able to recognize and record the sources of the artifacts that he collected. His notes for the 1901 collection identify the function, what he termed the "finding-spot," and often the owner and/or maker of each object. The 1906 collection, although it lacks such documentation, is accompanied by a list of prices, now in the ROM's Department of Anthropology, paid for the objects by the OPM. The close association between the objects in this group and those in the 1901 collection make it possible to identify the provenance, the function, and the maker of many of the artifacts in the 1906 collection as well.

The literature and strategies of art history, anthropology, and history contribute to this study. Art-historical methodology emphasizes the importance of the objects as primary data. To understand the society that produced the objects, ethnological literature is essential. A historical perspective elucidates the point of view of the collector and the unique situation at Bella Bella at the turn of the century. In the study of a collection made by a missionary, it is particularly important to be aware of the social, moral, religious, and intellectual context of the observer, whose descriptions and reports about "his Indians" were coloured by his belief in the primacy of his own way of life and thought, and his desire to dismantle and reconstruct Heiltsuk culture to conform to a Euro-Canadian, Christian model.

Having been made at a turning point in the history of the Heiltsuk people by an out-

Fig. 5. *The Reverend Dr. Richard Whitfield Large, missionary and medical superintendent at Bella Bella. From "Souvenir of Bella Bella, B.C." Courtesy Royal British Columbia Museum, Victoria. PN 16450.*

sider who lived at Bella Bella for an extended period of time, the R. W. Large Collection is ideally suited to illustrate three major concerns of native art studies: the meaning of the objects and their significance as documentation of a specific historical situation, the influence of the collector in the interpretation and organization of artifacts, and the role of the museum collection in shaping perceptions of First Nations art history.

The Large Collection can be read as a document of a specific period, a critical one in the history of the Heiltsuk people. At the turn of the century the move from Old Bella Bella ('Qélc) to New Bella Bella (Waglisla) was under way. 'Qélc had grown around the Hudson's Bay Company's Fort McLoughlin (1833–1843) and subsequent trading store (established 1853).[6] The remnants of five Heiltsuk-speaking tribal divisions, ˇXíx̌ís (down river people, i.e., people to the north), 'Qvúqvay̓aítx̌v (calm water people, named after 'Qvúqvaí, a village at Gale Creek),[7] Uẃíhitx̌v (people of the inlet), 'Uyalitx̌v (seaward people), and 'Isdaítx̌v (named after 'Isda, a village at Elcho Harbour) were amalgamated at this location by the early 1890s.[8] Fort McLoughlin had been dominated by the 'Uyalitx̌v, in whose territory it was. The 'Isdaítx̌v groups moved to McLoughlin Bay in the 1860s after the great small-pox epidemic; the Uẃíhitx̌v peoples came about 1881 with the establishment of the mission; the 'Qvúqvay̓aítx̌v arrived after 1891 after their principal village ('Qábá, or Kokyet, on Yeo Island) was destroyed by fire (see Figs. 3–4).[9]

Waglisla was laid out by the missionary Dr. J. A. Jackson and the Heiltsuk leaders in 1897 and the move to the new site was conducted and completed by the Heiltsuk with Large's help. The move emphasized the change in traditional Heiltsuk social structure and housing that had begun at 'Qélc in the early 1880s. The old village had been domi-

nated by the Hudson's Bay Company store, the great cedar-plank lodges lining the beach, and, later, the church. Small single-family houses eventually crowded the site. The new village was dominated by the physical and cultural structures of church, school, and hospital. Yet, as an HCEC study has pointed out (Hopkins, Martin, and Carpenter 1990), the grand new European-style houses at Waglisla were much larger than the single-family dwellings that had been built at 'Qélc. They could accommodate extended families and provide room for feasts and other gatherings,

Fig. 6. *South end of Bella Bella ('Qélc) in the 1880s. Traditional Heiltsuk houses and canoes can be seen in front of the fenced Hudson's Bay Company property (left and centre) and the mission property (right). Courtesy British Columbia Provincial Archives and Records Service, Victoria. Edward Dossetter photograph. PABC HP 33587, neg. no. B-3570 (AMNH photograph no. 42310).*

thus allowing the integration of old and new ways of life at Waglisla.

Although at Old Town many Heiltsuk had already adopted Christianity and begun to live in smaller households, and at Waglisla aspects of traditional culture continued, for Large the transplanting of the village symbolized evolution and improvement. His understanding of First Nations traditions was influenced by his religious beliefs and nineteenth-century evolutionist theory; he believed that Heiltsuk society was progressing from pagan to Christian, childlike to mature, and primitive to modern. But the artifacts that Large collected illustrate that, while the progressive Heiltsuk embraced new ways of living as they successfully adapted to the European cash economy and social norms, they did not completely abandon their indigenous art and culture. Large mentions twenty-five individuals who contributed to his collection. Other records show that many of these people were involved simultaneously in traditional institutions such as chieftainship, shamanism, and (modified) potlatching,[10] and in Euro-Canadian institutions such as the Methodist Church, the Epworth League, and the Bella Bella Cornet Band.[11]

The Large Collection can be read as an illustration of the concerns of the collector.

The first minister at Bella Bella, Reverend Charles M. Tate, lived in the village for four years. He was succeeded by a string of temporary missionaries, each of whom stayed only about one year (see Appendix A). Large was the first long-term Methodist missionary at Bella Bella and the first permanent doctor in the region. He established the hospital at Bella Bella and operated a summer hospital (which had been set up in 1897) at the site of one of the many canneries on Rivers Inlet to serve not only the Heiltsuk who spent the summers working there, but all of the fishermen and cannery workers—Euro-Canadian, Chinese, Japanese, East Indian, and First Nations—who came from all parts of the coast to that rich fishery.[12] Large's close association with the Heiltsuk as minister, physician, surgeon, administrator, justice of the peace, choirmaster, and teacher made his collection of artifacts and its documentation unique. The missionary doctor's interest in folk medicine, mythology, and archaeology is evident in his published writings, which are a primary source for this study. Unlike many ethnological collectors, Large spent years in one community and recorded specific, personal information rather than generalized "scientific" data. Also, as physician and surgeon, he had power in, and access to, aboriginal society beyond that available to many missionaries.

Large's collection can be read as an important document for the study of issues in First Nations art history, which has been hampered in the past by the assumption that aboriginal art is static through time, anonymous, and lacking in documentation (see Vastokas 1986/87). We know the exact time period of the collection because Large sent the pieces to the Toronto museum soon after he acquired them. Because many pieces appear to have been new when collected—and were probably made especially for Large—this period in some cases also defines the time of manufacture. As well as noting the place of origin of the object (the majority of the documented objects in the 1901 collection are from Bella Bella, and most of those in the 1906 group are probably from the village as well), Large could often record its owner, maker, and vendor. This specific information about place, time, and people makes it clear that Bella Bella art is neither static nor anonymous.

Five people mentioned in Large's 1901 documentation were makers of objects. Their works show particular personal variations and subjects within a historical style. Further, the life and work of two of these artists, Chief Robert Bell and Captain Carpenter, illustrate the adjustments that many Bella Bella people made to try to maintain aboriginal traditions while participating in the new society of this progressive Methodist village. Large's documentation allows Heiltsuk artists to be perceived as individuals; it also provides the key to the attribution of other works to these artists. For instance, Daniel

Mask. See Catalogue, No. 59.

Houstie's idiosyncratic version of the Bella Bella style can be recognized in a group of undocumented boxes and ceremonial objects in the 1906 collection. The personal histories of these Bella Bella artists make the Large Collection an important illustration of the role of the individual artist in historical native art studies.

While many traditional objects were no longer made for traditional use at Bella Bella because of the replacement of native ceremonies with Christian institutions, objects collected by Large indicate that Heiltsuk artists produced replicas of traditional paraphernalia and tools for sale, thus actively participating in the documentation of their own culture. Replicas and originals, old and new objects, traditional and novel forms coexisted and overlapped in Bella Bella between 1898 and 1906. All of these are authentic manifestations of specific responses to the cultural environment by individual Bella Bella artists, and their coexistence is evidence of the shift in that environment.

Missionaries had no training as ethnological observers and their bias against traditional native society and religion is well known; their writings and collections have therefore rarely been taken seriously as possible sources for native art studies. But Large's collection with its important documentation, which includes information about First Nations people as individuals, is evidence that missionary sources can indeed be as important as generalized ethnographic data to the study of native art history.

Notes

1. The Ontario Provincial Museum (OPM) began as a teaching collection for teachers in training at the Toronto Normal School (NS) in the 1850s. In 1896 the archaeological collection of the Canadian Institute was added to the Normal School Museum, and in 1906 the name was changed to the Ontario Provincial Museum. The OPM collections were transferred to the Royal Ontario Museum (ROM) in 1933, shortly after the Normal School Museum was closed down. The catalogue of these collections is called the Normal School catalogue. Most of the objects in the R. W. Large Collection still carry Normal School (NS) accession numbers (see Needham 1970).

   David Boyle was superintendent of the Canadian Institute's archaeological collection and moved over to the Normal School with the collection, much of which he himself had acquired and donated. Boyle was superintendent of the NS/OPM from 1896 until his death in 1911, and Provincial Archaeologist from 1886 until 1911 (see Killan 1983).

2. This topic is thoroughly discussed in a paper by Heiltsuk curator Pam Brown (formerly Pam Windsor) of the UBCMOA (Brown n.d.).

3. For a comprehensive discussion of the name Bella Bella and its applications, see Carpenter 1984.

4. ʾQélc can be translated as "having kelp."

5. Drucker, who spelled the village name Wʾkilíʾsla, translated it as "stream that spreads" (Drucker Papers).

6. Hilton (1990:319) agrees that the trading store was set up in the early 1850s, but Harkin (1988:286) gives the date as 1866. There is no doubt, however, that the community continued as a centre of commerce and as a funnel for Euro-Canadian goods entering the central coast. The store at ʾQélc was run as a branch of the Hudson's Bay Company store at Bella Coola from 1870 to 1883, when it was taken over by a local trader.

7. ʾQvúqvaí was commonly spelled Kokqui in English.

8. These regional groups incorporated many distinct Heiltsuk-speaking tribes. For example, the Yáláthitx̌v (Goose Island people) and the Uwígalitx̌v (Calvert Island people) were part of the ʾUyalitx̌v division of the Heiltsuk.

9. Jennifer Carpenter (HCEC), letter to the author, 28 August 1990. Although their head chief moved to ʾQélc in 1881 (Harkin 1988:242), most of the ʾQvúqvaýaitx̌v lived at their traditional villages for another decade. The remains of the houses in these once-populous settlements could still be seen in 1909 (Walbran 1909:46).

10. The complex system of formalized exchange known as the potlatch regulated the ranks, privileges, and responsibilities of members of Heiltsuk society. Its primary features were the display, before an audience, of inherited prerogatives (such as the right to use certain crests and masks) and the distribution of property to validate claims to new status (such as the assumption of a name, a marriage, or initiation into a dancing society). After provincial and mission-

ary pressures resulted in the banning of the potlatch by the federal government in 1884 (the law came into effect in January 1885), the form of the potlatch was modified as the Heiltsuk clandestinely continued this important institution.

11. By the 1920s, the band was known as the Bella Bella Concert Band.

12. The Rivers Inlet hospital had been built by the Methodist missionaries Reverend Thomas Crosby and Dr. A. E. Bolton at Wannock Cannery. After the hospital burned down in 1904, operations were transferred to Green's Cannery. The year-round Bella Bella hospital and its summer branch at Rivers Inlet were for many years the only medical facilities between Vancouver and Port Simpson.

2
SOURCES:
ART
HISTORY
ETHNOLOGY

THE OBJECTS

The most important sources of information for this study are the objects themselves. Large sent 284 items, 139 of which are now stored in ROM Ethnology. In addition, 5 undocumented items found in the Ethnology collections have been included in the catalogue because they are so similar in form, material, decoration, execution, and condition to the Large material as to be almost certainly part of that collection. For the first time since they were collected, these objects have been assembled, examined, and catalogued.[1] Similar objects have been placed together in the catalogue; there are 128 entries.

There are probably 113 stone and bone artifacts from Large's original 284 housed in the Archaeology collections of the ROM's Department of Anthropology. These items, which are not included in this catalogue, are listed in the Normal School (NS) accession records as tools, tool fragments, or gambling markers. Another 15 objects from the original collection were exchanged with museums in Haiti and Australia, and 10 items were not available for this study (see Appendix H).[2] Neither the 6 natural history specimens (sea-lion teeth and the underjaw of a wolf or dog) nor a pipe collected in Ontario in 1904 (NS 28249), which appear in the 1907 NS list of Large's collection, are part of the study, but they do illustrate the scope of the missionary's interests. Similarily, two related collections—other artifacts collected by Large in Ontario and a group of 22 Northwest Coast objects (9 of which are in ROM Ethnology) purchased from Large's widow, Isabella Geddes Large, in 1926—are part of this study only as illustrations of Large's collecting activities.

PUBLISHED SOURCES

The primary written sources for this study are R. W. Large's letters describing the success and importance of his mission. They appeared in the Methodist Church of Canada periodicals the *Missionary Outlook* (*MO*) and the *Missionary Bulletin* (*MB*) for the years 1898–1914.[3] The letters, intended to be inspirational and to encourage donations to the mission field, contain important information about the people of Bella Bella and their adaptation to their new situation. Large seems to have taken pleasure in reporting the daily activities of "his" Indians, by whom he was frequently pleased, often amused—and sometimes appalled. Naturally, he stressed the positive aspects of the people's "evolution" from "savagery" to "civilization," but his inclusion of descriptions of many aspects of traditional belief, and his willingness to record some of the setbacks as well as the successes of his mission, make Large's letters a useful source for the study of Heiltsuk history.

Very little has been published about the history, society, and art of the Heiltsuk people. It is surprising that they should be lesser known than the nations whose ancestral lands encircle them, especially since the Heiltsuk were influential in the spread of the hamatsa Winter Dance cycle and since their art marks the boundary between the two main artistic traditions of the Northwest Coast, the Northern and the Southern.[4] Martine Reid (1987:232) has also observed this paradox, that the Heiltsuk "occupied a pivotal position" among the Northwest Coast groups, and yet they "are perhaps the least known to anthropologists and other students of the culture." It is this shortage of documentation on the Heiltsuk Nation that makes the missionary records especially important.

Several archaeological investigations in the Bella Bella region (Borden 1975, Carlson 1976b, Hobler 1970, Simonsen 1973) have produced information on the history of Heiltsuk territory. While a discussion of the rich archaeological finds is outside the scope of this book, it is important to mention that excavations conducted by Simon Fraser University in the settlement area of the original Heiltsuk tribes have uncovered the oldest site on the coast, showing over 9000 years of continuous habitation. Investigations have established a cultural sequence in which evidence of traits encountered in early historic times (i.e., late eighteenth century) appears 1500 to 2000 years ago. A useful synthesis of the published historical material can be found in John Pomeroy's archaeological study, "Bella Bella Settlement and Subsistence" (1980).

The Heiltsuk first appear in European literature with the descriptions by George Vancouver and Alexander Mackenzie of their encounters with First Nations people in Milbanke Sound and Dean Channel in 1793 (Vancouver 1798, Mackenzie 1962). In the late eighteenth and early nineteenth centuries, the Heiltsuk were active in the profitable maritime trade, acquiring new materials and manufactured goods from European and American vessels in return for furs. An attack led by Chief Kaiete ('Qa'aít) on the American trading vessel *Atahualpa* in Sturgis Bay, Milbanke Sound, in 1805 is one of the few recorded incidents from the maritime fur-trade era that mention the Heiltsuk. The event, in which the crew of the ship and many Heiltsuk, including 'Qa'aít, were killed, was noted in the *Annual Register and Naval Chronicle* for 1806, according to Captain John T. Walbran of the Canadian Government Steamship *Quadra* (Walbran 1909:152–53). Interestingly, the story of the attack was also told to Walbran by Captain Carpenter, the lighthouse keeper at Dryad Point just north of Waglisla and one of the five Bella Bella artists represented in the Large Collection. Carpenter's wife was a descendant of Chief 'Qa'aít. The account demonstrates the vitality of Heiltsuk historical tradition in Large's time.

FIG. 7. *Bella Bella Hospital, Waglisla, with the hospital staff. Courtesy Royal British Columbia Museum, Victoria. Photograph by R. W. Large, from "Souvenir of Bella Bella, B.C." PN 16455.*

The period surrounding the building, in the winter of 1833/34, of Fort McLoughlin by the Hudson's Bay Company is documented in the writings of the traders William Fraser Tolmie (1963) and John Dunn (1844). In his journal for 1835, the trader John Work (1945) recorded two brief visits to the fort. Little else was written about Bella Bella and the Heiltsuk until the 1880s with the establishment of the Methodist missions described in Church publications by R. W. Large and by Reverend Thomas Crosby (1914) and Reverend C. M. Tate (1916, 1917). The annual reports of the Department of Indian Affairs (DIA) contain statistics and reports about Bella Bella from 1880 to 1918 that show the increasing control of the Methodist Church and the Canadian government over First Nations life.

Ethnographic literature treating the Heiltsuk as separate from the Kwakwaka'wakw is scanty. From the 1880s to the 1940s, anthropological studies of Heiltsuk society and ritual life were undertaken by Franz Boas, Ronald Olson, and Philip Drucker, all of whom stated that their information was fragmentary because the old culture was no longer remembered. My study illustrates that this common rationale must be questioned in light of enduring Heiltsuk traditions.

Boas visited Bella Bella very briefly in the 1880s and in late August 1897 with the Jesup North Pacific Expedition. When he returned to Bella Bella in November 1923, Boas was struck both by the transformation of the village and the tenacity of Heiltsuk traditional thought:

> The changes which have taken place since I was here the first time in 1886 are almost unbelievable. . . . Outwardly all the people are Methodists, . . . [but] their former Weltanschauung [world view] is still deeply anchored in them. [1969:281]

In the preface to his *Bella Bella Texts* (1928), however, Boas lamented: "The whole culture of the Bella Bella has practically disappeared."

Drucker, whose research was done in the winter of 1936/37, noted: "Native culture has been badly shattered in Northern Kwakiutl [i.e., Bella Bella] territory, where European influence, especially that of the missionaries, has been strong for the last sixty or seventy years." As a result, he wrote, his accounts of Heiltsuk ceremonials "are incomplete in many respects" (1940:201).

Olson observed the same cultural deterioration when he did research at Bella Bella in 1935 and 1949:

> The time when a complete picture of Bella Bella culture could be reconstructed has long since passed. Since about 1880, when they moved to their present location, the Bella Bella have been under constant pressure from the missionaries and members of the hospital staff to give up their old culture. The success of these well-meaning and devoted persons has been all too great, from the ethnographer's point of view. [1955:319]

Despite the perceived shortage of knowledgeable informants at Bella Bella, Boas compiled two books of Bella Bella stories, *Bella Bella Texts* (1928) and *Bella Bella Tales* (1932), and in *Tsimshian Mythology* (1916) he included some of the stories collected by Jesup Expedition member Livingston Farrand. A very brief description of the Heiltsuk clan and descent systems, class structure, and dance societies was published in *American Anthropologist* (1924). In this article, Boas concluded that the Heiltsuk, with four endogamous clans—Raven, Eagle, Killer whale, and Wolf—and the option of either matrilineal or patrilineal descent of crest affiliation and privileges, had a social organization that combined characteristics of the Vancouver Island Kwakw<u>a</u>ka'wakw to the south and the Tsimshian to the north.[5] Fragments of information about Bella Bella ceremonies are found in Boas' works on the Kwakw<u>a</u>ka'wakw, in particular "The Social Organization and the Secret Societies of the Kwakiutl Indians" (1897) and *The Religion of the Kwakiutl Indians* (1930). Boas described Heiltsuk social organization and ritual in terms of the institutions of the surrounding tribes while stressing the fact that the Cannibal dance

Fig. 8. *The hospital staff at Bella Bella (Waglisla). Isabelle Geddes Large stands at the right beside sons Gordon (top) and Richard Geddes (middle).* Courtesy Royal British Columbia Museum, Victoria. Photograph by R. W. Large, from "Souvenir of Bella Bella, B.C." PN 16456.

orders of the Kwakwa̱ka̱'wakw and aspects of Tsimshian dance ceremonies derived from the Heiltsuk in the first half of the nineteenth century (1987:426–27, 430, 651), again placing the Heiltsuk in a central position between the tribes to the north and south.[6]

Drucker's culture element lists (1950) also stress the geographic, social, and cultural centrality of the Heiltsuk. Heiltsuk technologies share traits with both northern and southern tribes and can be seen as intermediate between the two. Drucker's categories, however, are too simplistic to provide more than the most general type of information about the Heiltsuk. More useful is "Kwakiutl Dancing Societies" (1940), in which he describes some aspects of the ceremonies of the Heiltsuk, Oweekeno, and Haisla. Because the dance rituals of these adjacent language groups were very similar, information gathered about any one of them is relevant to the others.

Olson wrote about these three groups as well. In "Notes on the Bella Bella Kwakiutl" (1955), Olson collected information about the original Heiltsuk-speaking "village-tribes," including migrations, crest groups, hereditary ranked names, legends, and brief descriptions of marriage, shamanism, dancing societies, and kinship terminology. There is specific information about old village locations and survivals of indigenous culture, illustrated by the continuity of chiefs' names and ranks from generation to generation. Chiefly names, such as Kahyi't ('Qa'aít) and Wa'wiyala (Waúyala), discussed by Olson in 1955 are the same as those mentioned in Tolmie's accounts of Fort McLoughlin in 1833/34.

The works of Boas, Drucker, and Olson are the primary published sources of ethnographical information about the Heiltsuk. Michael Harkin's dissertation, "Dialogues of History: Transformations and Change in Heiltsuk Culture, 1790–1920," is one of the few recent studies of Heiltsuk history and culture (1988).[7] Other published sources used in this study of the Large Collection deal with the Heiltsuk only in passing and only as they relate to other Northwest Coast groups.

Historical and ethnographic studies of the Heiltsuk are not plentiful; even less has been written about Heiltsuk art. Bella Bella pieces are reproduced in many publications on Northwest Coast art, but to date no single publication has focused on the art of the central coast. Often the place of an artifact's collection rather than of its origin is what appears in museum records. Many Heiltsuk carvings are erroneously attributed to the Kwakwa̱ka̱'wakw, the Haida, the Nuxalk, or the Tsimshian, for the work of Bella Bella artists was admired and obtained (through marriage, purchase, potlatch, or warfare) by other tribal groups. Large's documentation of his Bella Bella collection is immensely useful in identifying these "lost" Heiltsuk works.

The Nuxalk were among those who acknowledged the superior carving skills of the Heiltsuk. According to Nuxalk tradition, this exceptional artistic ability resulted from the union, in the early period of the world, between a Bella Bella woman and Yulätimut, the most powerful of the four supernatural Carpenters who carved out of wood the bodies of mankind's ancestors. Many of the Heiltsuk are thought to be descendants of Yulätimut (McIlwraith 1948, 1:40, 269, 345). Methodist missionary Thomas Crosby was aware of the reputation of the Heiltsuk artists: "With the exception of the Hydas, the Bella Bellas are said to be more clever than the other Coast people in their own crafts, such as making canoes, boxes, and carving wood and stone" (1914:187).

The carved and decorated boxes mentioned by Crosby are examples of art works that were traded from Bella Bella to many other communities. "A large group of boxes and chests . . . originated in Bella Bella, although many of them were collected on other parts of the coast" (Holm 1976:42). Several masks obtained from other coastal groups, and catalogued accordingly, are now thought to have been made at Bella Bella. One such mask (AMNH 16/594) described as Haida (Swanton 1905, pl. 25) was later identified by Holm as possibly Heiltsuk (1976:42).[8] A spectacular transformation mask (CMC VII-B-20) collected by Dr. Israel W. Powell in 1879 on the Queen Charlotte Islands was originally catalogued as Haida. The CMC catalogue entry notes that Peter Macnair and Alan Hoover of the RBCM thought that the mask should be attributed to the Bella Bella on stylistic grounds, and it has appeared in at least one publication as such (Halpin 1986:51). Some pieces catalogued as Nuxalk (e.g., RBCM 218, a coffin box in the shape of a killer whale) also have Heiltsuk characteristics.[9]

The identification of poorly documented Bella Bella objects in museum collections is proceeding as scholars learn to distinguish between several North Wakashan and Nuxalk substyles. Holm has been the most important force in the attempt to differentiate Northwest Coast art styles by tribe, date, and artist. He has addressed issues of connoisseurship in native art studies (1981) and his study of Kwakwaka'wakw carver Willie Seaweed (1983b) is one of the few in-depth studies done to date of the work of a single native artist. Holm has identified certain combinations of forms that characterize some Bella Bella art works (1972, 1976). His notes on Heiltsuk objects in catalogues such as *Form and Freedom* (Holm and Reid 1975) and *The Box of Daylight* (Holm 1983a) further analyse Bella Bella style.

Just as Boas defined the structure of Heiltsuk society in terms of its neighbours, Holm defined Bella Bella sculpture in relation to surrounding groups:

> In an otherwise Bella Coola or Tsimshian-like face a large, somewhat flattened and nearly circular orb is defined by narrow upper cheek and underbrow planes. In more naturalistic masks this may be subtly modeled, whereas in more stylized faces its angularity and boldness approaches the Bella Coola form, but the Bella Coola cheek bulge seldom occurs. [1972:80–81]

Kerfed Boxes, Chest, and Dipper. See Catalogue, Nos. 37–39, 41.

In another article he stated:

> The Bella Bella country [is] an area that is particularly hard to pin down stylis-
> tically because the region of the Northern Kwakiutl [sic] speaking peoples is
> bounded by the strong stylistic areas of the Haida, Tsimshian and Bella Coola,
> and there is considerable merging of the art traditions. Styles seem to take two
> major directions, one . . . in which the sculptural planes are bold and distinct,
> and suggest a northern influenced Bella Coola-Kwakiutl approach, and the
> other a more naturalistic style very [difficult] to distinguish from Haida or
> Tsimshian work. [1976:41]

Holm found two-dimensional design easier to isolate. Speaking of the characteristic
style of a group of painted boxes that he believes were made at Bella Bella and traded
up and down the coast, he observed:

> The details of the style are quite easy to recognize. Some of the basic charac-
> teristics are very thin formlines in a wide open composition, extremely non-
> concentric, *small* inner ovoids and single hatching (that is, hatching in one
> direction only, usually from upper right to lower left) in the secondary U-forms.
> There are many other, more subtle, points of distinction, but this list should suf-
> fice to show that this can be seen as a distinct style of painting. [1981:178]

Peter Macnair, Alan Hoover, and Kevin Neary also briefly described the characteristics
of Bella Bella art in *The Legacy* (1980:37, 48–49). They, too, noted a change in the art
through time:

> Probably about 1865 certain changes in Northern Kwakiutl [sic] design began
> to occur. The majority of pieces produced from this time onwards seem to have
> been manufactured at the village of Bella Bella and appear to represent the out-
> put of that village-specific school of painters. [1980:37]

The Legacy (p. 149) is one of the few catalogues to discuss the work of an individual Bella
Bella artist who is known by name. This is Captain Carpenter (Du'kḷwayella), one of those
whose work was collected by Large. Carpenter is also mentioned in Walbran (1909:152)
and is the only artist in Large's collection to be documented outside Large's writings.

This is the study of a museum collection. Douglas Cole's *Captured Heritage* (1985) and Aldona Jonaitis' *From the Land of the Totem Poles* (1988) help to place Large and his collection within the context of the fever of acquisition that was so much a part of ethnological investigations on the artistically rich Northwest Coast.

Unpublished Sources

Unpublished written sources for this study were found in several archives. In the ROM Normal School file are letters to and from Large concerning the acquisition of his collections by the Ontario Provincial Museum. Letters about the cost and administration of the Bella Bella mission are among the T. S. Egerton Shore papers in the Archives of the United Church of Canada at Victoria University, Toronto. The Toronto Archives of the United Church also has a slim biographical file on Large and the Bella Bella mission, as does the United Church of Canada, B.C. Conference Archives, Vancouver. The latter repository also holds the "Bella Bella Mission Manuscript Journal" (Barner n.d.) which covers the period from 1880 to 1924, as well as files on other Methodist missionaries on the Northwest Coast during Large's time. Archival sources of ethnographic information are Boas' fieldnotes from 1923 and Olson's from 1935 and 1949. These notes contain names of individuals which are not included in the more "objective" published texts (Boas 1923, Olson 1955).

Copies of some of the above material are on file at the Heiltsuk Cultural Education Centre (HCEC) at Waglisla, which has an extensive archive on all aspects of the history and people of Bella Bella. The HCEC collects and maintains records of Heiltsuk oral and written histories, traditions, and language. It also has original manuscripts and copies of manuscripts pertaining to Bella Bella and the Heiltsuk Nation. Its photographic archive contains images of the village and vicinity, and an inventory of slides and photographs of Heiltsuk art. The contribution of the community of Waglisla was also very important to this study (see Acknowledgements). Reports of the death of Heiltsuk culture have certainly been exaggerated, for much traditional knowledge has been retained and the culture is ongoing.

Finally, the most important sources are the Heiltsuk art and artifacts in museum collections, most of which are unpublished. For this study, the Heiltsuk objects in the Royal British Columbia Museum, the University of British Columbia Museum of Anthropology, and the Canadian Museum of Civilization were examined. Of particular importance for this and all studies of Heiltsuk art is the HCEC collection of slides, photographs, and accession records (where available) of Heiltsuk art. Assembled by Jennifer Carpenter, co-ordinator of the HCEC, and Heiltsuk artist Robert Hall, it covers eighteen museums in North America. Although most Bella Bella pieces in these museums are not well documented, they provide the artistic context for Large's collection.

Notes

1. This book grew out of a Master's thesis written for the Department of Interdisciplinary Studies, York University, Toronto (Black 1988). See also Black 1989.

2. Because these ten objects are not stone and bone artifacts, it is assumed that they are not in the ROM's Archaeology collections.

3. The full runs of the *MB* and the *MO* are in the Archives of the United Church of Canada at Victoria University, Toronto. These publications also contain letters from other Methodist missionaries on the Northwest Coast including those of C. M. Tate and W. Raynor who served at Bella Bella.
   Large's son, Dr. Richard Geddes Large (who was born at Bella Bella in 1901) drew from his father's letters in the *MB* and the *MO,* as well as from his own experiences as a doctor at Rivers Inlet, Bella Bella, and Prince Rupert, for his book *Drums and Scalpel* (1968). R. G. Large (letter to the author, 15 December 1984) reported that his father's papers were destroyed in a fire at Port Simpson, so there are few other records of the missionary's activities.

4. For a discussion of two-dimensional design traditions of the Northern and Southern stylistic provinces, see Macnair, Hoover, and Neary (1980:27–42).

5. For a concise explanation of Heiltsuk clans and crests see Hilton 1990.

6. It can be argued that Heiltsuk descent systems were flexible in order to allow marriage with both northern matrilineal groups and southern groups which passed crests and privileges through the male line. The centrally placed Heiltsuk could extend their trade networks and access to resources throughout a wide region by this strategy. Jennifer Carpenter, personal communication, 1990.

7. Harkin uses ethnohistorical and anthropological strategies to define the relationship between Heiltsuk history and Heiltsuk aboriginal cultural categories and conceptual structures. It is interesting to note that Anton Kolstee, in his dissertation on Heiltsuk ceremonial music, similarly emphasizes the "strong relationships between Heiltsuk musical patterning and other systems of relationships in Heiltsuk culture"(1988:iii).

8. Holm (1976:42) says the mask "could be seen as either Bella Bella or Haida."

9. Similar difficulties with identification of regional styles can be seen in studies of the art of the

neighbouring Haisla. For example, a face mask (SAM 91.1.39) once published as Tsimshian has more recently been identified by Alan Sawyer as Haisla. When Sawyer attempted to establish a chronology for Haisla masks through analysis of the style of dated museum specimens, he was able to identify the characteristics of two Haisla substyles, but found that "distinct regional styles and the history of their gradual evolution" had been blurred as the result of the decline of the native populations after European contact and the resulting amalgamation of the remaining groups in a few major centres (Sawyer 1983:143–45). Similar factors, with similar effects, were no doubt present in Heiltsuk art.

3
MISSIONARIES AND COLLECTORS:
THE CONTEXT OF THE LARGE COLLECTION

FIG. 9. *Members of the distinguished Humchitt family of Bella Bella. Photograph by R. W. Large, from "Souvenir of Bella Bella, B.C." Courtesy Royal British Columbia Museum, Victoria. PN 16464.*

THE BELLA BELLA MISSION

The Heiltsuk population was ravaged by the smallpox epidemic of 1862. Survivors eventually moved to McLoughlin Bay to join those Heiltsuk already settled around the site of the old Hudson's Bay Company post (see Fig. 3). When Reverend Thomas Crosby visited the area in 1880 from his base at Port Simpson, he found the "Millbank Sound Indians . . . scattered in a number of villages within ten or fifteen miles of the Fort" (1914:183). In May 1880 Crosby sent William Henry Pierce, a teacher who was half Tsimshian, to start a school at Bella Bella. Reverend C. M. Tate and his wife arrived in September of that year and in November the first convert at Bella Bella, a man known as Bella Bella Jack, was baptized with the Christian name of Arthur Ebbstone (Large, R. G., 1968:8; Tate 1917:10). Tate wrote that at Bella Bella it had been his "privilege to witness some of the grandest transformation scenes that have ever taken place on this coast" (*MB* 2, no. 1[1904]:181). By 1884, when Tate left, he testified that the "material aspect of the village [was] entirely changed" and that one hundred people had been converted (*MO* 23, no. 2[1904]:35). Among them were Chief Charley of Bella Bella, the ʼUyalitx̌v chief Humpshet (Humchitt) and his people (see Fig. 9), and the young ʼQvúqvaẏaítx̌v chief known as Wockite from Milbanke Sound and his people (Crosby 1914:186; Harkin 1988:236).[1]

Some time in the 1880s Humchitt, the head Heiltsuk chief, moved into Bella Bella from his village about 11 km away. On Christmas Day, 1882, Humchitt gave a feast to which he invited all the people of Bella Bella and the surrounding villages.[2] At this feast hostilities that had existed between Humchitt and Chief Charley were resolved (*MB* 9, no. 1[1913]:77),[3] clearing the way for the amalgamation of the Heiltsuk villages.

"What incorporation into mission villages fundamentally meant," according to historian Rolf Knight (1978:244), "was an extensive (if not total) reorganization of Indian life." For example, marriage alliances were important means of transferring property and intangible forms of wealth such as names and ceremonial privileges, and serial "investment" marriages were the rule among the Heiltsuk chiefly class (Olson 1955). Mrs. Moses Knight of Bella Bella told Olson that the first missionary there (Tate) "took away all excess wives from the chiefs and kept them at the mission" (1955:343).

Despite such radical changes enforced by the missionaries, the presence of the Methodist mission and school and the prospect of medical facilities to come were strong incentives for the Heiltsuk to move into Bella Bella. That Heiltsuk reasons for moving to Bella Bella had little to do with the missionaries' agenda of social and religious reform is clear from the ethnographic and historical record. New forms of knowledge and wealth, and new forms of power—temporal, spiritual, and supernatural (náwálakv)—were sought by the Heiltsuk in the Methodist village. For example, because the Heiltsuk conceived of "the cause and cure of any sickness [as] simply different modalities of the same power," the Methodist missionary doctors were the logical healers for those threatened by new and often fatal diseases (such as smallpox, scarlet fever, measles, and whooping cough) brought about by the power of white people (Harkin 1988:199).

Dr. J. A. Jackson, the first medical missionary at Bella Bella, arrived in 1897. He initiated the relocation of the community to Waglisla because the site on McLoughlin Bay had become overcrowded and there was not enough land to build the single-family homes that the missionaries thought were essential to Christian life. The people's decision to move may have been precipitated by the destruction of Chief Núṅukvas's home, which had been built on pilings at the water's edge, in a severe storm. After this unfortunate event the Heiltsuk asked the resident trader to allow them to build on the large vacant section of land that the Hudson's Bay Company held in the centre of the village (Fig. 10). When he refused they decided to move to the new location (Gladstone n.d.; HCEC ms. CB 2a).

FIG. 10. *View of the north end of Bella Bella (Qélc) in 1884 shows that the great lineage houses seen in Fig. 6 were rapidly being replaced by single-family dwellings. The Hudson's Bay Company refused to allow the Heiltsuk to build on the vacant land around the trading store, seen here on the left. Courtesy British Columbia Provincial Archives and Records Service, Victoria. Chittenden photograph, 1884. PABC HP 10399, A-3977.*

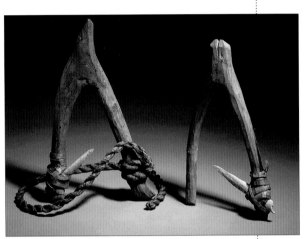

Fish Hooks. See Catalogue, No. 73.

Mrs. Moses Knight remembered that "many of the people were dissatisfied with the way things were" at McLoughlin Bay. "Some were resentful of the chief. . . . Among other things, they said he bit much too savagely in the Tanis dance" (Olson 1955:343).[4] The oldest chief did not make the move to the new village; he was still living at Old Town in 1903 (*MB* 1, no. 3[1903]:299), so perhaps the move also represented a change in the village hierarchy: "Model mission villages at times entailed as much a reorganization of local political power as anything else" (Knight 1978:245).

The chiefs had opposed the efforts of the first Heiltsuk convert to Christianity, Bella Bella Jack, to promote Christianity in the village but they permitted the foundation of a Methodist mission in 1880. Both the ʼUyalitx̌v chief, Humchitt, and the ambitious young ʼQvúqvaẏaítx̌v chief, Wockite, apparently trying to outbid one another, offered to pay Reverend Crosby piles of blankets and furs if he would send a teacher immediately to their villages (Crosby 1914:185–86). When Reverend Tate arrived at Bella Bella six months later, he was officially welcomed by the chief and allowed to live in Chief Humchitt's house for six weeks until the mission house was built (*MB* 7, no. 3[1911]:536).

One of the reasons for this change in attitude in 1880 may have been the surveys and other activities of the Indian Reserve Commission, which eventually resulted, in August 1882, in the allotment of twelve reserves for the Heiltsuk people living at Bella Bella and six reserves for the Heiltsuk (ʼQvúqvaẏaítx̌v) still living at the villages of ʼQábá (Kokyet) on Yeo Island and ʼQvúqvaí (Koqui) at the head of Gale Creek.[5] The Heiltsuk leaders may have hoped that an English-speaking missionary in the village would help them to interpret and deal with an increasingly regulatory government (a law prohibiting the potlatch was passed in 1884 and a series of restrictive fishing regulations came into effect in 1888 and 1889 [Stevenson n.d., pp. 95–98]). Many missionaries did support the native communities against the government. Tate sided "with the Indians in land claims" (*MB* 9, no. 1[1913]:76), and thought that the "church should be sure Indians get fair treatment and get enough land" (*MB* 6, no. 3[1910]:520). Tate and Dr. Horace C. Wrinch, a missionary to the Tsimshian based at Hazelton, believed that the fishery regulations were made to favour corporations and were unfair to the natives (*MB* 3, no. 3[1906]:815). Both spoke out on behalf of their villages.

Despite the generally favourable attitude on the part of the missionaries, some First Nations people thought that the missionaries were in league with the government to take away their land: "Some say there is a deep-laid scheme, part of it being to send the missionaries first to quiet the Indians, get them civilized, teach them it is wrong to fight, and to obey laws, etc., and then the settlers come in after and take possession of their territory," wrote Wrinch from Hazelton in 1909. "The outlook is not rosy [for the Indians]," he concluded; "the present time seems a great perplexity to them" (*MB* 6, no. 2[1909]:357).

The increasing non-native presence on the central coast and the establishment of canneries on the Fraser (1870), Skeena (1877), and Nass (1881) rivers and closer to home in Rivers Inlet (1882) and Namu (1896) created new problems for the Heiltsuk along with economic opportunities. W. H. Pierce (who started the Bella Bella school in 1880), when serving at Kishpiax (Kispiox) on the upper Skeena in 1904, indicated that there was a native awareness of the potential dangers of encroaching Euro-Canadian industry when he recorded that one of the non-Christian Tsimshian men brought three of his children to join the Methodist temperance organization, the Band of Hope, because he knew that the railroad construction would "bring bad white men, with their fire water, so he [wanted] his children to be prepared to meet them" (*MB* 2, no. 3[1905]:557). Knight observed that "many Indian leaders who opted for and led their followers into mission systems were undoubtedly moved by the need to find new defenses to the massive changes growing around them" (1978:245).

Three small specimens collected by Large between 1899 and 1901 relate specifically to the missionization of the Bella Bella people. A spinning disc (NS 23104) was collected from Arthur Ebbstone (1846–1903), also known as Bella Bella Jack, the first Bella Bella Christian. In the late 1870s, on their way back from a stint of seasonal work in the sawmills of Puget Sound, Ebbstone and another Heiltsuk man, George Blucher, had espoused Christianity at the Pandora Street Methodist Church mission hall for Indians in Victoria. Blucher soon gave up Methodism because it prohibited him from taking part in traditional ceremonies, but Ebbstone, who was perhaps not of the chiefly class and therefore not required to fulfil obligations within the dance and potlatch system, continued to profess Christianity in spite of the fact that some of the chiefs threatened to kill him (*MO* 23, no. 2[1904]:35). He kept a Bible, although he could not read it, and raised a flag on a pole outside his house every Sunday.[6] When Crosby first visited Bella Bella in 1880, it was Ebbstone who welcomed him. According to Reverend R. B. Beavis, Ebbstone lived "a consistent and Christian life and for many years was the efficient watchman of Bella Bella" (Beavis n.d.). When Large arrived at Bella Bella in December 1898, he found this "simple, warm hearted, unlearned Indian . . . still seeking to lead the people to Christ."

Ebbstone rang the church bell, made the fires, gave out the hymn books and Bibles,

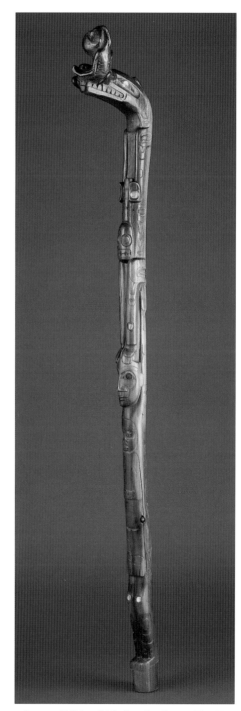

Cane or Talking Stick. See Catalogue, No. 61.

and showed people to their seats in the church (*MB* 1, no. 4 [1904]:418). These roles indicate that the mission enabled him to assume a new kind of power and prominence in Heiltsuk society. In fact, Harkin (1988:253) suggests that "for the Heiltsuk, the attraction of education was the opportunity to gain access to the missionary power," which is conceived of as a form of náwálakv (supernatural power).[7] In Harkin's interpretation, the Bible that Ebbstone brought from Victoria was an objective form of that power. When, shortly after his return from Victoria, Ebbstone went alone to the mountain behind the village to pray that a teacher would come to Bella Bella (Tate 1917:10), he was following a traditional method of acquiring náwálakv through seclusion and meditation. One kind of acquired náwálakv was the power of prophecy; the subsequent arrival of the teacher W. H. Pierce was an indication that Ebbstone had acquired that power. Ebbstone's new Euro-Canadian clothes were another sign of náwálakv—a changed appearance or new outward form. His new name and new pole (although a flag pole rather than a totem pole) were also traditional Heiltsuk indications of access to supernatural power and the change in social status that accompanies it (see Harkin 1988:232-33, 255). Ebbstone, and no doubt all of Large's congregation, fitted Methodist forms into Heiltsuk social and conceptual structures.

The other objects that recall the history of the Methodist mission are a "stone axe, probably a whetstone (klah-qua-bah'-la)" (NS 23126) and a "stone paint pot" (NS 23l30). Both were obtained from Reverend George Edgar of China Hat (Klemtu), a cordwood station on Swindle Island north of Bella Bella. Along with Bella Coola, Rivers Inlet, Kokite (Kokyet), Nolo (ʼNúlú), Namu, and Goose Island, China Hat was part of the original Bella Bella mission field in the 1880s (*MB* 8, no. 3[1911]:1311). Edgar was sent there as a teacher in 1897. By 1900 when Large opened the new church at China Hat, it was an "earnest Christian village" of 120 Kitisoo Tsimshian and Heiltsuk-speaking ˇXíx̌ís people who occupied fifteen houses and ran two trading stores (*MO* 20, no. 2[1901]:35).

Edgar was a Tsimshian from Hartley Bay whom the Indian Agent considered "an example of what civilization and a practical training will do among the Indians" (DIA 1906:247). The first Heiltsuk (ˇXíx̌ís) Christian at China Hat, Jim Starr (1848–1918), had impressed Reverend Crosby by travelling 160 km to Port Simpson to get nails to finish "the little church he was building all by himself for his people, in faith that the missionary would come to them soon" (*MB* 2, no. 4[1905]:812). Starr and his wife (Fig. 11) moved to Bella Bella when the mission was established there and became Large's greatest supporters and truest friends (*MB* 1, no. 2[1903]:233). Alfred Brown, a Heiltsuk Christian from Bella Bella, later went to China Hat as a missionary-teacher, so the close association

FIG. 11. *Mr. and Mrs. James Starr, active members of the Methodist Church at Bella Bella. Courtesy Royal British Columbia Museum, Victoria. Photograph by R. W. Large, from "Souvenir of Bella Bella, B.C." PN 16470.*

between the Methodist villages was maintained (*MB* 9, no. 1[1913]:78).[8]

When Large moved to Waglisla early in 1901, "a large number" of people were already living there (*MO* 20, no. 2[1901]:47). The new village was much admired by George Morrow, the Indian Agent:

> The Bella Bella Indians deserve special mention for their pluck and persever-
> ance as shown by them a year or two ago when they removed from the old vil-
> lage of Bella Bella, about two miles further north on the reserve. They have
> built a fine village, good houses, a church, an hospital and a school, in fact work
> has been accomplished by the Indians of this village in two years that it has
> taken many years to accomplish in other places. [DIA 1903:297]

In 1906 it was reported that the buildings of Bella Bella were splendid and sanitary conditions were good. The people, all of whom were at least nominally Methodist, enjoyed good health, although it was admitted that there was an exceedingly high death rate due to tuberculosis. Their attendance at day school was fair, they were industrious and progressive, and they exhibited favourable temperance and morality. Reverend B. C. Freeman compared the model Christian village of Bella Bella with the "heathen" Kwakwaka'wakw village of Newitti, "where steamboats do not call," where families were "blighted," and the people's lives seemed "hopeless" because, unlike the Bella Bella people, they did not have "a teacher to guide them" (*MB* 2, no. 3[1905]:578).

By 1907, with a population of 318, Bella Bella had become the second largest Methodist village on the coast.[9] Among the residents, Large counted "20 rough carpenters, 10 boat builders of very credible boats, 1 lighthouse keeper, 4 wood carvers, 2 silversmiths, 2 small store-keepers, a banker who lends money to other Indians at 50% interest, [and] 2 young men who count fish at canneries during the season." There were sixty-three "good houses," a steam sawmill (native-owned and operated), a recreation hall, a day school, a mission house, a hospital (the only one between Nanaimo and Port Simpson), a wharf, and a warehouse. A plank walk 6 m wide ran through the village and was lit by oil lamps on winter nights (*MO* 26, no. 2[1907]:6; Fig. 12). By 1909 there were five well-stocked native-owned stores. At Christmas, Large noted with pleasure, that these establishments displayed

> in more or less pro- and con-fusions,—oranges, apples, nuts, candies, toys,
> gum, fire-crackers, candles for illuminating the windows, soda water, prize

FIG. 12. *On the main street of Bella Bella (Waglisla) in 1913. The boardwalk and the "grand new houses" built in European style can be seen in the background. Courtesy Royal British Columbia Museum, Victoria. McKenna Land Commission photograph. PN 12397.*

pop-corn packages, onions, potatoes and cabbage, dress goods, notions and staple groceries—with tissue paper bells, chains and garlands over-hanging all. [*MB* 6, no. 3(1910):515]

The eighteen-piece Bella Bella Cornet Band (Fig. 13) was one of the best on the coast and furnished music "for all weddings, funerals, village feasts and other celebrations" (*MB* 8, no. 1[1911]:1303).[10] There was a choir of between twenty and thirty well-rehearsed voices, and an active branch of the Methodist Epworth League. The Bella Bella people contributed substantial amounts of money and free labour to the church, school, and hospital.

Three years after Large went to Bella Bella he sent his first Northwest Coast collection to the Toronto Normal School Museum (see p. 15, n. 1). Although he did not record his reasons for making this collection, a review of the intellectual climate of the time and of the activities of artifact collectors at Bella Bella and elsewhere on the coast will illuminate some of his concerns and place his collection within the context of the scramble for artifacts that characterized the museum period of anthropology (see Stocking 1985; Cole 1985).

FIG. 13. *The Bella Bella Cornet Band. The photograph appears to have been taken on board a ship, perhaps en route to a band performance or musical competition. Courtesy Royal British Columbia Museum, Victoria. Photograph by R. W. Large, from "Souvenir of Bella Bella, B.C." PN 16471.*

Whistle. See Catalogue, No. 68.

Intellectual Climate

In August 1897, a year and a half before Large arrived in Bella Bella, the village had been visited by the members of the Jesup North Pacific Expedition: Franz Boas and Harlan I. Smith of the American Museum of Natural History (AMNH), and Livingston Farrand of Columbia University.[11] On his way from the Skeena River to Rivers Inlet, Boas spent only a short time at Bella Bella, but Farrand, accompanied by native scholar George Hunt of the Kwakw<u>a</u>ka'wakw village of Fort Rupert, stayed in the village for the rest of the summer to study the social organization of the Heiltsuk (Boas 1974:110–16).[12] Boas seems to have preferred to work in the traditional village of the Oweekeno at Rivers Inlet rather than in the Christianized and rapidly changing community of Bella Bella. Hunt's role probably included that of interpreter, although Boas mentioned that Hunt (who was Kwaḱwala-speaking) had trouble with the Heiltsuk language (1932:vi–vii).

The expedition was organized and financed by Morris K. Jesup, the president of the board of trustees of the AMNH, to investigate the Asiatic origins of the North American Indians and their migration routes from the old world (as well as, of course, to collect artifacts for the museum). The question of the origin of the aboriginal peoples of North America figured prominently in evolutionist debates of the nineteenth century; the AMNH hoped that scientific study of the physical characteristics of the Northwest Coast people and documentation of their culture through collections of mythology and artifacts would provide some answers.

The approach taken by the Jesup Expedition was a relatively new one for ethnologists. In the first half of the nineteenth century knowledge of the indigenous peoples of North America had been gathered by dedicated amateurs loosely associated with museums. Boas was instrumental in bringing ethnology into the realm of professional science. He stressed the importance of empirical, inductive fieldwork. All the minute details of the daily life of a people, as well as their art, their ceremony, and their mythology, were important. If possible, this information was to be obtained from native informants in their own language. But, although Boas recorded the histories and the traditional beliefs and technologies of native communities, he chose not to document the modernization going on in villages such as Bella Bella.

At the turn of the century there was an urgency to this collection of information about the indigenous peoples. In 1903 Boas predicted that the North American tribes would be extinct within twenty years (quoted in Hinsley 1981:277). It was certainly true that the Northwest Coast native communities that had survived the epidemics and the social and political upheavals of the previous fifty years were changing rapidly. The "pure" aboriginal culture longed for by early twentieth-century ethnologists was increasingly hard to find, if indeed it had ever existed.[13]

According to the nineteenth-century doctrine of Social Darwinism, the death of North American native culture was inevitable; the weak and primitive native societies would naturally be consumed by the superior, more advanced civilization of Europe. In 1878 the American evolutionist Lewis Henry Morgan stated that the American Indian must be understood not as a racial category but as a savage state of human culture (quoted in Hinsley 1981:150). Boas and the other expedition members were determined to salvage as much of this disappearing phase of culture as possible.

In Toronto at this time David Boyle was guiding the Ontario Provincial Museum (see p. 15, n. 1) in the establishment of an ethnological collection. Boyle's personal interest was archaeology, but his admiration for the ethnological collections in European museums prompted him to advertise for artifacts in 1900. "A stream of letters soliciting donations flowed out of his office to various museums and to religious missions all over the world" (Killan 1983:111). Boyle's letters brought results and in 1903 a room was set aside in the Toronto museum for ethnological contributions. The *Annual Archaeological Report,* which Boyle had been publishing since 1887 (Killan 1983:111), now included articles by both Boas (1906) and Large (1905).[14]

Large's contributions to Boyle's project were in the tradition of the dedicated amateur ethnologists of the nineteenth century. Missionaries had long been encouraged in this role. For example, in 1851 the American philologist William Walden Turner advised the secretary of the Smithsonian Institution that the only men suitable to study the "mental idiosyncrasies" of the Indians were the missionaries who spent long years among them, "qualified by education and sustained by motives of benevolence" (quoted in Hinsley 1981:50). Large was better educated than many of his fellow missionaries and, although an amateur in an increasingly professional field, he was interested in contributing to the developing Canadian anthropological collections. Part of his motivation was no doubt financial; Methodist publications such as the *Missionary Outlook* and the *Missionary Bulletin* reveal that fundraising for the construction of mission buildings was a preoccupation for Large and his fellow Methodists. Nevertheless, despite his isolated position at Bella Bella, he was aware of the intellectual currents of his time and, like many of the others associated with the British Columbia missions, he was informed about some of the concerns of the new science of anthropology.

As amateur observers, missionaries concerned themselves with current debates

concerning the origins, migrations, and impending fate of aboriginal peoples. Professor E. Odlum, a former missionary to Japan, pondered the origins of the British Columbia natives. Writing to Crosby in 1910, he stated: "The Indians of the Alaska and British Columbia coasts are, in my humble opinion, asiatic and largely Japanese" (Crosby 1914:399).[15] Reverend B. C. Freeman, who served at Skidegate from 1893 to 1903, wrote a tract entitled "The Origin of the Haida in Alaska," in which he outlined a theory of migration to the Queen Charlotte Islands (Freeman n.d.). The Haida creation story, in which the first men were fathered by Raven and born from a shell on the beach at Naikun (Rose Spit), was never part of the scientific discussion.

Odlum saw the Indians as artless, living simply off the land and sea: "They are true children of nature and are as independent of artificial aids from Caucasian civilization as it is possible to be. The forest, seashore and open ocean give them all they need for food, shelter and clothing." They were "saturated and gifted with imagery and ornate speech," and they were "the most natural congregational singers" (Crosby 1914:399). The highly developed food-gathering technologies of the First Nations were overlooked and their elaborate arts were seen as natural talents of a simple people. Similarly, Reverend Frank Hardy, who succeeded Freeman at Skidegate, found "no splendor of an ancient civilization, no natural history, no wealth of language and literature, but rather the remnant of a barbarous race" on the Queen Charlotte Islands, the ancestral territory of the Haida. Today, Haida art and culture are respected and admired, but Hardy was of the opinion that "the race is not fit for absorption, and is moving towards extinction" (*MB* 3, no. 3[1906]:504, 831).

Other missionaries thought that the civilizing power of Christianity was the agent that would prevent the extinction of the natives by bringing them to maturity. In 1899 the British Columbia Indians were described in a *Missionary Outlook* column as "without any well-defined ideas of God or religion . . . without civilization," and it was concluded that "until the Gospel reaches them, theirs is a truly savage life" (*MO* 18, no. 2[1899]:33–34). The state of "civilization," which involved European ideals of work, thrift, cleanliness, dependability and humility on the part of those of the lower classes, was conceived of as a condition of Christianity. Native survival was thought to be "a question of elevating the race" (*MO* 24, no. 10[1905]:223).

The missionaries shared with Morgan and other evolutionists the idea that the aboriginal peoples were on a lower rung of the evolutionary ladder: "In regard to the duties and responsibilities of civilization, the Indians are children, and for a time, have to be treated as such," instructed the *Missionary Outlook* in a column titled "Our Question

Mask. See Catalogue, No. 60.

Drawer." "The object of schools, Indian institutions, etc. is to train them up to be men and women" (*MO* 18, no. 1[1899]:5–6). The missionaries at Bella Bella do not seem to have questioned this. Tate referred to the natives as "these simple-minded people" (*MB* 6, no. 3[1910]:519). Dr. W. Raynor, who filled in for Large from November 1906 to June 1907, cautioned, "We should not forget that in dealing with the Indians we are dealing with children" (*MB* 4, no. 2[1907]:554).

Large himself stated that the Indians "resemble children" (*MB* 1, no. 1[1903]:83); they had "not yet the higher mental recreations within their reach" (*MO* 20, no. 3[1901]:55). But even if he was sometimes amused at "the blundering way in which they advance," he was certain that they were making progress—in his terms. He viewed their enthusiasm for new technology in the form of gasoline-powered boats as a positive "stage in their evolution" (*MB* 6, no. 3[1910]:516–17), and was confident that they would eventually outgrow their "superstitions." Nonetheless, Large seems to have recognized that the rapid changes at Bella Bella were stressful and problematic. The Heiltsuk people were, he thought, "in a dangerous period between a lower and a higher civilization" (*MB* 5, no. 4[1909]:713). Large's biases and his ignorance of the complexities of Heiltsuk culture are apparent in these opinions. It is significant, however, that Large recognized that the Heiltsuk people of Bella Bella, among whom he lived for twelve years, were in a period of cultural *change* rather than in decline.

COLLECTING AT BELLA BELLA

By the time Large arrived at Bella Bella, the village had been visited by a number of artifact collectors. In 1875 James Swan of Port Townsend sent a shipment, which included Bella Bella artifacts, to the Smithsonian Institution. The collection had been acquired through a Hudson's Bay Company trader at Victoria and included "ancient relics" (mainly stone tools) as well as "imitation[s] of old relics" such as wooden halibut hooks, wood and bone tools, spears, paddles, and whistles.[16] The Smithsonian also received a Bella Bella wooden and copper dance fan (NMNH 20636) from Swan in 1877 (see No. 51) and a group of beautifully carved model poles (NMNH 74743–74747) in December 1884 (Cole 1985:46). The well-carved "imitations" indicate that there was an active curio trade at Bella Bella before and during the residency of the first missionary (1880–1884).

In only an hour, on 13 September 1881, J. Adrian Jacobsen, who was collecting for the Royal Ethnographic Museum (Museum für Völkerkunde) in Berlin, was able to purchase a number of important artifacts at "the impressive principal village of the Bella Bella." He was particularly impressed with a chief's seat and "since it was not possible to buy the piece, . . . ordered a similar one from the most renowned wood carver among the Bella Bella" (MfV IVA 2475–2477). A cedar canoe was also purchased, perhaps from the same carver, as well as "numerous artistically carved wooden clappers and rattles," "a carved chief's staff," and a "beautifully carved food box" (Jacobsen 1977:10). It appears that both old and new carvings of high quality were readily available for purchase at Bella Bella at this time.

J. Adrian's brother, Fillip Jacobsen, also travelled to Bella Bella to collect artifacts. He was there in 1884 and again in 1893 when he purchased a house frontal pole (RBCM 3) from a chief at Old Bella Bella as well as a large collection of old masks and ceremonial objects now in the Royal British Columbia Museum (Cole 1985:67).

The Indian Commissioner for British Columbia, Dr. Israel W. Powell, was an active collector for both American and Canadian museums. (The transformation mask he collected on the Queen Charlotte Islands in 1879 has been mentioned on p. 23.) In 1883 the AMNH received a 9-m canoe from him. Although there is some confusion about the origin of this canoe, its decoration is in the Bella Bella style; Cole (1985:84) strongly suggested that it is the one that Powell mentioned having seen near Bella Bella in 1879. The Heiltsuk masks and cedar-bark head rings acquired by the AMNH from George Hunt in 1899 (AMNH 16/4736, 16/4740, 16/4732–4735) may have been collected by Hunt at Bella Bella in 1897 during the Jesup Expedition. A mask from Bella Bella (AMNH 16/962) was purchased for the AMNH by Boas in Victoria in 1894. Lieutenant George T. Emmons sent Bella Bella objects to the AMNH in 1884 and 1893, and to the Museum of the American Indian in 1885 (NMAI 11/3866–3868).[17]

In 1897 George A. Dorsey and James Deans, working on behalf of the Field Columbian Museum (now the Field Museum of Natural History [FMNH]), raided two burial grounds at Bella Bella, taking skeletons and a coffin box (Cole 1985:173–75).[18] At the time Large was not yet in the village, but later he would certainly have come into contact with collectors such as Dr. Charles Frederick Newcombe, who provided the Field Museum with Bella Bella artifacts in 1903 and 1906 (FMNH 19938, 19978, 85058), and Emmons who again sent Bella Bella objects to the MAI in 1906 (NMAI 9749, 9772).

Model Totem Poles. See Catalogue, Nos. 20–21.

COLLECTING BY MISSIONARIES

A contemporary Haida chief has said that "the church sold dancing gear . . . to museums and built churches with the money" (Low 1982:35).[19] It is true that many Northwest Coast missionaries were involved in the artifact market. But they rarely mentioned it in their writings, and it is not clear whether money earned from sales of art and artifacts went to the native people, the missions, or the missionaries themselves. (According to the *Western Methodist Recorder*, missionaries were very poorly paid [Barraclough 1902:5].) Neither is the method of acquisition always discernible. Artifacts may have been purchased by the missionaries, given as donations to the fundraising efforts of the missions, and/or traded for medical or other services.

What is clear is that missionaries were active and enthusiastic artifact collectors and that the nature of their collections was determined to a large extent by First Nations people who controlled the collecting process. Unlike anthropological collectors, missionaries did not have well-defined collecting strategies. They took what was available in their villages and what the people chose to offer them.

Some of the objects became available because of radical changes in native life enforced by the missions; others were newly made and indicative of contemporary native concerns. Indeed, traditional arts such as wood and silver carving and basketry were promoted by the missionaries. At the yearly fall fair at the Methodist village of Kitamaat, for example, prizes were awarded for the best cedar-bark mats and baskets woven in the traditional manner (Raley 1904a). As well as being a factor in the Methodist ideal of pious industriousness, indigenous skills were seen as a means by which First Nations people could become Canadian workers. "The Indian who is able, with rude tools, to carve skilfully totem poles in slate, stone, and wood, or execute graceful designs on silver and gold," wrote Reverend George H. Raley, "with modern tools and careful technical training will make a skilful mechanic, carpenter, and joiner" (Raley 1917:6).

One of the first missionary collectors was Thomas Crosby. Crosby arrived at Port Simpson in 1874 and the next year sold material to James Swan, the agent for the Smithsonian Institution. Crosby apparently maintained "a sort of museum" at Port Simpson, where he displayed some of the poles and ceremonial objects discarded by the newly Christianized Tsimshian. He seems to have actively sought customers, for he persuaded native craftsmen to repaint an old pole and house front so that they would be more attractive to museums (Cole 1985:22, 29–30). In 1908 George Heye of the Museum of the American Indian purchased a large collection from Crosby, who was then at the

Fig. 14. *Tsimshian stone mask
acquired by the collector Alphonse
Pinart from the missionary at
Metlakatla on the Nass River.
Courtesy Musée de l'Homme, Paris.
MH 81.22.1.*

Coqualeetza Residential School at Sardis. Large had heard that the collection was a good one and urged Boyle to purchase it for the OPM. Boyle went to British Columbia to see the collection, which he pronounced "not large but comprehensive," and made what he thought was a good offer for it, but Crosby turned him down. One assumes that the "extravagantly high" price Crosby was asking for his artifacts was paid by Heye.[20]

In the early 1880s, the cooperative store at the Anglican missionary William Duncan's model village of Metlakatla sold argillite and silver carvings to tourists who stopped there on the way to Alaska.[21] Duncan also "reintroduced old crafts such as hat-making which might find a market locally or as curios in Victoria" (Usher 1981:144). The remarkable "sighted twin" stone mask (Fig. 14) now in the Museé de l'Homme, Paris (MH 81.22.1), was purchased by Alphonse Pinart, a French traveller, amateur anthro-pologist, and artifact collector, from "a protestant pastor" at Metlakatla, no doubt William Duncan (Cole 1985:52).[22]

Anglican missionaries associated with the London-based Church Missionary Society sent artifacts home to England. For example, in 1898 the British Museum in London pur-chased a shipment of forty objects, including a model of a Haida house, from Reverend Keen of Masset (BM 1898:1–40).[23] Reverend R. H. Hall of Alert Bay seems to have been an active collector. He sent a number of shipments to the Church Missionary Society and also to the Pitt Rivers Museum (Cole 1985:292, 232, 186).

Some missionaries were occasional suppliers of material to the professional collec-tors. A priest at the Nuu-chah-nulth village of Nootka (Yuquot) solicited artifacts on behalf of J. Adrian Jacobsen, who after his 1881 visit to Bella Bella (p. 42) continued to travel and collect artifacts on the coast until 1883. The Reverend P. Charles at Clayoquot (another Nuu-chah-nulth village), helped Newcombe acquire native objects in 1903. In 1905 the MAI received material from Reverend S. S. Osterhout, who was the Methodist missionary on the Nass River (1893–1898) and at Port Simpson (1898–1903) (Osterhout n.d.), and the Denver Art Museum has a small wooden ladle with a carved skull in the bowl (DAM 1942.251/QBB-3-G) that was collected by a woman missionary at Bella Bella in the winter of 1896/97 (perhaps Miss Reinhardt, a schoolteacher, who stayed alone at the mission through the winter of 1895/96 or 1896/97). A shaman's whistle and charm in the NMAI were acquired by Emmons, probably in 1885, from a Reverend Tait (NMAI 11/3859–3860). This is probably C. M. Tate, because the pieces are described as Bella Bella (see p. 78).

Other missionaries were themselves major collectors. Dr. Horace C. Wrinch was the Methodist missionary at Hazelton from 1902 to 1936 (Wrinch n.d.). His collection of 363 objects, made between 1900 and 1930, is in the Canadian Museum of Civilization.[24] The Collison collection now in the University of British Columbia Museum of Anthropology (UBCMOA) was amassed by Reverend W. H. Collison, the Anglican missionary at Metlakatla, Kincolith, and Masset, and his son, Reverend W. E. Collison (UBCMOA 1975:35; Cole 1985:243). Collison assisted Emmons with his collecting as well.

Reverend George H. Raley, while serving with the Methodist mission at Kitamaat, Port Simpson, and Sardis, acquired a collection of about 800 pieces (now in the UBC-MOA) which he sold to Colonel Victor Spencer, a member of a prominent British Columbia family, in 1934 for display in Vancouver (Matthews 1934). Raley seems to have looked on the artifacts he collected as decorative curiosities, a view no doubt shared by many missionary collectors. For example, three old tánís masks that Raley acquired (UBCMOA A1882–A1884) had been taken from the burial cave of a Kitlope shaman about 1897. At the Kitamaat mission, they were displayed as curios. Raley (1902b) wrote that the masks "worn by the cannibals, though rather gruesome, grace the walls of the study at the mission house." At Port Simpson, where he moved in 1907, Raley operated some sort of store that sold artifacts in connection with the mission. Reverend C. S. Reddick, travelling with Raley on board the mission ship *Udal* in 1909, mentioned that at China Hat (Klemtu) "Mr. Raley had picked up a few bones [boxes?] for his curiosity shop" (Matthews 1934; UBCMOA 1975:32). Unfortunately, Reddick does not elaborate. A comment by Raley suggests that spoons were perhaps a specialty of the shop: "There is no finer curio collection than one of Indian spoons—wooden, bone or horn, ivory and silver; plain, painted, or carved . . . they make most unique souvenirs" (*MO* 21, no. 7[1902]:146).

The collecting of myths as well as objects was emphasized by professionals such as Boas, but only a few missionaries recorded native legends and beliefs. Crosby (1914:100–111) published a group of stories collected by his daughter, Jessie.[25] Ralph Maud (1982:16) observed that these were "slender offerings," neither collected nor presented in the rigorous manner prescribed by Boas. Reverend J. C. Spencer (Methodist) of Bella Coola published an unusually comprehensive list of dances and feasts, excerpted from a booklet entitled "The Potlatch" (*MB* 3, no. 3[1906]:486–88). Reverend D. Jennings (Methodist) of Port Essington wrote a short explanation of Tsimshian crest names and divisions (*MO* 20, no. 4[1901]:79). Because this kind of specific ethnological information is rare in missionary publications, Large's records and anecdotes about the traditional beliefs of the residents of Bella Bella, along with his collection of objects from the village, are particularly valuable for the study of turn-of-the-century culture in a Christianized native community.

Ladle and Wooden Skull. See Catalogue, No. 50.

Large's Northwest Coast Collections

Large sent three lots of objects to the Ontario Provincial Museum. His first shipment from Bella Bella arrived in Toronto at the end of 1901 and was entered into the Normal School catalogue as numbers NS 23101–23193 on 1 January 1902. There were ninety-two objects in this shipment, of which sixty are still in the Ethnology collections of the Royal Ontario Museum's Department of Anthropology. Large sent four more boxes of "Indian specimens" to Toronto in September 1906 along with an inventory/price list. This shipment is not as well documented as the first because Large planned to "inspect the specimens" during his stay in Toronto on his way to New York City. (He was on furlough from Bella Bella from November 1906 until June 1907 and spent most of his sabbatical visiting American medical facilities.) The shipment was received by the museum in October and Large did visit Toronto that winter, but there is no record of any additional information about the objects from Large. In a letter to David Boyle of the OPM he wrote: "Some [of these specimens] are duplicates, but others quite rare and I was much pleased to find they had not yet been picked up."[26] These objects were catalogued in November 1906 as numbers NS 27847–27977. Fifty-nine of the objects are in ROM Ethnology. On 23 November 1906, just before he left Bella Bella, Large wrote to Boyle that he had

> just packed another couple of boxes with some odds and ends I was able to collect. When the people found I was going home for a visit they brought out everything pretty much they had. I did not think there was as much in town, and some of the specimens are very good ones.[27]

Although the letter reveals how Large acquired much of the collection (he acquired what the Heiltsuk were willing to let him have), no information was enclosed with these boxes either, because Large planned to be in Toronto himself to help with the unpacking. The OPM accession list notes that Large's third shipment was part of the October 1906 purchase, but the artifacts were not catalogued until April 1907. They were entered as numbers NS 28196–28256, and nineteen of these objects are in ROM Ethnology. ROM 28307 (No. 117 in this catalogue), a wooden stick described in the accession list as "for drying nets, etc.," was probably also part of this shipment. Its catalogue number is not in the same sequence as the others (it is a little farther along in the list) but Large is named as the source.

Five undocumented objects in ROM Ethnology that should, on stylistic grounds, be included with the documented objects in Large's collection are: No. 40 (kerfed chest), No. 77 (engraved bone hook), No. 50 (wooden ladle and carved skull, which fit together to form one piece), and No. 41 (kerfed chest).

When Large was in Toronto in the winter of 1906/7 he entered into a new agreement to collect exclusively on behalf of the Ontario Provincial Museum.[28] On his return to Bella Bella he attempted without success to acquire another pole and commissioned models of a fish trap, a bear trap, and a canoe in the process of construction, and a model of an old Indian house from Bella Bella carvers. These, with descriptions of the technology that they illustrated, were offered to the museum, but for some reason the arrangements were not completed.[29]

Large reluctantly left Bella Bella in 1910 and moved to Port Simpson where there were suitable schools for his children. His association with the Toronto community continued. In June 1919 C. T. Currelly of the ROM wrote to Large, requesting his help in obtaining a life-size Haida group for display. Large had seen such an exhibit at the Smithsonian Institution in 1915 and admired it, but by July 1919 it was becoming increasingly difficult to arrange for such work. The old Haida carver from whom he would have liked to commission the group had died in June 1919.[30]

At this time, Large had "a fairly good collection" that he was thinking of selling, preferably to a Canadian museum. Although he had been approached to sell it elsewhere, he wanted to give Currelly the first option to buy, perhaps because of his earlier agreement with the OPM. He planned to be in Toronto from September to December 1920, during which time he hoped to meet with Currelly and arrange the details.[31] But Large died (at the age of forty-seven) at Prince Rupert on 20 August; the fate of that particular collection is not known.

It included masks, rattles, clappers, paddles, clubs, argillite poles, spoons, boxes, stone implements, a witchcraft box, and a stone mirror, probably the one illustrated in Emmons' *Slate Mirrors of the Tsimshian* and labelled as having been obtained from Large (1921:12). "Sixteen stone pieces, etc., Indian curios collected by Dr. R. W. Large, British Columbia" were purchased from Mrs. Large in 1926 by the members' committee of the ROM.[32] The Raley Collection at the UBCMOA contains four Bella Bella objects that were obtained from Large: a feast ladle collected in 1908, twin masks, and a raven rattle (UBC-MOA 6713, 2120 A–B, 1760). [33]

Model Totem Pole. See Catalogue, No. 24.

THE PRICES OF ARTIFACTS

Large believed that he was gathering the last examples of the old way of life at Bella Bella. On the subject of commissioning models and replicas, he said in 1907: "the old ones who really know how to make those things are fast dying off,"[34] and in 1920 he said that the traditional carving and painting skills would "soon be a lost art with the young people." As the demand continued and the supply was thought to be dwindling, the prices of the artifacts increased. Large said that his last collection—the one that he offered to Currelly of the ROM in 1920—was expensive, "as there have been a number of American and Canadian collectors in the field."[35]

Other factors affected the prices of artifacts. One was the state of the Heiltsuk economy—people sold artifacts when they needed cash. "The fact of the matter is that the Indians have made so much money at fishing, trapping and making things for tourists of late, that it has been practically out of the question to get them to undertake such work as you desire," wrote Large from Port Essington with regard to the proposed commissioning of the life-size Haida group. At the same time, Large noted that the coastal economy changed rapidly: "From present appearances the salmon run this year will be small, and as the prices of skins have dropped considerably, prospects are better of getting the Indians to do some work [carving] at reasonable rates."[36]

The fluctuating income of the natives influenced their willingness to sell. Large was able to purchase two house posts from 'Qélc for Franz Boas of the AMNH in 1900 (AMNH 16/8379, 16/8380; see Figs. 23–24), and presumably the matching poles for the OPM (Nos. 18–19), for $20 a pair—the owners needed money then and had to sell.[37] When the OPM asked Large to acquire another pole in 1907, however, he could not persuade the owners to sell the pole that he wanted because they had no need of cash at that time. There were so few poles left in the area that Large thought he would have to travel to the Queen Charlotte Islands in order to buy one.[38]

Although it was perhaps still a luxury rather than a necessity,[39] the Heiltsuk at this time were well aware of the value and uses of money. During the summer they worked for wages at the canneries, the men fishing and the women cleaning and packing fish.[40] Dr. Raynor noted that the Heiltsuk were "spoken of very highly by their employers . . . and are in great demand, especially by the cannery managers" (*MB* 4, no. 2[1907]:552). According to Large, some men "made as much as $20 to $25 a night" during a season that lasted up to four weeks (*MB* 2, no. 2[1904]:282). Two other types of employment for cash in and around Bella Bella were boat building and hand logging. Wood carving and silver work were the chief sources of income for some, who sold their work to other natives as well as to curio collectors.

The sale of art work could be very lucrative. At Bella Coola, Dr. J. C. Spencer related that a "very clever" wood carver and silversmith renounced Christianity, "went back among his heathen friends," and was able to make a "considerable amount of money [carving] such things as headdresses, masks, whistles, etc." for native ceremonies (*MB* 1, no. 1[1903]:94). The curio trade could be profitable as well. "Although they have not yet fully learned the value of their wares, anxious curio-seekers are rapidly teaching them, and it is now not uncommon to be asked twenty-five dollars for a basket or a hat," commented one visitor to the coast (*MO* 28, no. 1[1908]:35). For a basket, Crosby asked as much as $50 to $80, which was thought to be very high.[41] The Kwakwaka'wakw woman's hat from Fort Rupert (No. 6) in Large's collection was considerably less. It has a price of $5 painted inside the brim. In 1909 Large noted that a Bella Bella woman paid $5 for an "extreme picture hat something of the Gainsborough style" which was ordered from a catalogue (*MB* 6, no. 3[1910]:515), so perhaps the Kwakwaka'wakw hat was priced at the going rate for fancy hats.

The materials from which artifacts were made seem in some cases to have been more important than the artifacts themselves in establishing value. Boyle thought that Crosby's asking prices of $4 and $5 for plain stone axes were very high, but Crosby was under the impression that many of his stone artifacts were made of jade. Boyle said they were slate and therefore not worth "more than one-tenth to one-twentieth part of what he asked."[42]

The ROM's Department of Anthropology has a list of the prices paid for Large's 1906 collection (Appendix F). The least expensive pieces, at 25 and 50 cents, were the gambling stones, the small baskets, the "war club handle" (adze handle, No. 111), and the little wooden bird from an old mask (No. 49). The crudely made "yew wood box, old model" (No. 44) was also only 50 cents; it may have been commissioned by Large to illustrate the old technology, and this low price may therefore indicate that those who did this kind of rough carving to order did not value their work highly. Spoons, including old ones carved from mountain-goat horn, were 75 cents, but stone axes, bone bark beaters, and other implements were $1. New silver jewellery was more expensive, ranging from $2 for a small brooch (NS 27885) to $6.50 for two large bracelets (No. 92, ROM 27884/906.2.2). Carved stone pile drivers (Nos. 122–23, NS 27916, 27918) were $4 each, as were copper bracelets (NS 27913, No. 85), one of which was thought to be made of native copper, and an elaborate cedar dance hat (No. 55). Curiously, one of the dance masks (No. 48) was only $3, the same price as the painted cooking box with tongs (Nos. 37, 109) and the small "scalloped edge dance implement 'official sceptre'" (No. 46). Perhaps the dance wand was relatively expensive because it was a valued ceremonial object. Two argillite poles (Nos. 22–23) were costly: one was $6.50, the other $5. The "high crown dance hat" (No. 7) and a carved cane (probably the "carved ceremonial wand," No. 64) were each $10. Since both the hat and the cane are complex pieces, the price may reflect the skill that went into their manufacture. The "carved box used for dance masks, etc." (No. 36), which is a large, much weathered, but beautifully carved chest, was also $10. The "war spear" with a "carved whale rib point" (No. 65) is the most expensive object at $20. The high price may reflect the size and complexity of the piece and the rarity of the carved whalebone.

It is interesting to compare these prices with those paid by the Smithsonian Institution to James Swan for his 1875 collection of Bella Bella objects. Gambling stones and plain spoons were then worth 30 cents apiece. A large painted box could be had for $1.50, but stone hammers and whalebone bark beaters were $2.80. Four wooden masks cost $7.80. A beautiful wooden mask with an attached painted parchment cape was the most expensive single item at $6. Swan's water bucket and ladle cost $1.65 whereas Large's (Nos. 38–39), which are very similar, cost $4. Between 1875 and 1906 it can be seen that prices increased but that the relative values of objects remained the same. Stone and bone pieces were expensive compared to masks. This reflects a bias identified by Cole: "Jacobsen sought bone and stone objects—a general nineteenth-century preference implying antiquity and one not fully appropriate to the Northwest Coast" (Cole 1985:63).

It has been claimed that the missionaries used the money from the sale of artifacts to build their churches (Low 1982:35). This may have been the case at Bella Bella. Large's writings make it clear that the Heiltsuk people contributed considerable labour and money to the establishment of the mission and hospital buildings.[43] It is probable that some of the proceeds from the sale of traditional artifacts formed part of that contribution.

Notes

1. Chief Charley of Bella Bella was the second-ranked chief of the ʼWúyalitx̌v tribe of the Heiltsuk. The first-ranked ʼWúyalitx̌v chief was Humshett. There are many versions of this historic Heiltsuk name. Drucker, for example, spells it "Hamtcit" (see other spellings in nn. 2, 3). In Heiltsuk orthography it can be rendered "Haémzit" and translated roughly as "the one to go to for food" (John Rath, personal communication, July 1986). This important hereditary name is now used as a surname by a chiefly lineage in Waglisla. The name Wockite is no doubt an anglicization of the name of that chief's ʼQvúqvaẏaítx̌v village. According to Harkin (1988:236), this chief had the name Waúyala.

2. Tate gives the date of the "feast of reconciliation" as 1882 (Barner n.d.). In 1883 Humchitt gave a second reconciliation feast when another chief joined the village (Harkin 1988:243). Chief Humchitt died in 1885. His heir, Chief Moody Humchitt, sponsored a feast in 1892 when the ʼQvúqvaẏaítx̌v moved to Bella Bella after the fire at ʼQábá. At this feast the ʼQvúqvaẏaítx̌v chief, who may have been Robert Bell, announced his intention to convert to Christianity (McKervill 1964:47, Harkin 1988:243–45). One of the five Heiltsuk artists named by Large, Bell became head chief at Bella Bella.

3. Humchitt became the leading chief at Bella Bella. The Department of Indian Affairs listed the Bella Bella chiefs in 1897–1899: "first chiefs—Boston Humpsit [Humchitt], Kittee; second chiefs—Charley Tihe, Housty, Nu-nu-cus [Núṅukvas] and Carpenter" (DIA 1899:591).

4. Mrs. Knight was referring to a part of the tánís ceremony when the dancer, who was possessed by the Cannibal spirit, rushed wildly at members of the audience and bit them on the arm, removing a piece of flesh. Although it looked spontaneous, this part of the performance, like the entire Winter Ceremony, was carefully prearranged. Those attacked had the special right to be bitten and were paid for their participation. The dancer surreptitiously used a small, sharp knife to cut the flesh.

    The chief who "bit much too savagely in the Tanis dance" was perhaps Chief Charley. A one-time rival of Humpshet, he was opposed to the move to Waglisla (Harkin 1988:250), so he may have been the old chief who was still living at Old Town in 1903.

5. The Heiltsuk reserves are listed as follows: Bella Bella and the burial ground on Denny Island, Hoonees (Roscoe Inlet), Quartcha (Roscoe Inlet), Noota (Roscoe Inlet), Clatse (Roscoe Inlet), Echo (Elcho, Dean Channel), Kisameet (Fisher Channel), Howeet (Hunter Island), Kunsoot (Denny Island), Jajustus (Kajustus, Denny Island), Werkinellek (Goose Island), and Yellertlee (Goose Island). The ʼQvúqvaẏaítx̌v reserves are listed as: Kokyet (Ellerslie Channel), Grief Island (Ellerslie Channel), Kyarti (Ellerslie Channel), Neekas (Ellerslie Channel), Tankeah (Tankeeah, Seaforth Channel), and Koqui (Seaforth Channel) (DIA 1900:110–13).

6. Ebbstone's flag was apparently intended to indicate "God's Day [and] call the people to worship" (Neilson 1981). Neilson says it was a white flag. Harkin (1988:232) assumes it was a Union Jack because Reverend Crosby and his crew of native evangelists flew this flag from the stern of their canoe when they first visited Bella Bella in 1880 (Tate 1917:10). Methodist missionary accounts of conversion are rather standardized and often mention a flag as a symbol of the new Christian. Charlie Amos (Wahuksqumalayou), a Haisla man who was converted at the

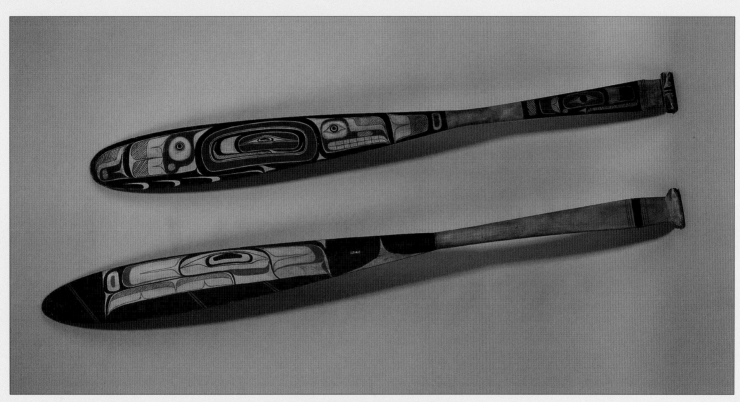

Paddles. See Catalogue, Nos. 25–26.

Methodist Indian mission in Victoria, carried home a British Ensign to Kitamaat in 1876. Raley (1902a) referred to Amos' flag as "God's Letter." The use of national flags in this context underscores the connection between religious and political control of First Nations populations.

7. An example of the substitution of one kind of power for another can be detected in W. H. Pierce's account of the conversion of Chief Walter Kaal of Kispiox. Kaal brought a war club that had belonged to his great-great-grandfather to the church. "Now I want to lay it at the feet of Jesus," he said, "and I want the missionary to give me a Bible in its place" (*MO* 28, no. 5[1908]:103).

8. Alfred Brown had assisted Large in the hospital and had "learned to give anaesthetic very well under the doctor's direction" (*MO* 22, no. 9[1903]:203).

9. The population for 1905 was given as 327. In 1907 it had declined to 318, and in 1909 to 315 (DIA 1905:68; 1907:44; 1909:38).

10. This quotation is from an article titled "Music Among the Coast Indians of Northern British Columbia," written by Large's wife, Isabella Geddes Large (*MB* 8, no. 1[1911]:1302–4). Large and his wife were both talented musicians. She was "a brilliant pianist" and a Fellow of the Ontario Conservatory of Music (Large biographical file). He was an accomplished baritone soloist (*MB* 3, no. 1[1905]:117). The Heiltsuk obviously shared their talent and enthusiasm for music making.

11. For a fuller discussion of the Jesup North Pacific Expedition and its members, see Jonaitis 1988:154–213.

12. Some of the myths recorded at Bella Bella by Farrand appeared in *Tsimshian Mythology* (Boas 1916:883–88) and *Bella Bella Tales* (Boas 1932) but he did not publish anything on Heiltsuk social organization.

13. J. Adrian Jacobsen, collecting for the Royal Ethnographic Museum in Berlin, visited the Tsimshian village of Kitkatla after he had visited Old Bella Bella in 1881. He pronounced Kitkatla to be the first "real Indian village" that he had seen. Unlike Old Bella Bella, it was remote and pagan and "therefore not influenced by modern culture" (Jacobsen 1977:13).

14. In the *Annual Archaeological Report 1903,* an article titled "The Killing of Moostoos the Wehtigoo" is attributed to Large in the table of contents but the article itself has no by-line. The article relates the proceedings of a trial, held in Fort Saskatchewan and in Edmonton in 1899, of a band of Cree hunters accused of killing a companion because he was possessed by the spirit of the man-eating monster, the Windigo. In Garrad (1987:38) the author of the article is given as J. R. Boyle. Given the subject matter of the piece, Large was not likely the author.

15. Interest in the possible Asiatic origins of the Northwest Coast peoples persisted. Some years later Dr. G. H. Darby, who became the missionary doctor at Bella Bella in 1914, was awarded a fellowship in the Royal Anthropological Society for his work, in collaboration with a British doctor, on the incidence of the Mongolian spot (a birthmark common to Asiatic peoples) among the coastal Indians. With statistics on blood types that he had collected over the years at Bella Bella he was able to "add tangible evidence to the theory that the North American Indians are related to the Mongolian race" (McKervill 1964:99).

16. SI 4686. The Hudson's Bay trading store at Bella Bella may have been the original source of Swan's material.

17. Slides of Heiltsuk objects in the NMAI are on file at the HCEC.

18. The coffin box is probably FMNH 51988, a slide of which is on file at the HCEC.

19. The Haida chief may have been referring to the Anglican Church at Masset or the Methodist Church at Skidegate. The Roman Catholics, the Presbyterians, and the Salvation Army also had missions on the Northwest Coast. The Anglican missions were directed by the Church Missionary Society in London, England. For an outline of missionary activity on the Northwest Coast, see Fisher 1977.

20. R. W. Large to David Boyle, 23 November 1906 (NS file); David Boyle to R. W. Large, 8 October 1906 (NS file).

21. In 1862 Duncan moved a group of Christian Tsimshian from Fort Simpson to the old Tsimshian village site of Metlakatla where he established a utopian, European-style community (see Usher 1981).

22. The unsighted mate to the "sighted twin" mask was collected at Kitkatla in 1897 by Indian Commissioner Dr. Israel W. Powell and is now in the CMC (CMC VII-C-329). For a discussion of these remarkable works of art and the discovery that they are in fact two halves of a single Tsimshian transformation mask, see Duff 1975:160–67.

23. Douglas Cole, personal communication, 1993.

24. See Hall 1983.

25. J. Adrian Jacobsen (1977:72) mentions that he met Crosby in 1881 and heard from him a story about the power of the Indian doctors.

26. R. W. Large to David Boyle, 26 September 1906 (NS file).

27. R. W. Large to David Boyle, 23 November 1906 (NS file).

28. OPM to R. W. Large, 14 February 1907 (NS file).

29. R. W. Large to OPM, 22 November 1907 (NS file).

30. R. W. Large to C. T. Currelly, 23 June 1919 (NS file).

31. R. W. Large to C. T. Currelly, 21 July 1920 (NS file).

32. There are actually twenty-two objects (ROM HN 656–677) catalogued as obtained from Mrs. Large in January 1926. Nine of these are in ROM Ethnology (HN 659, 663–664, 670–671, 674–677).

33. Large offered a collection to the Provincial Museum in Victoria as well. C. F. Newcombe wrote to Large on 17 November 1912:

    Enclosed is a list of articles in your Indian collection which, I think, are desirable for the Provincial Museum. You will see that it includes the greater part and that those specimens not listed could still be useful as a nucleus of another set.

Will you kindly let me know the value you put on [the collection]. If it is satisfactory, I will send the money at once. I ask you to reply at your earliest convenience.

Articles from Bella Bella on the list include two fish traps, a black hooked-nose mask, model canoe, a "killer whale crest," two charms, and an assortment of stone tools (Newcombe n.d.). Museum records do not show these objects as part of the RBCM's Heiltsuk collection. Either Newcombe omitted the source in his records or Large sold the collection elsewhere.

34. R. W. Large to David Boyle, 22 November 1907 (NS file).

35. R. W. Large to C. T. Currelly, 21 July 1920 (NS file).

36. R. W. Large to C. T. Currelly, 21 July 1920 (NS file).

37. R. W. Large to Franz Boas, 26 November 1900, AMNH 1900 (file 1900-15).

38. R. W. Large to David Boyle, 22 November 1907 (NS file). The situation in 1911 must have been different again, for in that year C. F. Newcombe was able to collect four house posts in Bella Bella (BM 11.696.1–11.696.4; Jacknis 1991:276–77).

39. This was the case at Skidegate in 1906. Reverend Hardy wrote that the Haida "get their living so easily and cheaply that money is more of a luxury than a necessity. Accordingly, labour is hard to get unless the wages are tempting" (*MB* 3, no. 3[1906]:499).

40. Heiltsuk women's life and work at Namu and other canneries were documented in an exhibition, "Cannery Days: A Chapter in the Lives of the Heiltsuk," curated by Pam Brown for the UBCMOA (summer 1993).

41. David Boyle to R. W. Large, 8 October 1906 (NS file).

42. David Boyle to R. W. Large, 8 October 1906 (NS file).

43. In 1909, for example, the Heiltsuk gave eight hundred days' free labour to build the new church at Waglisla. In addition, the men donated $500 in cash and the women $200 (*MO* 29, no. 4[1909]:79).

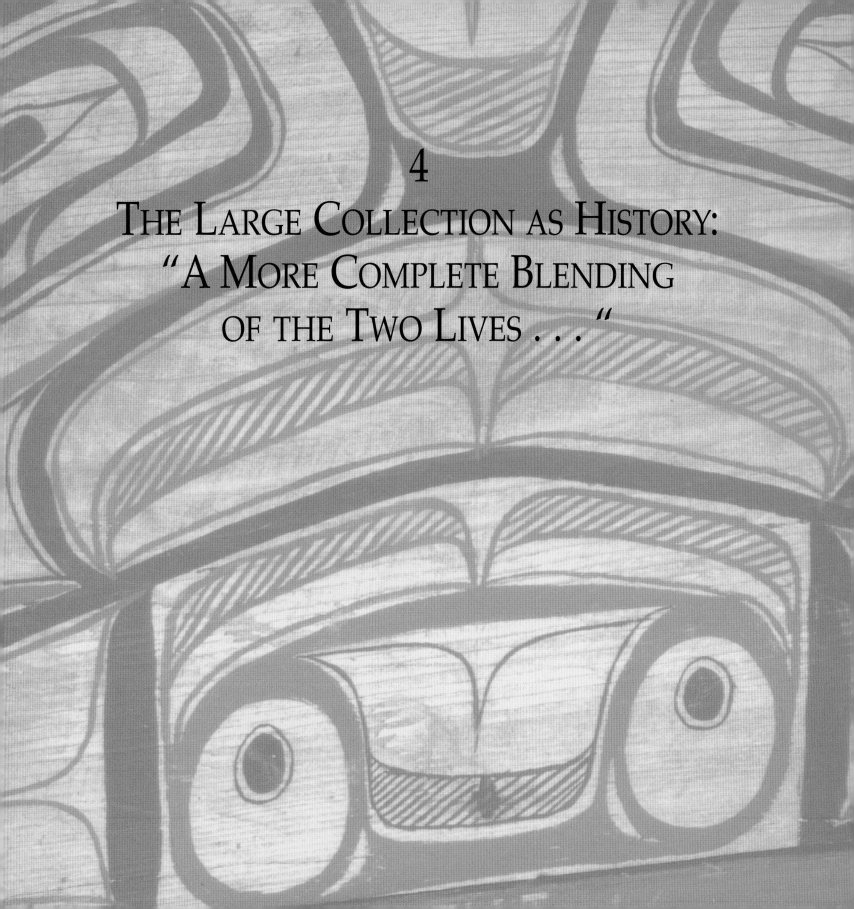

4

THE LARGE COLLECTION AS HISTORY:
"A MORE COMPLETE BLENDING
OF THE TWO LIVES . . ."

T he Large Collection as a whole is a record of turn-of-the-century Bella Bella, a village that maintained many Heiltsuk traditions while rebuilding itself as a model Methodist community. The collector wanted to illustrate the progress that the people of his village had made in the twenty years since their conversion to Christianity. Much of the collection is, in the missionary's words, "odds and ends," and yet remnants, such as the parts of the shaman's coronet, the chiefs' spoons, the dance paraphernalia, and the old house posts, embody aspects of a continuing tradition. Feasts went on in a modified form, skills were maintained and used in new contexts, and the Heiltsuk struggled to combine the old and the new.

Tools and Technology

When Large arrived in British Columbia in 1898 he was already aware of the efforts of Ontario's Provincial Archaeologist, David Boyle, to promote the collection and study of archaeological artifacts in Canada. The young doctor had sold or donated 149 objects, mainly from Simcoe and York counties in Ontario, to the newly established archaeological section of the Toronto Normal School Museum in July 1897 (see p. 15, n. 1).[1] Through Boyle's *Annual Archaeological Report* Large would have been familiar with the curator's scientific methods and objectives, which are clearly delineated by Boyle's biographer, Gerald Killan, with reference to Boyle's own writings:

> In his first *Archaeological Report* Boyle did not clearly articulate his motives for emphasizing function and working methods but did so in subsequent publications. His primary reason was to study technological evolution, to trace man's progression from the most primitive tools and technology to the "miraculous" engines and tools of the late nineteenth century. With this end in view, he urged the preservation of "not only perfect and highly finished specimens of all kinds, but the very rudest in form as well, and especially those on which the workmanship appears to be incomplete. The former may serve to exemplify the lower types from which the ideally perfect weapon or tool was evolved." The second reason for making "a close and patient study of function and working methods" was "to understand the modes of thought, manners of life, and conditions of early society. . . . To learn the uses of [artifacts]," he explained, "is to arrive at a knowledge, not only of how the ancient people lived, but of how

they thought which is of even greater importance, for if we can ascertain this we are on the highway to an understanding of much that it would be extremely interesting to know relative to aboriginal mental development, and consequently valuable as a contribution to the history of our race in its progress from the rudest to the highest and most refined manifestations of humanity." [Killan 1983:107–8][2]

Many of the objects and fragments of objects that Large sent from Bella Bella to Boyle must have been intended to illustrate these evolutionist concepts. A large portion of the collection (57 per cent) consisted of undecorated tools, fragments of tools, fishing gear, and gaming pieces, most of which are now in the ROM's Archaeology collections and were unavailable for this study (see Appendices G and H). This material, which included playing discs, spinning discs, gambling stones, paint stones, stone hammers, axes, bone chisels, stone knives, fishing sinkers, fish hooks, pile drivers, and fragments, may indeed be of the "rudest in form" and some may be "incomplete," for those objects that are of interest because of their completeness or decoration are among the 144 objects stored in the Ethnology collections of the ROM's Department of Anthropology that are the focus of this study.[3] Among the objects in ROM Ethnology, however, there are pecked stone and shaped bone artifacts that, if not ancient, illustrate ancient tool-making techniques and stone-age technologies of the Northwest Coast that were being replaced by "the 'miraculous' engines and tools of the late nineteenth century." Their obsolescence may account for their availability to the collector.

It appears that many of these tools, such as the "canoe awl" (No. 115) that was used to determine the thickness of canoe hulls, were no longer in use in turn-of-the-century Bella Bella. The Heiltsuk, who had been famous canoe-makers, had replaced their seagoing canoes with sail and gasoline boats. By 1911 the Indian Agent Iver Fougner was able to report that there were more gas boats in Bella Bella than in all of the other villages in his agency put together (DIA 1911:203).[4] As the commercial fishery replaced weir fishing the pecked stone pile drivers used to drive stakes into the river beds for fish traps (Nos. 122–123, NS 27916, 27918) were no longer needed. The Heiltsuk owned and operated a sawmill by 1903. Sawcut lumber replaced split and adzed planks in house building. Large was misinformed about the uses of tools such as the chisels used to rough-finish wood (Stewart 1984:35; Niblack 1890:282), which he described as "stone axes, with handles, as used in getting cedar boards from trees" (No. 121, NS 27860), and the stone mauls (No. 123, NS 27919, 27920, 27922) which are catalogued as "stone war

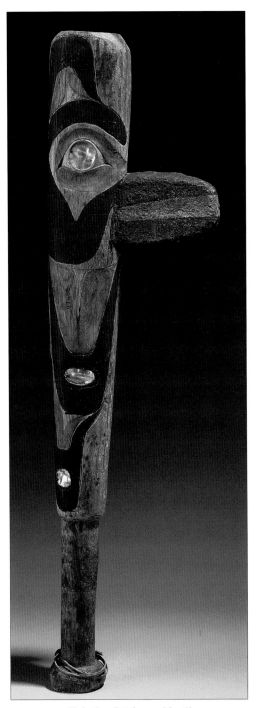

Club. See Catalogue, No. 63.

clubs." His confusion about the function of common, indigenous tools implies that he had not seen them in use. Among the tools that are described in the NS catalogue as "old time" or used "in early days" are a whalebone bark beater (No. 108), a mussel shell knife (No. 107), a leister spear (No. 81), and two halibut hooks (No. 74, NS 28210). These tools no doubt were collected to show the technological evolution of the Heiltsuk.

Many of the tools that Large collected were probably still in use; the Heiltsuk continued to fish and gather food for their families using some traditional tools and techniques despite the modernization of their community. In 1907 when Bella Bella was well established as the second largest Methodist village on the coast displaying many European-style amenities and technological "improvements," Large noted that the Heiltsuk supported themselves by fur-sealing, trapping, and fishing, as they had always done (*MO* 26, no. 2[1907]:6). Their involvement in the commercial fishery and other remunerative jobs such as hand logging, although new forms of economic production, did not fundamentally change their ancient pattern of seasonal movement in search of resources.[5] "This is the season of the year when the people are on the move," wrote Large in April 1902. "Since the New Year they have been trapping, logging, getting fish eggs, halibut and seaweed and now they are leaving for the fur-sealing at Goose Island" (*MO* 21, no. 6[1902]:126).

Large observed and recorded the methods of gathering herring eggs on branches and of using a herring rake (*MO* 21, no. 6[1902]:126; *MB* 6, no. 1[1909]:16). His accurate description of a small bone chisel (No. 110) as a "bone implement for removing inner bark from hemlock" implies that the edible inner bark, or bast, of the tree was still gathered at Rivers Inlet in mid-June using this "piece of whale-rib with sharpened end." Two observers in the 1830s recorded how bast was used: "They . . . take the tender rind from the inside bark of the hemlock tree and pound it into cakes, which they dry in the sun" (Dunn 1844:251); the Kummuchquetoch (Kimsquit) people traded "some cakes made from the inner bark of the hemlock" at Fort McLoughlin (Tolmie 1963:252).[6]

Two stone hammers (NS 23106, 23181) were found at Goose Island (Yáláthi), a seaward island about 30 km from Bella Bella where the fur seal was still hunted in May and June as it had been before the amalgamation of the Heiltsuk groups at Bella Bella. Goose Island was the home of the Yáláthitx̌v before they joined, perhaps as early as 1835, with other Heiltsuk-speaking groups (Mitchell 1981:83; Olson 1955:320). The area was designated as Bella Bella reserve no. 12 (Yellertlee) in 1882, and it continues to be an important Heiltsuk camp. By Large's time the seal hunt had become a commercial activity, and the missionary doctor thought that it was "a very dangerous way of making a little money, as they go far out to sea in their sail-boats [and] a gale might spring up almost any time" (*MB* 2, no. 4[1905]:81). The hunters usually got from two to three hundred seals, which sold for $8 to $13 each in 1900 (*MO* 19, no. 9[1900]:198).

The seasonal movements of the Heiltsuk, like many of their continuing traditions, worried the missionary. Despite the fact that valuable seal skins were donated to the church building fund, Large was distressed by the conditions at the outlying camps such as Goose Island where a serious epidemic broke out in 1900. "When they leave their village they do like to drop indolently into the old life of filth, smoke and overcrowding," he lamented (*MO* 19, no. 9[1900]:198). Sanitary conditions were not his only concern: "They throw off all restraint when they leave the village, and Sabbath in the camps . . . is not kept as it should be" (*MO* 20, no. 7[1901]:151).

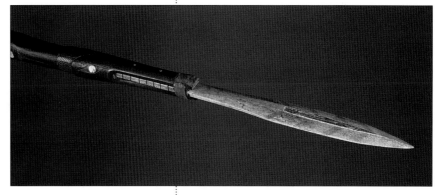

Spear. See Catalogue, No. 65.

Similar temptations were offered by the many canneries on Rivers Inlet where Heiltsuk people worked during the fishing season. The first Rivers Inlet cannery had been built in 1882 after Reverend Tate called attention to the great salmon runs there (Simonsen 1973:27–28; Walbran 1909:424). In 1897 Reverend Crosby and Dr. A. E. Bolton built a hospital near Wannock Cannery. After the Bella Bella hospital was opened in 1902, the Rivers Inlet facility was maintained as a summer hospital because of the increasing seasonal population on the inlet. In 1909 there were seven canneries in operation on Rivers Inlet, with an average of 335 workers each, "including sixty Indian women, 100 boats with two men each, fifteen white men and sixty Chinese" (*MO* 29, no. 10[1909]:235). Crosby observed: "heathen people and Christians for hundreds of miles along the coast, also Chinese, Japanese, and a number of white men, visit and work" at the canneries (Crosby 1914:193). Conditions on the inlet troubled Large, who with his family was in residence at the Rivers Inlet hospital during the summer season, because the "high tension" among the different groups was aggravated by alcohol and gambling (*MO* 19, no. 9[1900]:198).

Large complained that because the cannery stores made a profit from the gamblers, the canneries didn't discourage them (*MO* 19, no. 9[1900]:198). Under the influence of the mission at Bella Bella, the Heiltsuk had apparently renounced this traditional, popular form of recreation. Large was able to state: "Only certain tribes gamble, and I am glad to say the Port Simpsons, Kitamaats, and Bella Bellas [all Methodists] do not do it, neither have I seen one of them under the influence of liquor" (*MO* 19, no. 9[1900]:198). His statement is supported by the Indian Agent, Iver Fougner, who found the Bella Bella to be "amongst the most moral and temperate Indians on the coast" (DIA 1911:203). Gambling paraphernalia—four sticks that were originally part of a set of forty or fifty used in the game of lípa (No. 82), eleven gambling discs (NS 27924–27930, 28230–28232, 28247), twenty-eight gambling stones or sets of gambling stones (NS 27943–27965, 28225–28229), and two "sealbone gamblers" (NS 27908–27909)—make up 17 per cent of Large's collection, and may have been included to illustrate "aboriginal mental development" of the Indians.[7] In 1905 a Japanese cannery was opened across the bay from Waglisla, and Large hoped that it would be a permanent business where "more employment will be provided for the people within a mile of home" (*MB* 3, no. 1[1905]:116) and where, no doubt, Large could keep his eye on them.

Many of the "old time" tools of the Heiltsuk who lived at Bella Bella had been replaced by modern ones, but traditional skills survived and were put to use in new ways by the missionary. The elaborate new Bella Bella church, with its red and yellow cedar wainscotting, arched windows, and decorative steeple was constructed at no cost to the mission by the men of Bella Bella, as was the schoolhouse, which also had an elaborate spire, and the mission house (Fig. 15), which boasted five bedrooms, a study, an office, a dining room, a kitchen, a pantry, and such decorative details as "set in bookcases with glass doors above and cupboards below on either side of the study grate."[8] Traditional skills were used to make replicas, probably intended for museum display, that would illustrate old technologies and show the "technological evolution" of the Indians. Five one-piece halibut hooks with bone barbs and twisted cedar rope lines (No. 73) were new. These were probably made for Large's collection, as examples of this common central-coast form, to complete his inventory of Heiltsuk fishing technology. A roughly made, unpainted bent bowl is designated "yew wood box, old model" (No. 44).[9] An "old time halibut hook and sinker" (No. 71) was made by Daniel Houstie and an "old time Indian

FIG. 15. *Large's home, the fine five-bedroom mission house at Bella Bella (Waglisla). Like the other mission buildings, it was constructed free of charge by the Heiltsuk people. Courtesy Royal British Columbia Museum, Victoria. Photograph by R. W. Large, from "Souvenir of Bella Bella, B.C." PN 16465.*

cradle" (No. 11) was made by Enoch. Other new objects made by known Bella Bella artists using traditional skills, material, and subjects are discussed in Chapter 5, "Five Bella Bella Carvers."

The availability of cloth and ready-made containers at the Bella Bella stores and through mail-order catalogues meant that the working of cedar bark in Large's time was not as common as it had been twenty years earlier. Tate reported in 1883 that "basket-making and mat-weaving are steadily prosecuted" by the women while at the Goose Island camp (*MB* 9, no. 1[1913]:80), but by 1897 Indian Agent Charles Todd observed that the Indians in the Northwest Coast Agency, which at that time included Bella Bella, had "lost most of their old-time employments, such as . . . making moccasins, baskets, mats, hats, fish lines, etc." He attributed this to "the many better paid employments furnished by the white men" (DIA 1897:89). The working of cedar bark became a tourist industry. A traveller on the coast observed in 1908 that some Indian women were "adding to the family incomes by making mats, baskets and hats of cedar bark, cedar roots, and grasses." The missions encouraged this industry. It has already been noted (p. 45) that Reverend Raley promoted basket and mat making at Kitamaat by awarding prizes for these arts at the annual fair. From Kitamaat Raley went to Port Simpson where his influence can be detected in the program at the Crosby Girls' Home. "Basket weaving and the making of straw picture frames, boxes, weaving, etc." were introduced and a sale of the work was planned. In particular, the school wanted "to revive interest in the art of basket weaving, an art which the younger Indian is prone to neglect" (*MO* 29, no. 12[1909]:286).

Basketry was the province of women, and at least one of the baskets in the collection was obtained by Mrs. Large. Her name is written (twice) on the bottom of No. 3. Mrs. Large was active in the mission, particularly with the women of the community. When she called on them in their homes she found them "sitting around on the floor while things are in pretty much the same untidy state that existed in the old Indian houses" and concluded that they were "quite satisfied to live in the old untidy ways of the past." The women controlled the households and were "careful to keep alive the old heathen customs, particularly in regard to the births, marriages, etc." (*MB* 2, no. 3[1905]:591). This traditionalism was seen as a problem by the missionary, so steps were taken to involve the women in the work of the church. At first they were not enthusiastic about attending church-sponsored activities, but by 1903 they were becoming interested in Mrs. Large's Ladies' Aid group. The women met every Wednesday afternoon at the mission house to do sewing and knitting, which would be sold to raise funds to build the new church (*MB* 1, no. 1[1903]:83; *MB* 2, no. 3[1905]:592).

It seems that the women were encouraged to make either Indian baskets and mats or European-style sewn articles, but at least one woman at Bella Bella was able to combine the two traditions. The "slipper case representing frog" (No. 10) is the only Bella Bella object in the Large Collection attributed to a woman. It combines Heiltsuk materials (woven cedar bark and painted cedar) and form (a puppetlike frog, reminiscent of the articulated figures used in potlatch and dance performances) with European materials (printed cotton) and function (slipper container) to produce an object that is typically Heiltsuk in its inventiveness and humour. "The Bella Bella made many funny little monsters, apparently for no reason but to amaze people with the artist's imagination," observed Holm (Holm and Reid 1975, fig. 25). Despite its hybrid nature, the slipper case embodies this distinctly Heiltsuk sensibility. And the frog is a particularly suitable motif to express it. That the bag's contents would have been "eaten" by the frog seems to allude humorously to the animal's legendary greediness (Harkin 1988:166). As well, the frog's ability to exist in two forms (tadpole and frog) and to cross the boundary between two environments (water and land) is mirrored in the bag's incorporation of two traditions and two different worlds.

The mats and baskets in the Large Collection are plain, everyday objects that, like the bark beaters, illustrate the old way of life. But the hybrid nature of the slipper case is perhaps more typical of Large's modern village than the other more traditional basketry objects in the collection.

Frog-Shaped Bag. See Catalogue, No. 10.

Details of Bark Mats.
See Catalogue, Nos. 8–9.

Baskets. See Catalogue, Nos. 3–5.

Ritual Dances and Feasts

The potlatch was, the missionaries believed, the primary barrier to native assimilation and "advancement," reinforcing as it did indigenous social organization, marriage and inheritance conventions, mortuary customs, economic systems, and power structures, and providing a format for feasting and dancing. Northwest Coast missionaries had been vocal in their condemnation of the potlatch and were influential in its official suppression by the 1884 amendment to the *Indian Act* known as the "potlatch law," which banned not only the potlatch, but the "tamananawas" dances of the Winter Ceremonies.[10] Despite official prohibition, though, the Heiltsuk continued these fundamental Northwest Coast institutions in disguised and modified forms. In 1901 the Bella Bella people wished for "a more complete blending of the two lives—the old and the new" (*MO* 20, no. 3[1901]:54). Large was concerned about this blending of old and new as it manifested itself in "overshadowings of the old potlatch" in his nominally Christian village:

> A man gives a party and calls his friends to dine with him. They come dressed in their best, and a blessing is probably asked upon the food, and all goes well til the after-dinner time. Then some one gets up, perhaps, and gives a new name to the giver of the feast, and he, in turn may distribute some small gifts, hand-kerchiefs, dress goods or spoons. The departing guests carry home with them food, and it may be a more generous supply is given to the head chiefs. . . .
>
> One of their number dies and a tombstone is purchased. This must be placed in position at the grave. The firemen and the brass band are paid to do the work, and paid handsomely, and there is a feast afterwards, and perhaps gifts distributed in memory of the departed. Food, blankets, dishes and clothing will generally be burned at the grave of the deceased, not once only, but several times. . . .
>
> A couple wish to get married. The friends come to the minister who talks the matter over with them, gives a little advice, the banns are called on three successive Sundays, and they are then married according to Discipline. But quietly, in many cases, a present of money or goods has been given by the groom or his parents to those of the bride, according to old established usage. [*MO* 20, no. 3(1901):54]

It is obvious from this report that the important milestones of Heiltsuk life continued to be marked in traditional ways. The assumption of new names and ranks still had to be validated by giving away goods to witnesses, appropriate marriage payments continued to be made, and funerary traditions were maintained.

When Dr. Raynor was in Bella Bella while Large was on furlough in the winter of 1906/7, he found it "rather difficult to enlist the co-operation of the people in the Christmas entertainment" because

> they were having [a feast] nearly every day for three weeks before Christmas and New Years. [These were] tomb-stone feasts . . . given by the friends of someone who had died the previous winter. As there had been several deaths from whooping-cough, there were necessarily many feasts. These were all quiet . . . there was no potlatching.

Raynor did not attend any of these memorial feasts, which, although no "potlatching" was detected, were in fact forms of the traditional mortuary potlatch that was held about a year after death. At that time the formal mourning of the widow ended, the new holder of the deceased's name was recognized, and a monument—now a tombstone rather than a mortuary pole—was erected (Harkin 1988:59). Raynor did go to a wedding feast—that of Tommy Hunt. "The band rendered some splendid music," he reported, "after which we partook of a very excellent dinner." Then, after making a brief congratulatory speech, the missionary judiciously "left them to enjoy the afternoon in their own way" (*MB* 4, no. 2[1907]:549–50). If the enjoyment involved some form of potlatch, he did not see it.

Not only did the feasts continue at Bella Bella in a modified form, but Heiltsuk chiefs participated in more elaborate feasts and potlatches in other communities. Reverend Dr. J. C. Spencer of Bella Coola wrote in 1906 that the Bella Coola people had never given up their old customs and as a result their community was "a sort of rendezvous for Indians from Christian villages who really wished to attend or receive goods through the potlatch. . . . We regret to say that almost this whole tribe, together with the Kimsquit and Talio tribes, began feasting and dancing early in October and finished late in January" (*MB* 3, no. 3[1906]:485–88). Spencer went on to list ten types of potlatches that were "reasons for ceremonious feasting and dancing" at Bella Coola. At Namu cannery (where many Heiltsuk people worked) an "old-time" dance was given on the occasion of the death of one of the principal chiefs in 1906 (*MB* 3, no. 3[1906]:796)

Hat with Four Rings. See Catalogue, No. 7.

and at Kitamaat in 1907 the "feasting and potlatching" started in November and continued until Christmas (*MB* 4, no. 3[1907]:673).

At these feasts, a Heiltsuk chief may have worn a hat like the woven spruce root "high crown dance hat" or four-ringed chief's hat (No. 7). This may have been made as a replica for Large; it appears to be new and lacks an inner cap that would have kept it on the head. The inner cap is characteristic of hats made to be worn.

Food for the feasts would have been presented in huge dishes such as the one in the shape of a beaver, which was made by Captain Carpenter (No. 42), and the beautifully made canoe-shaped "large food box" (No. 43), which exhibits the precise carving (representing a bear) and black patina of an old artifact. Two large feast bowls that were used by Chief Moody (Humchitt) of Bella Bella in 1890 at "the feast of the hereditary chief" are now in the collection of the Canadian Museum of Civilization (CMC VII-EE-37–38). Olson (1935, 1949:21) noted that two huge dishes representing a wolf and a sea lion were given by the Bella Bella to the Hartley Bay people when "they came to comfort the Bella Bella people in the drowning of an Eagle [clan] man." These references indicate that feast bowls were used at potlatches in Bella Bella during the mission period. Although in 1888 Niblack observed that "wash bowls are used as receptacles for food, and are taking the place of the native wooden bowls" on the Northwest Coast (1890:337), traditional containers were preserved at Bella Bella and brought out for important feasts.

The spoons that Large collected were also associated with traditional feasts at Bella Bella. The three that were collected in 1901 are catalogued as "chief's horn spoon[s]" (Nos. 98–99) and "chief's spoon, very old" (No. 100). They were obtained from important Heiltsuk chiefs Herbert Humchil (Humchitt),[11] Bob Lawson (1858–before 1909), and Nooneyuas (Núṅukvas, 1835–1904). They would have been used and distributed by the chiefs at parties with "overshadowings of the old potlatch." Eight other spoons that Large sent to the Ontario Provincial Museum in 1906 may also be connected with "feasting and potlatching."

Ceremonial objects make up only about 15 per cent of the collection.[12] Large was firm in his opposition to any revival of the "old-time songs and dances" that had been officially stopped by Reverend Tate at Bella Bella in 1880 and (theoretically) in all communities by the "potlatch law" of 1884. One such revival was attempted in the winter of 1901 when, to Large's distress, many of the members of his Christmas choir danced with "painted faces [and] fantastic costumes." Lamenting the fact that the people could return so easily to their "past lives," the missionary cancelled the planned Christmas festivities to illustrate that, in his view, they were not compatible with indigenous ceremonies (*MO*

20, no. 3[1901]:54. At least one convert was permanently alienated from the Church by this kind of censorship. In Bella Bella during the missionary Dr. George Darby's time (1912–1959), "one man who had been very active in the church was still in a petulant huff, years after he had been reprimanded by a former missionary for engaging in an ancient ritual not in keeping with Christian practice and belief [and the doctor] was never able to persuade him to come back" (McKervill 1964:44). The reprimanding former missionary may have been Large.

Large described five examples of dance paraphernalia collected before 1902 as the products of neighbouring non-Christian groups; even so, they are typically Heiltsuk objects, and other collectors obtained similar paraphernalia at Bella Bella in the late nineteenth century. Ceremonial material of this type may not have been brought to Large because the Christianized Heiltsuk were supposed to have given up their "old time" institutions about twenty years before he arrived in the village. George Hunt collected at least four cedar-bark head rings from Bella Bella (AMNH 16/4732–4735), and cedar-bark rings from Bella Bella are also in the National Museum of the American Indian (NMAI 4603), the National Museum of Natural History (NMNH 20686), and other museums. A red cedar-bark head ring (No. 53) and neck ring (No. 54) collected by Large are, however, described by him as "used by the Fort Rupert Indians" rather than by the Bella Bella people. It is likely (but not certain) that these cedar-bark rings were collected at Fort Rupert and not at Bella Bella.[13] No matter where the rings were actually obtained, Large's documentation should be read as contrasting the Christian Heiltsuk, who as far as he knew no longer used these symbols of the spirits, with the non-Christian Kwakwaka'wakw of Fort Rupert who, in 1901, were still openly performing dance ceremonies.

Red cedar bark is a sign of the sacred season of the Winter Ceremony, the first and most prestigious of two separate dance cycles in the ceremonial year. It was a time when the spirits came close to the village and the secular order was replaced by the supernatural. The Heiltsuk Winter Ceremony is called the Shaman's (ċaíqa) series. A second, separate ceremonial cycle, the Returned from Heaven (dhuẃláx̌a) ritual, was performed after the ċaíqa series was over and the secular order had been reinstated.[14] A third ceremony, the dog-eating dance (nuɫəm), was distinct from the other two (Hilton 1990:318–19). After these dance cycles were banned, they continued to be held in secret, often in a condensed or combined form.

Three documented masks are associated with a non-Heiltsuk group although they were collected at Bella Bella. Like the cedar-bark rings, they were used in the outlawed dances. A mask made by Bella Bella carver Daniel Houstie is described by Large as "used by Interior or Stick Indians" (No. 57), and two masks collected from a man named Solomon at Bella Bella (Nos. 58–59) are identified as "Stick, Sinash [Siwash] (or Interior Indian)."[15]

The grotesque mask by Houstie, however, is a common Heiltsuk type. Similar heavy masks with exaggerated features (such as long, hooked noses, wide, rectangular mouths with protruding lips, heavy brow and cheek ridges, prominent eyes, and dramatic painting) are found in several collections from Bella Bella (McM 1984.5, Fig. 16; AMNH 16/4736; NMAI 5/9833, 9749; NMNH 217408). The ROM (1976:16), Drucker

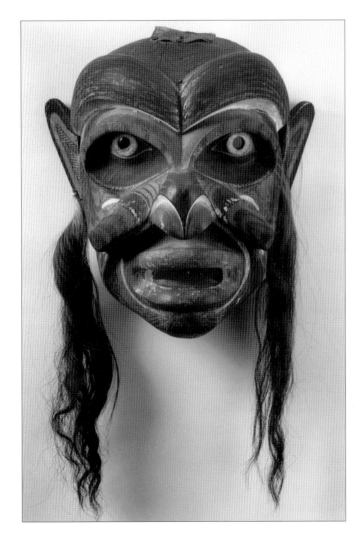

FIG. 16. *A distinctive Heiltsuk mask type, this grotesque mask is thought to represent the Wild Man of the Woods, or p̓k̓vs. Courtesy McMichael Canadian Art Collection.*
McM 1984.5.

(1965, fig. 3), and Hilton (1990:318) have published this mask as Bukwús (Heiltsuk pƙvs), or Wild Man of the Woods, whose dance was one of the ranked dances of the Returned from Heaven (dhuẁláx̌a) series (Olson 1954:248).

Pƙvs is a forest dweller, and it may be this characteristic of the spirit that caused Large to associate the mask with the Interior tribes, once sometimes called "Stick Indians" by the coastal peoples. The word means "tree" or "wood" in Chinook, and "is universally applied by certain Northwest Coast tribes to any Indians from the interior, i.e., to those who live back in the woods" (Hodge 1910:636). It is unlikely that the Wet'suwet'en and Chilcotin, who were the closest inland tribes to Bella Bella, would have made or used such a mask. McIlwraith states that the Carrier (Wet'suwet'en) lacked the rich ceremonial life of the coastal tribes (1948, 1:18), and according to Drucker the Bella Bella had little or no contact with the inland groups (1965:110). Large's attribution of this mask to a group other than the Heiltsuk is misleading, for it is a Heiltsuk prerogative that was made at Bella Bella by a Heiltsuk carver in the Heiltsuk manner.[16]

There is, however, a specific etymological and conceptual correlation between the Heiltsuk Wild Man of the Woods (pƙvs) and non-Heiltsuk people (those excluded from Heiltsuk culture) that may explain Large's curious description of Houstie's mask. Pƙvs is a wild man, devoid of culture, who exists outside of Heiltsuk civilization and outside of the Heiltsuk (human) social order. Pƙvs is also the name for the Heiltsuk "orphan class" (xamala), made up of slaves and others without social standing, titles, or access to resources. "Not merely of low status, pkvs were in a real sense outside the social order altogether," explains Harkin. "They were excluded from Heiltsuk symbolic life almost completely, and as such constituted a class of virtual non-persons" (1988:40–41). In this sense, the First Nations of the interior, with no position within Heiltsuk society and culture, would be pƙvs. One wonders if Houstie had attempted to explain this complex concept to Large, without success. Whatever its basis, Large's description of the pƙvs mask as "used by Interior or Stick Indians" is oddly appropriate.

Although Solomon's masks do not represent the Wild Man of the Woods (pƙvs), they are also identified as "Stick, Sinash [Siwash] or Interior Indian" masks, and are also typically Heiltsuk. No. 59 resembles old Heiltsuk masks that were used in the Returned from Heaven (dhuẁláx̌a) dance cycle, such as RBCM 10, which was collected at Bella Bella by F. Jacobsen in 1893. No. 58, which at one time had eye flaps that could be moved up and down to make the eyes appear to open and shut, may be associated with the sleep-causing (K!ya'LkyaLamas) dance, a prerogative held by an important Bella Bella lineage (see No. 2). Another suggestion is that the masks were meant to represent peo-

Mask. See Catalogue, No. 57.

ple of the Interior.[17] The Nuxalk dance of the Supernatural Charmer features a series of dancers who exhibit the masks, clothing, and distinctive characteristics of various groups such as Tsimshian, Bella Bella, China Hat, and Cowichan (McIlwraith 1948, 2:217–18). It is possible that the Heiltsuk, too, owned a similar dance that represented neighbouring tribes which Large might have classified as Stick or Siwash. Drucker (1940:215) records that a minor dhuw̓láx̌a spirit that was represented in one Heiltsuk dance "is a Stick Indian spirit (aLasiml) who dances with feathers, bows and so on."

The masks that Large collected from Solomon appear to be old, but most ceremonial objects in the collection were new when they were collected, and might have been made especially for Large's collection. Perhaps by this time (1906) there were few traditional artifacts left in the village, but it is more likely that the Heiltsuk were unwilling to sell paraphernalia associated with dance ceremonies. The Bella Bella shaman's whistle and charm (NMAI 11/3859–3860) that Emmons acquired from Reverend Tait, or Tate, were given to the missionary by "the last shaman of the village, only under the condition that they would never be permitted to be seen by any of the natives."[18] The Bella Bella insisted on the proper handling of ritual objects for many years after the rituals were officially stopped. McIlwraith records an incident that took place in 1921. The death of the wife of a Bella Coola man was attributed to the man's having sold a sacred carving. The carving should have been destroyed but was instead sold to a government agent who let uninitiated people see it. The Bella Bella concluded that the vendor would suffer a disaster. The subsequent death of his wife was believed by the people of Bella Coola to have been caused by "the thoughts of the Bella Bella." This incident hindered McIlwraith's attempts to collect artifacts at Bella Coola (1948, 1:697).

Probably because the Methodist Heiltsuk still placed great value on sacred dance objects and ancient family prerogatives and kept these matters secret from Large, much of the ceremonial material in Large's collection is fragmentary and lacks any indication of its original context. It is therefore difficult to reconstruct the extent of the survival of the Heiltsuk dance ceremonies and other traditions in the new village of Waglisla.

With professional interest, the doctor recorded Heiltsuk treatments for illness (primarily those which involve sympathetic magic) and the techniques and results of witchcraft. As a physician, Large was interested in the "spirit possession" of true shamans whose curing powers come from an encounter with a spirit. But he was also aware of the conceptual analogies between the curing shamans and the dancers of the Winter Ceremony, known as the Shaman's (c̓aíqa) series, whose "spirit possession" was the result of initiation in dance societies. Large distinguished between three kinds of shamans, explaining that the "spirit enters doctors, man-eaters and dog-eaters" while they are voluntarily wandering in the mountains or forests and "gives them power" (*MB* 5, no. 4[1909]:707–8). He did not elaborate on these rituals. Missionary opposition to the dance rituals and Heiltsuk secrecy surrounding these traditions meant that Large would have known little else about the various shamans and their initiations.

Nevertheless, Large's brief descriptions of Heiltsuk Winter Ceremonies have some basis in fact. Olson, for example, noted:

> A shaman is called glugwall, literally one who has or controls a spirit power (glu'gwi). The word tsaika [čaíqa] also means a shaman, but with the meaning that he can perform sleight-of-hand. This last title is used mainly in connection with the Tsaika dance series which is sometimes called the "Shaman's Series." [1954:250]

According to Drucker, some initiates in the Shaman's (čaíqa) series were eaters of human or dog flesh. The initiate, he wrote, was made maniacal because of lack of food during his confinement in the forest, and "rushed back to the village to tear pieces of flesh from the arms of those he met, or to seize a live dog and rend it to pieces, eating portions of it." Drucker explains that the man-eaters are Cannibal or tánís dancers, the most highly ranked of the čaíqa series, the dog-eaters are nuɫəm dancers, and what Large called "doctors" are true, rather than ceremonial, shamans (Drucker 1940:208–11).

Large described "a demonstration of the Indian doctor's power" but, with his limited knowledge of Heiltsuk ceremonialism, was unable to provide a meaningful context for the event. The formal nature of the performance and the presence of an audience, however, suggest that it was a supernatural display in a Winter Ceremonial performance. Large wrote that two "doctors" (in this case, čaíqa) sat opposite one another in a dance house. One had in his hand a piece of stalactite crystal (a symbol of spirit power). When he rubbed his hands together, the crystal disappeared, to reappear in the hands of another "doctor" across the room. A challenge was issued to those who doubted the magic displayed, whereupon a "woman fell writhing to the ground as if shot, and vomited blood and bloody froth." This reaction was apparently caused by the crystal having been magically thrown into the body of the woman, perhaps because she questioned the shamans' powers, for when the stalactite was again seen in the hands of one of the "doctors," the woman miraculously recovered (*MB* 5, no. 4[1909]:694–95).

Small Wooden Bird. See Catalogue, No. 49.

Once again, Large's descriptions are lent credibility by later anthropological writings. The men who magically manipulated the powerful crystals may have been "healers" (hailĩkila) who had the ability to transfer spirit power to, or remove spirit power from, dancers or members of the audience. (The woman who "fell writhing to the ground" may have been so affected.) These ceremonialists were described by Drucker in connection with the Heiltsuk Returned from Heaven (dhuẁláx̌a) series of dances:

> A healer has the power to enter the room of any dancer, and can cause the inspiration ("put power on") or drive out the spirit of anyone. His insignia is a two-ply headband of cedar bark mounted with curved, upward-projecting spikes of copper (apparently similar in style to the bear-claw or goat-horn coronets of more northerly shamans). [1940:211]

This description suggests that the "two copper head ornaments" (No. 56) collected by Large were part of a healer's dance coronet. "In present day Bella Bella," writes Harkin, the hailĩkila "is remembered and performed as the most important dance" of the dhuẁláx̌a series" (1988:46).

Another artifact collected by Large and associated with the Winter Ceremonials is the "doctor's floating stone" (NS 27966). Large described how this or a similar stone might have been used:

> Sometimes they relate the miracles performed by these strong men of the Indians' past. A popular one was to make a stone float. The stone was first passed around for the people to weigh and examine, and then a piece of light material, which is found on the mountains, of the same shape and size, was cast on the water and floated. Jim Wise [1827–1907] brought me one of these secretly and explained the trick. [MB 5, no. 4(1909):696]

It is clear that, although the dances were supposed to be a thing of the past, ceremonial objects such as the "doctor's floating stone" were kept secret from the uninitiated.

According to Drucker (1940:203), making a stone float was one of the tricks called "shamans' magic" that were shown by novices in certain minor dances of the Shaman's (c̓aíqa) series. At Bella Bella this trick was shown on the second night of the Kinkla'klah dance (Olson 1955:342).

The ceremonial objects that Large collected are fragments of larger objects and/or of elaborate sets of dance paraphernalia and the missionary was not able to document the complex structure of meanings, prerogatives, wealth, and exchange that they represent. Typical of the fragments is a "bird from dance mask" (No. 49), a small, unpainted, simple carving that appears to have been part of a nineteenth-century artifact. Although there is nothing in Large's collection that might explain the original context of this fragment, a comparison with a Chief of the Sea (K̲umugwe') mask (UBCMOA A3634) suggests that the fragment might have been attached to a similar mask. The UBCMOA mask is surmounted by a rotating starfish, on each arm of which sits a small gull. It was collected from the Kwakw̲ak̲a'wakw of Fort Rupert (Tsax̲is) but was originally a Heiltsuk prerogative (Hawthorn 1967:242). According to Olson (1954:248), Monster-under-the-sea, or K!u'magwa (K̲umugwe'), was the spirit shown in the eighth-ranked dance of the Heiltsuk Returned from Heaven (dhuẇláx̌a) series.

The "copper rattle" (No. 51) is a very simplified version of a complex nineteenth-century Heiltsuk object type. Large's rattle is an unpainted cedar disc with a handle. At the top is a rough triangle of folded copper which encloses noise-makers. It is clearly a less complex version of a dance fan collected from the Heiltsuk in 1877 (NMNH 20636, see p. 42), the circular body of which is painted with a face design. The dance fan has two triangular pieces of folded copper attached to the top, like ears, and two wooden handles. A similar roughly triangular shape made from folded copper, this time without disc or handle, is seen in a rattle collected by Dr. Darby at Bella Bella after 1912 (UBCMOA A1111). A comparison of these three objects shows the simplification in the form of a ceremonial object associated with a loss of traditional culture, but at the same time indicates that the essential structure of the object survived despite the Christianization of the village. Copper rattles may have been retained because of their association with ceremonies for the naming of children. Among the Kwakw̲ak̲a'wakw, rattles used in such ceremonies were made either of the metal copper or of wood in the shape of a Copper, the distinctive copper plaque that is a unit of wealth on the Northwest Coast (Hawthorn 1967:148). As mentioned earlier (p. 67), the women of Bella

Rattle. See Catalogue, No. 51.

Bella, despite outward signs of modernization, were careful to maintain Heiltsuk traditions. Important family ceremonies such as the naming of a child would have been slow to change.

Large kerfed chests like the "Indian carved box, for dance masks" (No. 36) were the "valuable property of a wealthy person, used for storing ceremonial regalia and wealth items" (Stewart 1984:85). Such containers may also have figured in the Heiltsuk Cannibal (tánís) dance, which

> Was begun in the same way as a major potlatch (dlíala; given in conjunction with a mīL'a [dhuẁláẋa] dance)—by arranging a marriage. The bride brought with her a "box of dances" (tukwanutcàLī, "goes at her side"). A box of Shamans' dance regalia was bound with cedar withes, instead of the red cedar bark used for a mīL'a dance box. [Drucker 1940:208]

Both the worn condition of No. 36 and its complex and precisely carved design imply that it is older than most of the other artifacts Large sent to the OPM. Weathering of the wood has produced a dark patina and there is little trace of the original black, red, and blue paint. It is possible that this chest had been used as a coffin. Large wrote: "About Bella Bella I have seen [burial boxes] laid in niches of the rocks, in almost inaccessible places that had to be reached by ladders" (1905:100). At least one burial box was removed from a Bella Bella burial ground and sold to a museum (by Dorsey and Deans, see p. 43). Like most missionaries, Large would have strongly disapproved of graverobbing by collectors. Unfortunately, because the chest is part of the 1906 collection, its source is not known. In style the chest resembles those of the northern coast, and at least one important Heiltsuk family had prerogatives that were obtained through marriage with the Tlingit. Although the chest is culturally Heiltsuk, we cannot assume that it was made or collected at Bella Bella.

PROVENANCE: OBJECTS FROM OTHER COMMUNITIES

A notation signed "T. F. M." (probably T. F. McIlwraith, who became keeper of the ROM ethnological collections in 1925) at the beginning of the Normal School catalogue list of Large's 1906 collection states that because "Large was at Bella Bella, . . . probably all his material is from there." It has been demonstrated that most of the ceremonial objects Large collected correspond to aspects of specific Heiltsuk dance and/or feast parapher-nalia recorded by Large and his contemporaries or by ethnologists who visited Bella Bella more than twenty years after he left the village. However, an object such as the carved chest shows that all of the objects that were collected by Large cannot be uncon-ditionally attributed to Heiltsuk carvers. Another ceremonial object that may have orig-inated outside Bella Bella is the "carved slate knife" (No. 45), which is engraved with a picture of a Nuu-chah-nulth wolf, or a dancer in a Nuu-chah-nulth wolf mask and cos-tume. Large associated the ceremonial objects in his 1901 collection with the Fort Rupert Kwakwaka'wakw and tribes of the interior; this may have been the case with the 1906 group as well.

We know that some objects were collected at Bella Bella from people who had brought them from other communities. The Hyda (Haida) basket (No. 1) was collected from Alfred Wilson (1865–1935), whose family had lived on the Queen Charlotte Islands; the O'wekeno (Oweekeno) walking stick (No. 32) was obtained from Timothy Hunt (1860 or 1867–1922), whose family came to Bella Bella from Rivers Inlet. Other objects, such as the argillite poles (Nos. 22–23) that were not made by the Heiltsuk, may have been pur-chased at Bella Bella from people who came to the hospital, or in other communities. The Bella Bella and Rivers Inlet hospitals served a huge area and Large estimated that only one-quarter of his hospital patients were from the village (*MB* 3, no. 3[1906]:800). As a minister and medical officer, Large visited many other places, such as Steveston, Bella Coola, Owikeno Lake, Kimsquit, Klemtu (China Hat), Hartley Bay, Metlakatla, Port Simpson, Kincolith, Lakalzap (Greenville), Skidegate, the Skeena River, and the west coast of Vancouver Island (*MB* 2, no. 1[1904]:132–34; *MB* 5, no. 1[1908]:703–8). The exis-tence of "foreign" artifacts in what is essentially a collection from one location illustrates the problems of provenance and classification that arise in undocumented collections from the Northwest Coast, where the language groups are closely related artistically and culturally and there has been constant mobility between them through trade, intermar-riage, and the transfer of tangible and ritual property.

The presence in the collection of objects from outside Bella Bella may indicate that some types of objects were not available to Large in his own village but were readily available elsewhere. This may have been the case with the silver he collected. We know that by 1907 there were two silver carvers in Bella Bella, one of whom, Fred Anderson (*MB* 6, no. 1[1909]:9), was "a very good carver in silver and gold" and made bracelets for Vancouver dealers. He must have been successful at this, for he was able to build a very large and many-windowed residence at Waglisla (Large n.d.; Fig. 17). Anderson was a member of the Bella Bella Cornet Band and had some contact with Large. (Mrs. Anderson underwent eye surgery at the Bella Bella hospital in 1908.) The jewellery that Large sent to the OPM in 1906 (Nos. 92–93; NS 27884–27885, 27887) may have been made by Anderson or the other Bella Bella silver carver, but the jewellery in the 1901 collection is from Fort Rupert (Nos. 90–91) and an Alert Bay carver called Oliver (Nos. 86–88). The silver brooch from the Fraser River (No. 89) in the shape of a salmon is probably a souvenir from Steveston, an enormous fishery and cannery complex at the mouth of the Fraser River. Large worked at the Japanese hospital there in the summer of 1898, and again shortly after his marriage at Vancouver in May 1899 (*MO* 18, no. 7[1899]:146).[19]

In at least one case, Large's notation of the provenance of an artifact expands our knowledge of the little-understood regional styles and artifact types of the central coast. He noted that a "carved eagle" plaque (No. 27) came not from Bella Bella but from "Kimsquiet" (Kimsquit), a mixed Heiltsuk ('Isdaítx̌v)–Nuxalk village at the head of Dean Channel. It was obtained from Paul George, who was probably related to King George, one of the two old chiefs who governed Kimsquit.

FIG. 17. *This splendid house was built at Bella Bella (Waglisla) by the silver carver Fred Anderson. Courtesy Royal British Columbia Museum, Victoria. Photograph by R. W. Large, from "Souvenir of Bella Bella, B.C." PN 16466.*

Silver Brooches. See Catalogue, Nos. 86, 88–89.

The only white visitor known to have been at Kimsquit in the 1860s reported that the inhabitants were "the most uncivilized natives he had ever met" (Gough 1984:201) and that they continued to resist "civilization." After the smallpox epidemic of the 1860s, people from the Kimsquit settlements along Dean Channel congregated at the mouth of the Dean River, but that village was shelled by a British gunboat in a disciplinary action in 1877. The shelling was in retaliation for the supposed harbouring by the Kimsquit of Oweekeno fugitives wanted for the murder of survivors of an American shipwreck. Heiltsuk chief Charley Hemsett (Humchitt) was involved in the operation, as were George Hunt of Fort Rupert and Alfred Dudoward of Port Simpson. Chief Humchitt's participation is thought to have had something to do with a long-standing feud between the Heiltsuk and the Oweekeno (Gough 1984:199–204). At the turn of the century the Kimsquit people were living in a small village of old-style communal houses at the mouth of the Kimsquit or Salmon River. The population had declined from seventy-eight in 1899 to sixty-three in 1908, and the chiefs had repeatedly but unsuccessfully petitioned the Indian agent to find suitable orphaned or deserted children for the tribe to adopt in an attempt to reverse this trend (DIA 1899:263; 1907:31). The Heiltsuk maintained ceremonial ties with the pagan Kimsquit despite opposition from Large. In 1905 the people of Bella Bella were invited to Kimsquit, ostensibly to work on a new road, but in reality to receive repayment for gifts given at the funeral of the principal Heiltsuk chief (Chief Robert Bell, who died in 1904). Large discouraged the trip and was pleased to hear that the road work was in earnest and the celebration was mild (*MB* 3, no. 2[1905–6]:252).

The Kimsquit plaque (No. 27) is an adzed cedar disc about 60 cm in diameter, representing an eagle. It is one of the few objects documented as coming from Kimsquit, and it is an unusual artifact. There is one other like it—an octagonal plaque (described as a shield in the UBCMOA catalogue) collected at Bella Bella by Dr. Darby (UBCMOA A1363; Fig. 19). The two plaques are similar in motif and form. They are also probably similar in function. They may illustrate an artistic convention and artifact type from the region between Bella Coola and Bella Bella, the ancestral lands of the ʼIsdaítx̌v people.

The head of the eagle on the ROM plaque was carved separately and nailed on so that it projects upward from the disc. The bird's body is painted with black and silver-blue paint, and the body design is arranged inside a deeply incised oval at the centre of

Fig. 18. *Kimsquit women with a harvest of herring eggs drying on racks. Courtesy Royal British Columbia Museum, Victoria. Photograph by R. W. Large, from "Souvenir of Bella Bella, B.C." PN 16472.*

FIG. 19. *Eight-sided plaque, representing an eagle, collected at Bella Bella by Dr. George Darby. Courtesy University of British Columbia Museum of Anthropology, Vancouver. UBCMOA A1363.*

(*Facing page*) FIG. 20. *Memorial painting, representing an eagle, from a grave house on Dean Channel, between Kimsquit and Bella Bella. Courtesy Royal British Columbia Museum, Victoria. PN 4582 (detail).*

the disc with the wings, tail, and legs arranged around the oval. The pigment has run in places; the wood is darkened and has a raised grain, so that the plaque appears weathered.

The UBCMOA plaque is eight-sided rather than round. An eagle's head projects upward from the top of the plaque and the body of the bird is indicated by a black oval shape outlining a stylized human face. Wings, shoulders, and tail are separate shapes and contain unconnected ovals and knifelike feathers. The legs are simple, straight U-shapes ending in lines and circles indicating talons. The design is executed in red and black paint. Darby's and Large's plaques are the same size (50.8 cm and 61 cm high, respectively) and while the styles of painting and the shapes of the plaques differ, the artifacts are obviously two versions of the same object type.

According to the UBCMOA catalogue, Darby's plaque is "possibly a model of a crest, mounted on a house front." It appears to be a copy of a memorial painting, representing an eagle, that was attached to a grave house on Dean Channel at, or near, Kimsquit (Fig. 20). Although the memorial painting is rectangular and fills the area under the eaves over the door of the house, the elements of the design are found on the eight-sided plaque. The head of the eagle has been carved separately and projects upward from the top of the board. The body of the bird is a painted oval which contains two eye-and-brow shapes at the top, and although the details in the old photograph of the house are not clear, a central stylized face is suggested. The legs end in stylized talons and the tail is indicated by three feather forms. The arched wings are painted with geometric shapes—two rows of U-forms connected with wavy lines and long, knife-shaped feathers with black tips. Along the top of the wings and under the eagle's head runs a heavy black line. All of these motifs, stylized and simplified, are seen on the UBC-MOA plaque.

The style of the attached eagle's head on Large's plaque (No. 27), the UBCMOA plaque, and the Kimsquit memorial is very similar to the eagle's head that projects from a house-entrance pole (CMC VII-D-18) that was collected at Talio, a village on South Bentinck Arm, which borders on 'Isdaítx̌v territory. The eagle on the pole holds a sun disc in its talons; another Talio house-entrance pole shows the same motif—an eagle holding a sun disc (CMC VII-D-400). Large's plaque may combine the eagle and sun in one object.

A comparison of Large's plaque from Kimsquit (No. 27) with the UBCMOA plaque and its prototype, the Kimsquit grave-house painting, suggests that the plaques represent a regional artifact type from the territory of the Heiltsuk-speaking 'Isdaítx̌v,

Circular Plaque with Carved Eagle's Head. See Catalogue, No. 27.

between Bella Bella and Bella Coola. Kimsquit was a mixed Nuxalk- and Heiltsuk-speaking village with close ties to the people of Talio and Bella Coola, and with Heiltsuk cultural characteristics such as grave houses (see Fig. 21), which were not used by the Nuxalk (McIlwraith 1948, 1:18, 453). The plaques suggest the existence of a distinctive

'Isdaítx̌v motif, which incorporated or influenced some Talio artistic conventions. The variety of styles found in Bella Bella art may be in part the result of the amalgamation of Heiltsuk groups, each of which had a distinctive stylistic tradition.

Such stylistic amalgamations have been detected in other areas of the Northwest Coast. In a study of Tlingit art, Alan Sawyer found that each dialectic subdivision of the language group had a distinctive style. The situation among the Haisla groups of Douglas Channel was, he suggested, analogous: "It appears evident that the wide variety of styles found in Northern Wakashan masks reflects the distinctive art traditions of the many groups that once inhabited the region" (1983:143). While there are other reasons for the variety of styles we recognize as Heiltsuk (such as differences in date, function, artist, and owner), regional artistic conventions would certainly be important in a diverse community such as late nineteenth-century Bella Bella.

FIG. 21. *Heiltsuk grave houses at Old Grave Point, near Bella Bella (ʼQélc). Courtesy Royal British Columbia Museum, Victoria. Photograph by R. W. Large, from "Souvenir of Bella Bella, B.C." PN 16469.*

Shamans and Healing

When Large was in Toronto in the winter of 1906/7 he entered into a new agreement with the OPM. He would collect not only artifacts but "myth and folklore" exclusively for that museum. A letter to Large from an unnamed OPM official (Boyle or William F. Brodie, the curator) refers to the new arrangement between the missionary and the museum:

> I think we are safe in regarding the matter closed, so far as your authority to purchase is concerned and so far, also, as the collection of myth and folklore goes. Hereafter, however, we shall feel that we are on better footing and I shall be much pleased to learn that after you return to Bella Bella you will find time to devote some attention to the editing of your myths and other superstitions as you have gathered [in] this work amongst the natives.
>
> Of course I am unable to say to what extent the remuneration for this work will go but this is something that can be arranged by mail between you and Dr. Colquhoun [Deputy Minister of Education].
>
> I hope you will have an enjoyable time while you are gone and I shall fee[l] easy indeed to know that you are not likely to make any bargain with American Institutions, for supply of information or material of a more tangible kind.[20]

Although Large told the OPM that he had recorded "myths and other superstitions" of the Heiltsuk, the only scientific account of Northwest Coast indigenous practices that he published was a short article in the *Annual Archaeological Report* of 1904 entitled "Mortuary Customs in British Columbia" (R. W. Large 1905), in which he described the treatment of the dead, types of burial, the burning of food at the grave, and the alleged eating of corpses by the Cannibal (tánís) dancers. In his letters to the *Missionary Bulletin* and the *Missionary Outlook* he related his experiences with Heiltsuk shamans and his observations of native medicine and sympathetic magic. The cases that he described were selected to "reveal some phases of Indian character and belief" (*MB* 1, no. 2[1903]:232).

For instance, to cure haemorrhage of the lungs some expectorated blood was mixed with pitch and wrapped in four pieces of copper. These were then inserted in four sharpened sticks and placed in the stems of water lilies, which were left submerged in water (*MB* 1, no. 2[1903]:231).

Irregular breathing in a child was thought to be the result of the expectant parent's having seen an animal gasp for breath, heard the noise of a pump in a boat, or drunk bottled soda water or water near a land otter's house. There were appropriate cures for attacks related to each of these circumstances (*MB* 5, no. 4[1909]:705–6). The parents of a child who was having spasms and could not breathe thought that, because the child's face was purple during the attacks, the illness had been caused by the child's having watched its mother inflating and deflating a purple balloon for the child's amusement. When the child's face was washed in fluid in which the purple balloon had been soaked, the attack passed. Large preferred to believe that it was medicine he prescribed, rather than the parents' treatment, that had cured the child (*MB* 3, no. 1[1905]:115).

An old woman with a stiff neck revealed to Large that her condition had been caused by looking at a mask of a beaver when she was a young woman. Her father had wanted her to do this so that she would not turn her head around to flirt with the young men (*MB* 1, no. 2[1903]:227).

Large frequently mentioned the powers of the Indian doctors, particularly those who worked evil magic.[21] "Evil boxes" (mestachie boxes, or medicine men's boxes) were used to precipitate illness and death. A piece of the victim's clothing or spittle was taken and placed in the box and kept in contact with putrid matter; "the person from whom it was taken was doomed," Large wrote. "One can hardly over-estimate the power for evil this box had on the Indian mind. To lose a portion of an undergarment was often accepted as a death sentence." Large was present at the opening of one "evil box" at a public meeting in the Bella Bella firehall. Speeches were given and the box was opened. It contained bits of rags, a bottle of liquid, which was said to be poison, a piece of a coat, and some animal bones. When the objects were passed around for identification, "the scene was almost like searching for your dead in the morgue after some great calamity." Large had heard a lot about such boxes and was surprised by how little this one contained. The missionary was given the box with the request that the contents be washed and sunk in the sea (*MB* 5, no. 4[1909]:699–704, 711–12; 1, no. 2[1903]:229–30).

An "evil-throwing" doctor was thought to be able to cause death by magically projecting pieces of stone or bone into the body of the victim. Large reported a number of instances of death and disease that were allegedly caused by these doctors.

In one case, a Bella Bella man had gone to live at China Hat because he was sure that the death of one of his children had been caused by one of the chiefs. The family, while out in a canoe, had passed the chief sitting on the shore. "As they passed, the Chief made a motion with his hand, and he[the father] is quite sure that this motion of [the chief's] arm sped the weapon that killed the child" (*MB* 5, no. 4[1909]:694).

In another case, a young man violated some of the rules of the dance, so as punishment the chiefs killed the man's mother. An "old woman witch doctor" was given a piece of bone or stone from a collection that was kept for such purposes and she blew it into the victim through a knothole in the house. A stick was thrown on the roof of the house to let the inhabitants know what had been done. The victim "vomited blood in three days and was dead in two weeks" (*MB* 5, no. 4[1909]:693–94).

Large had a special interest in these Heiltsuk "superstitions": they were fascinating evidence of the world view that he was trying to reform, and as a doctor he was often in competition with traditional Heiltsuk medicine.

> The old-time Indians of the coast still believe to a greater or less extent in the power of the medicine men and witchcraft. Others, more advanced, still try decoctions made of roots and herbs. Still others pin faith to patent medicines. The missionary has to enter into competition with one or more of these rivals, and win confidence and retain it. [*MB* 1, no. 3(1903):300]

A successful medical treatment by Large could further the cause of the mission. For example, Large cured the wife of an important Heiltsuk chief by a simple operation (the chief thought his wife's illness had been caused by an "evil disposed doctor"). The chief, who had given Large "considerable trouble" in the past, thereafter became one of his most active supporters (*MB* 1, no. 2[1903]:232).

In 1903 there were two "old-time doctors" at Bella Bella who were "quietly treating some of the sick ones and keeping alive the old superstitions," such as burning food at the graves. The practice of witchcraft was an indictable offence, punishable by one year's imprisonment, and Large threatened to report the Heiltsuk doctors to the government if they "did not stop misleading the people." At one point Large seemed to think that his efforts were successful: "They promised to stop their practices entirely, and so far as we have been able to learn have kept their promises" (*MB* 1, no. 2[1903]:233). Dr. Raynor, who filled in for Large in the winter of 1906/7, seemed to agree: "The old medicine man is a thing of the past in Bella Bella" (*MB* 4, no. 2[1907]:550). In 1909, however, Large wrote that "in almost every death in the tribe, witchcraft by the older ones is supposed to figure, and nearly every sickness brings the dread of it." He noted that death was thought to be caused by "giving poison or injurious substances in food, casting a spell and projecting a foreign body into the vitals, the use of the evil box, [or] contact with inhabitants of the spirit world" (*MB* 5, no. 4[1909]:692–93). The missionaries

Stone Baton. See Catalogue, No. 45.

were apparently not as successful against the shamans as they had earlier believed. In 1908 one of the "old-time doctors," Dr. Charley (Owekeno Charley), was "secretly practicing at odd times," but Large could not catch him because "his patients screen him, and he pays his visits at night" (*MB* 5, no. 1[1908]:18). The Heiltsuk preferred to keep their options open and sought medical assistance from both kinds of doctors, each with his area of expertise (see p. 31).

The second "old-time doctor" at Bella Bella was Dr. Sam (1821–1906?), from whom Large acquired two crudely carved walking sticks (Nos. 31, 33) and a "stone playing disc" (NS 23122). Sam was a man of high rank—he was related to Chief Charley and was a well-known shaman who is mentioned in the fieldnotes of both Boas and Drucker.

Sam received his supernatural power on Calvert Island. While hunting there, his feet sank into solid rock. Not until the following day, when he heard the cry of the Cannibal spirit and received his power, was Sam able to free himself (Drucker Papers).[22] After an epidemic struck the Heiltsuk, Sam began to exercise that power and became an important doctor. His effectiveness is evident in a story related by Boas in which Sam was consulted by a family when their son did not return from a hunting trip. Sam put a shirt belonging to the boy under his pillow and in his sleep saw that it was full of blood. From this dream he knew that the boy had become ill while away from home. Further, he knew the reason for the illness. Sam explained that "the ghosts had hit" the boy, that is, the illness was caused by contact with the dead. ("If the anima [soul] goes to the land of the dead, the person will die; if it goes part of the way, the person will become sick but recover" [Olson 1935, 1949, quoted in Harkin 1988:147].) According to Large, Dr. Sam died suddenly of a haemorrhage in 1906 after eating jam at Solomon's house.[23] Two years later, his "wonderful magic powers" were still talked about in Bella Bella (*MB* 5, no. 1[1908]:18).

Chief Jim Noonaquos, or Nooniquas (Núṅukvas, 1835–1904; Fig. 22), from whom Large acquired the "chief's spoon, very old" (No. 100), may also have been a practicing doctor. He cured Old Dick (General Dick?) of a severely inflamed finger by cutting off the first joint to extract a piece of copper, which had caused the illness (*MB* 5, no. 4[1909]:699). The chief's old spoon seems to support his connection with shamanism. The bowl is of mountain-sheep horn and the carved bone handle suggests a land otter. There are two Tsimshian spoons with land otter motifs in the Portland Art Museum (PAM 48.3.261 and 48.3.739). They were collected by Axel Rasmussen, who thought they belonged to a medicine man because of the land otter motif—the animal is a powerful spirit helper (Gunther 1966:27).

Large's records of Heiltsuk medicine and shamanism are unique in missionary writings of the early twentieth century. Large's professional interest resulted in an extensive collection of information, and although he was obviously biased against the preservation of Heiltsuk beliefs and was confident that "an intelligent knowledge of disease will free them from all dread of witchcraft" (*MB* 5, no. 4[1909]:712), his collection of "superstitions" contributes to our understanding of how "the old and the new" coexisted in Methodist Bella Bella at the turn of the century. It is ironic that a man so intent on eradicating Heiltsuk culture should have left one of the few written records of the survival of traditional medicine and shamanism at Bella Bella.

FIG. 22. *Núṅukvas and his wife were photographed in their canoe at Bella Bella (ʾQélc) in 1889 while paddling out to the steamship* Barbara Boscowitz, *which was in the harbour unloading freight. Courtesy Royal British Columbia Museum, Victoria. PN 12390 (detail).*

MYTHOLOGY

The study of myths and legends was a long-standing interest of Large's. One of his collections was a group of thirty-nine drawings by Kwakwa̲ka̲'wakw artist Charlie George, Jr. (RBCM 15863–15901).[24] Most of these illustrate a Blunden Harbour tale about the ancestor/hero Soogwilis. As a child, the artist had been a patient in the Bella Bella hospital and had made the drawings for Large. In 1951 the drawings and the legend were published by Large's son, Dr. Richard Geddes Large, who wrote that his father "showed an intense interest in the folklore and customs of the native people" (1951:9).

In a letter to Boas in November 1900 concerning the two interior house posts he was sending to the AMNH, Large said that he had "not had time as yet to work on their legends &c. but am hoping for more leisure shortly."[25] He never did collect the legends; apparently his schedule left him little room for this proposed ethnological work. He had office hours from 10:00 a.m. until 1:00 p.m. on weekdays and made calls and attended to emergencies in the afternoons. Every Sunday morning he held a prayer meeting at 7:00 a.m. and preached at 7:30 a.m. On Saturday afternoons and evenings Bible study classes were held. There was another preaching service on Tuesday night, a prayer meeting on Thursday night, and "practice for Christmas" on Monday, Wednesday, and Friday nights. "So with the exception of these few engagements," wrote Large with characteristic wit, "I have all the evenings to myself" (MO 18, no. 4[1899]:81).

Another impediment to Large's study of myths and legends was his lack of knowledge of the Heiltsuk language. He must have known some Heiltsuk in order to carry out his medical and legal duties, and he did include the Heiltsuk terms (as he understood them) for stone hammer ("hous'te") and stone axe ("klah-qua-bah'-la," an attempt to render íháqvabálá, which means adze) in his catalogue notes, but it is unlikely that he spoke the language well. Nevertheless, although Large did not record any Heiltsuk legends, some of the artifacts he collected are in themselves concrete records of Heiltsuk mythology.

No doubt Large intended to provide the "legends &c" associated with the two house posts that he sold to the OPM in 1901 (Nos. 18–19). They come from the same house as the AMNH poles and, like them, one represents a bear with a small figure in its raised paws, and the other a killer whale.[26] The bear on the AMNH post (northeast corner post; AMNH 16/8379, Fig. 23) holds a bear cub, whereas the bear on the ROM post (southeast corner post; No. 18) holds a small human figure. These posts may illustrate the common bear-mother tradition. A Heiltsuk version of this story, "the bear who car-

ried away a woman," was collected by Boas and Hunt in 1923. It tells of a young woman who stepped on bear's dung while out picking berries and cursed it. A bear appeared, "elaborately dressed in black bear skin and with thick cedar-bark head and neck rings and also arm and leg rings, and a man's face carved on the shoulders of his blanket."

This is the "cannibal dancer of the bear," who abducts the woman. She gives birth to four bear-children and is eventually rescued by her brothers, taking with her "the cannibal dancer's whistles and ornaments [and] the carving box which contains other kinds of cedar bark ornaments," and thus obtaining the rights to certain Cannibal (tánís) dances and ceremonial privileges (Boas 1932:67–69).

The killer-whale posts are not easily associated with a known Heiltsuk legend, but they also seem to depict a human/non-human duality, for the small face in the lower fluke of the AMNH post (northwest corner post; AMNH 16/8380, Fig. 24) is a whale and on the ROM post (southwest corner post; No. 19) it is a human face. The whales face downward with their heads away from the centre of the house and their tails toward the centre. Large dorsal fins rise from their bent backs to support the squared longitudinal timbers of the house.

The two killer-whale posts appear to be the same ones shown in a sketch of a potlatch house drawn for Drucker by his informant Moses Knight in 1936/37, but unlike the AMNH and ROM posts, the killer whales in Knight's drawing face toward the centre of the house. The caption for the sketch reads:

> Posts and screen of a potlatch house (Istetx Bella Bella). These Killer Whale posts are used for the potlatch following a performance of the dluwulaxa [dhuẃláx̌a] society. The screen behind which the novices and masks are kept is shown extending between the posts. Society members are seated before it, and dance officials in the circle before the door through which dancers pass. [1940:209, fig. 2]

There is photographic evidence of a third killer-whale post (Fig. 25) in the American anthropologist Viola Garfield's collection of Northwest Coast photographs (Garfield 1949). The post was photographed at Bainbridge Island, Washington, in 1908. Garfield was told by the owner, Mrs. Alfred F. Woolsey, that the post had been cut down sometime between 1900 and 1905 by her father while he was working on the coast for the Alaska

FIG. 24. *House post in the form of a killer whale. The dorsal fin forms the roof beam support. The post stood at the back of the house (northwest corner), opposite the bear post AMNH 16/8379. It was sold by Large to Franz Boas in 1900. Courtesy Department of Library Services, American Museum of Natural History. AMNH16/8380, neg. no. 42853.*

Steamship Company. It was brought south, repainted, and installed on the lawn of his house where it stood as a decoration until it was destroyed in a storm. Although Garfield's notes give no indication of the post's original provenance, it is intriguingly similar to the ROM and AMNH killer-whale posts (Black 1992).

In August 1897 when the posts at 'Qélc were photographed for the AMNH, the house, which stood on the beach in front of the church, was in ruins.[27] It was being used to store canoes (still protected by woven cedar-bark mats) and European-style boats. When the house was photographed by Newcombe and by the Alaskan photographers Winter and Pond[28] just before the poles were taken down in 1901, all that remained of it were the two main beams.[29] The house was identified, presumably by Boas, as "Bella Bella house #1,"[30] but it is difficult to see from photographs of the village taken around 1900 which house it might be.

Only one other object in the collection, a speaker's staff (No. 64), appears to illustrate a Heiltsuk myth. Large described the staff as a "carved ceremonial wand," but did not record the meanings of the figures on the staff. They are (from top to bottom) a long-billed bird, a sitting wolf or dog (?) holding a small standing human, two doglike animals on all fours, and three standing humans. All these figures, intertwined and standing on each other's shoulders, ultimately rest on the brim of a large ringed hat worn by a person holding a digging stick. This complex arrangement of interlocking figures relates to a typically Heiltsuk origin myth recorded variously as the story of Tsḷŭ'mqǎlǎqs, "the mother-of-dogs" (Boas 1897:401–3; 1932:33–46); "the dog's wife (a Bella Bella story)" (McIlwraith 1948, 1:642–45); "the wolf children story" and "the origin of the Heiltsuk, or the dog husband" (Olson 1955:32–33; 1940:89–90); and the "dog-husband tale" (Drucker 1965:68). Although the recorded versions differ in details, the basic story concerns a Heiltsuk woman who gave birth to four dogs. This is one of the versions recorded in *Bella Bella Tales*:

> She used to go digging clams on the beach in front of her house to get food for her children. Now the young dogs began to grow up. At night when it was low water, she went down to the beach carrying a torch, and dug clams. Then she heard a sound like the singing of many children. Tsḷŭ'mqǎlǎqs wanted to know who the children were. She put her dig-

FIG. 25. *Killer-whale post acquired between 1900 and 1905 and moved to Bainbridge Island, Washington. Courtesy Special Collections Division, University of Washington Libraries. Viola Garfield photograph, U.W. 13655.*

ging stick into the ground, took off her cape, and hung it over the stick.
[In other versions she also put her hat on top of the stick.] Thus she
made it look like a person. Then she went to see who was singing. She looked
through a hole and saw now that her children were all boys. . . . Only the
youngest one put on his dogskin in time [and thus remained a dog] before the
woman had taken the skins and thrown them into the fire. [Boas 1932:33–34;
38–39]

This version, told by Ō'dzē⁵stalis in 1895, connects this dog-mother myth with the origin
of the Winter Ceremonies.[31] It goes on to involve the sons of Tsḷǔ'mqǎlǎqs in the story of
the supernatural Cannibal-at-the-North-End-of-the-World, Báxvbakváláṅusiwa, and the
origin of the 'Uyalitx̌v tánís dance society (Boas 1932:39, 44). Tánís initiates are possessed and abducted by the spirit of Báxvbakváláṅusiwa, whose associates, a quartet of
long-beaked cannibal birds, appear as masked dancers in ceremonies marking the initiates' return to, and reintegration in, Heiltsuk society. This connection may explain the bird
on the top of the staff. Its beak seems too long for Raven, a common Heiltsuk crest. Perhaps
it represents the huxwhukw, one of the cannibal birds associated with Báxvbakváláṅusiwa.

Many of the objects that Large collected illustrate the situation at Bella Bella in the
first decade of the twentieth century, when traditional and modern ways coexisted in
Bella Bella. The collection includes pecked stone tools such as the "mortar, representing
frog" (No. 119) that, if not ancient themselves, were made by ancient methods in forms
that are thousands of years old, as well as novelties such as a painted clam shell (No.
128). Some new objects, such as the "yew wood box, old model" (No. 44) and the "high
crown dance hat" (No. 7), are replicas of "old-time" artifacts, while others, like the "slipper case, representing frog, made by Bella Bella woman" (No. 10), imbue traditional
form and material with new function. Bella Bella was a rapidly changing community
between 1898 and 1907. Objects old and new, traditional and novel were all available to
Large. He collected not only traditional old artifacts, which would illustrate the ethnology of the nineteenth-century Heiltsuk, but also new objects and replicas that would
reflect the diversity of the modern Methodist community that Bella Bella had become
during his tenure. In doing so, he left a valuable record of Bella Bella art and of the community that produced it.

Talking Stick. See Catalogue, No. 64.

Notes

1. Large may have collected some of these objects as early as August 1892. This is the date noted for a brass ring (ROM 892.2.1) included in a list of fifteen additional York County objects from Large that were entered in the Normal School catalogue in 1902 (ROM 25006–25020). Between 1891 and his enrolment in medical school in 1893, Large was a schoolteacher, perhaps in Simcoe County. He worked on behalf of the Methodist Church in the Bradford district (*MO* 19, no. 2[1900]:36).

2. Killan quotes the following sources: *Annual Archaeological Report,* 1894/95:25, 29, 33; D. Boyle, "Archaeological Remains: A Factor in the Study of History," *Transactions of the Canadian Institute,* series 4, vol. 1, 1889/90.

3. This total includes five ROM X-numbered objects (Nos. 40, 41, 50, 77), which are very likely part of Large's Bella Bella material; "X" numbers were given to those objects lacking provenance and collection information.

4. Bella Bella was part of the DIA's Bella Coola Agency at this time.

5. Knight cautions against "discovering past social practices woven into new contexts: . . . In certain spheres, as in much social life, in domestic economy and even in some jobs in the cash economy (such as pelagic sealing) there was continuity of traditional patterns. However, the claims that traditional work and social practices were *typically* carried over more or less unchanged into industrial work are specious" (1978:178). See also Harkin (1988:290).

6. Traditionally, the inner bast would have been removed by a mussel shell, perhaps similar to No. 107.

7. The missionaries associated gambling with violence and alcohol. Its association with slavery might also have been a factor in their opposition to gambling games such as "lahal":

    > It was not uncommon for a Bella Coola to lose his freedom by gambling. At lahal especially, a player who had exhausted his goods not infrequently wagered his children or in extreme cases, himself. If he lost, his children, or himself, became the property of the winner. Unless speedily repurchased by some relative, such slaves were usually sold or given away at the first opportunity to a member of a foreign tribe, since it was considered improper for a man to hold a member of his own tribe in servitude. [McIlwraith 1948, 2:159]

    Lahal, a spirited game in which opposing sides must guess which hands conceal specially marked gaming pieces that are passed rapidly and secretly back and forth, is still popular on the Northwest Coast (see Holm 1987:40).

8. R. W. Large to T. E. Egerton Shore, 13 October 1910 (Shore Papers).

9. The NS catalogue entry was copied incorrectly from the inventory price list as "new wood box."

10. For discussions of the nature of the Kwakwaka'wakw potlatch, its suppression, and its ultimate survival, see Sewid-Smith (1979), Cole and Chaikin (1990), and Jonaitis, ed. (1991).

11. Perhaps this is Bertie Humchitt (1881–1914?).

12. The count of the total number of this type of object in the collection is not precise because the purpose of some carvings, such as the wooden figures collected from General Dick (Nos. 15–17, 29) and the walking sticks from Timothy Hunt (No. 32) and Dr. Sam (Nos. 31, 33), is not clear.

13. Large's 1906 collection contained a "head dress (cedar bark)" (NS 28204), which may have come from Bella Bella. It was traded to the Australian National Museum in 1907.

14. 'Caíqa ceremonies dramatize spirit possession by powerful and dangerous earthly elemental forces. In contrast, the dhuẃláx̌a—variously translated as "once more (come) down (from heaven)" (Drucker 1940:205), "heavenly" (Harkin 1988:3), and "coming down again" (Hilton 1990:318)—demonstrates the validating relationship between the Heiltsuk chiefs and the ancestral spirits in the world above. For further discussion and interpretation of Heiltsuk ceremonies, see Drucker (1940), Harkin (1988), and Hilton (1990).

15. Sinash is a misspelling of Siwash. Both Stick and Siwash are derogatory terms. "To call a man a "Carrier" [Interior Indian] was and still is an insult," wrote McIlwraith (1948, 1:18). According to LaViolette (1973:113), "some westerners believe that a tribe of SIWASH Indians actually did exist, and in some cases it is used as a neutral designation for Indian. But Indians consider it derogatory and opprobrious." These terms would not be used today but in Large's time they were current. The language barrier, the lack of ethnographic knowledge, and prevailing ethnocentric attitudes meant that many non-Indians did not know the proper names for native villages and language groups.

16. Prerogatives are inherited ranks and privileges, both tangible (such as masks, regalia, and totem poles) and intangible (such as names, dances, songs, and rights to resources), the rights to which are validated through potlatching.

17. Alan Hoover, personal communication, 1986; Bill Holm, letter to the author, 5 February 1986.

18. MAI collection record, 1922, on file at HCEC. It is interesting that Tate thought that the shaman he knew at Old Bella Bella was the last in the village. In Large's time, more than twenty years later, there were two Indian doctors in Bella Bella, said to be the last in the village (see p. 92).

19. See also the R. W. Large Biographical file.

20. OPM to R. W. Large, 14 February 1907 (NS file).

21. "'Good' shamans, i.e. those who do not practice evil magic, are called he'likuXu ('healers'). 'Bad' shamans, workers of evil magic, are called da'sgyu" (Olson 1955:338).

22. Harkin points out that in Heiltsuk mythology, "supernatural powers [are] obtained in ways very similar to hunting, and often indeed in the act of hunting." The connection between spirit power and the hunt is demonstrated in the c̓aíqa which "symbolically objectifies and manipulates" the relationship between men and animals, life and death, hunter and hunted (Harkin 1988:131–32).

23. "Glass was suspected" in the jam. Apparently, this was a method of revenge against witchcraft (*MB* 5, no. 4[1909]:693). Boas (1923:263–66) says that Sam died of influenza in 1918, which con-

tradicts Large's information. Narratives of spirit-power acquisition are formalized; it is possible that similar accounts of the experiences of two different Heiltsuk shamans have merged.

24. I am indebted to Randal Macnair for the catalogue information about these drawings.

25. R. W. Large to Franz Boas, 26 November 1900 (AMNH 1900).

26. A ROM Department of Ethnology publication labels the bear post as a "bear mother house post," but wrongly describes the killer-whale post as a "salmon house post" (ROM 1976:24, 21).

27. AMNH negative numbers 42852–42855.

28. Lloyd Winter and E. Percy Pond operated a commercial photography studio in Juneau, Alaska, from 1893 to 1943. They specialized in views of Alaska and left an extensive photographic record of the Tlingit and Haida.

29. The Newcombe photographs are RBCM, PN 143 and PN 482. The Winter and Pond photograph is Alaska State Library PCA 87-1350 (see Wyatt 1989:134).

30. Stanley A. Freed, letter to the author, 30 January 1986.

31. In other versions, two children remain dogs or wolves and two are transformed into humans (Boas 1932:41–42, 44).

5
Five Bella Bella Carvers

The Heiltsuk were respected carvers, canoe builders, and box makers in the nineteenth century.[1] The works collected by Large show that those artistic traditions continued into the twentieth century despite the great cultural changes that had taken place. Among the unnamed Bella Bella tradesmen listed by Large in 1906 were two silversmiths, four wood carvers, and a lighthouse keeper (see p. 35). Of the twenty-five individuals named by Large in the 1902 accession list, five are identified by the missionary as makers of objects: Chief Robert Bell, Captain Carpenter (the lighthouse keeper), Enoch, General Dick, and Daniel Houstie. Additional information in Large's letters and other archives about the lives of these men (see Appendix C) illustrates that Bella Bella art can no longer be viewed as the production of anonymous, undifferentiated craftsmen.

The lives of the artists, particularly Chief Bell and Captain Carpenter, testify to the adjustments that many Bella Bella people made to try to maintain native traditions while participating in the new social and religious order of their progressive Methodist village. Large's documentation allows the Bella Bella artists to be perceived as individuals, but, more than that, because his collection is the only one from Bella Bella that has such documentation, it is the key to the identification of other works by these artists. Daniel Houstie's idiosyncratic version of the Bella Bella style, for example, can be recognized in a group of undocumented boxes and mysterious ceremonial objects in Large's 1906 collection.

Most of the works by Houstie and the other artists mentioned by Large were new when they were collected between December 1898 and December 1901 (only the 1902 accession list mentions artists' names). Some, such as the decorated paddles made by General Dick and Daniel Houstie, appear to have been standard tourist-trade objects. Others may have been commissioned by the missionary to illustrate what he thought was a way of life on the threshold of extinction. While the functions of the originals of these objects are now unclear in many cases because of the lack of detailed ethnographic information about the Heiltsuk, the research for this study has suggested that Houstie's works are replicas of traditional household and ceremonial objects rather than novelties. Works by Bell, Carpenter, Enoch, and Dick also appear to follow traditional models, and suggest that Large was initiating this kind of production as well as gathering older artifacts when they were available.

Chief Robert Bell (1859–1904)

The four objects that Large obtained from Chief Robert Bell are indicative of the variety of style and workmanship in Bella Bella art at the turn of the century. A finely carved and painted wooden club (No. 62) depicts three Heiltsuk crest animals, Wolf, Bear, and Whale; the black and brown painting and three-dimensional treatment of the figures recalls traditional Heiltsuk sculpture. The wolf holds a small human figure in its paws and may refer to the story of the wolf-mother, or dog-mother, a uniquely Heiltsuk legend (see p. 99). Both the wolf and the human figure have "masks" over their eyes, a feature found on many Bella Bella ceremonial objects. Bell's lively carving has compact, rounded figures with small-scale detailing. The painting is varied—each figure is treated in a different manner and the artist makes use of solid colour, irregular hatching, and unpainted areas to emphasize the individuality of each element.

The club may have been used in the Winter Dances that continued in a modified form in Bella Bella and the surrounding communities despite opposition from the missionaries. The War dancer, the most highly ranked dancer in the Returned from Heaven (dhuẃláx̌a) series, carried a club that was carved with a lineage crest (Olson 1954:248; Stevenson n.d., p. 68). The whistle made by Bell (No. 68), although it is not decorated with traditional formline designs, is solid and functional. It may also have been intended for ceremonial use, but it and two roughly made and painted boxes (Nos. 35, 40) were probably made for sale to Large or to steamship passengers who stopped at the village.

Historians of aboriginal arts associate disintegration of form with loss of function. Such a decline is thought to be characteristic of the art of societies undergoing extreme and rapid cultural change. For instance, Drucker found "no evidence of any important modification of stylistic patterns during the historic period other than their gradual deterioration through disuse toward the end of the last century and the early decades of the present one." He attributed this decline to "loss of interest due to the rapidly accelerated acculturation of the Indians and to their nearly complete missionization" (1955:178–79). Deterioration in workmanship may, however, also reflect a change in the artist's health or personal situation. Both social and personal factors may explain the inconsistency in the work that Large acquired from Bell.

When Large made his first collection, Bell was the head chief of the village, the owner of Robert Bell and Co. general store, and an officer of the Bella Bella Cornet Band (*MB* 3, no.1[1905]:113).[2] Bell does not appear in Bella Bella records until after 1900. Probably he was from the ʼQvúqvaẏaítx̌v village of Kokyet (ʼQábá) on Yeo Island and

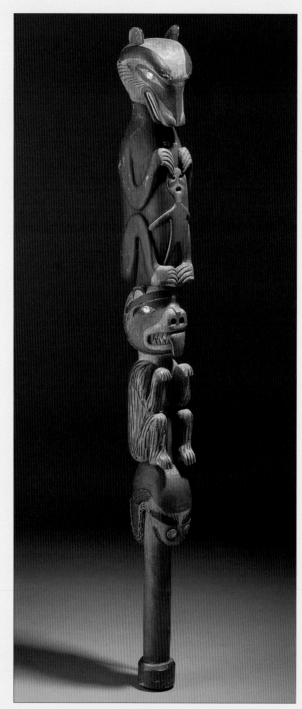

Club or Talking Stick. See Catalogue, No. 62.

moved into Bella Bella when a fire destroyed 'Qábá in 1891 (Beavis n.d.). Bell would have been over thirty years old at the time of the move, having spent his life in a village that resisted missionary influence. Reverend Tate tells of visiting 'Qábá from his base at Bella Bella and trying to stop a Cannibal (tánís) dance that was being performed there. Even though the missionary was locked out of the dance house and forced to leave the village, he took credit later for "having stopped the biting [of the tánís dancer] at Kokite," because "some time afterwards this whole tribe gave up their heathen practices [and] moved in a body to Bella Bella" (*MB* 8, no. 1[1911]:920).

'Qa'aít, the first-ranked 'Qvúqvaẏaítx̌v name, was held by Chief Bell. That chiefs of this name were mentioned by Vancouver (1798:2:276) writing in the late eighteenth century, by Tolmie (1963:294) and Dunn (1844:251) writing in the 1830s, and Boas (1897:430) writing at the turn of the century, signifies the continuity of Heiltsuk traditions embodied by the chief. Between 1897 and 1901 Bell succeeded Boston Humpsit (Humchitt) as head chief of Bella Bella. Olson's comment (1935, 1949:34) that, on the occasion of Chief Moody's father's marriage, Robert Bell performed as the sleep-causing (Kḷya'LkyaLamas) dancer, is the only reference to Bell's participation in Heiltsuk ceremonies in the ethnographic literature, but he must have been active in the traditional life of the 'Qvúqvaẏaítx̌v and the amalgamated Heiltsuk at Bella Bella.[3]

When Bell became chief, he apparently supported the missionary's efforts to curtail traditional ceremonies. Large was pleased by a notice that was "printed in large type on a sheet of cotton and posted on the main street when the head chief and band president was to be married." It read:

> The officer of the B.B.C.B. will give a real good time when Christmas Day will Held, and his band boys will also try give a splendid time, and now I wish you all, Ladies and Gentlemens of B.B. to get ready when the time will held. any person not feel well I wish they try to make themselves better now. No old fashioned doing will be given I hope everything will be ready when time come.
> —From the Officer of the B.B. Cornet Band. Robert Bell.

Large reported that the event, which probably took place in 1902, was "free from all old customs" (*MB* 3, no. 1[1905]:113).

On 19 August 1904, Bell died at the age of forty-five.[4] At the time of his death, he is thought to have had difficulties (possibly financial ones) associated with his store. The chief's death was marked by some of the "old customs," for according to Dr. J. C.

Spencer, the Bella Coola were invited by the Bella Bella in 1904 "to celebrate the death of a chief." The feast, which involved people from China Hat, Kitamaat, and Kimsquit, lasted two weeks.[5] The Bella Coola chiefs reciprocated by inviting some of the celebrants to their village where they gave away "with much ado, about 400 pounds of biscuits and a large amount of tea and jam" (*MB* 2, no. 3[1905]:595).

Bell held important positions in both traditional and Europeanized Bella Bella society. He had made rapid transitions—from old customs to Christianity, from a somewhat traditional village to a new, modern one, and from chief to business man. Adjustment to all these changes seems to have been difficult for Chief Bell. It must have been so for many of the Heiltsuk.

Captain Carpenter (1841–1931)

A man called Carpenter was recorded in the 1881 Canada Census as living at Bella Bella with his family (most of whom did not use English names). Captain Carpenter was, like Chief Bell, 'Qvúqvayaítx̌v. He was a second-ranked chief at Bella Bella (DIA 1888:480).

When Mrs. Carpenter died in the winter of 1904/5, Large commented that the chiefs "would get her tombstone," and in return the chiefs received a sloop and a sealing boat made by Carpenter and his son. Large was told that Mrs. Carpenter asked that her possessions not be burned on the grave, but be distributed to her "friends," the chiefs (*MB* 2, no. 4[1905]:821–22). This implies that the arrangements were more Western than they actually were. Rather than mementos to friends, such settlements were likely a continuation of Heiltsuk potlatch traditions in a form that the missionary did not oppose.

Carpenter's wife, who was a woman of high rank and a descendant of Chief 'Qa'aít (see p. 19), was buried in the grave house built for Chief Bell and was probably related to him. When Carpenter wished to remarry, Large suggested that he court the widow of the chief (*MB* 2, no. 4[1905]:821). A marriage to a relative of one's deceased wife would have been an appropriate Heiltsuk arrangement. That Large's suggestion was in line with Heiltsuk traditions of dynastic marriage may have been coincidence. On the other hand, it may indicate an attempt to accommodate selected indigenous social institutions. Perhaps it is Chief Bell's widow and her son who were photographed by the missionary with Carpenter at the Dryad Point lighthouse (*MB* 6, no. 1[1909]:10; Large n.d.).[6]

The chiefs of the northern tribes employed someone to make and repair canoes, masks, and other ritual objects, and "this man they call the Carpenter," according to Dunn (1844:291). Captain Carpenter's English name denotes his occupation of carver and canoe and boat maker.[7] Carpenter built a large canoe that was exhibited at the Fisheries Exhibition in London, England (Olson 1935, 1949:10; Tate n.d., p. 29), and, according to Reverend Tate, he also built a twenty-three-metre-long canoe that is now in the AMNH (*MO* 8, no. 2[1888]:2). He successfully adapted his considerable canoe-making skills to build sailing boats, which were much admired for their craftsmanship (*MB* 6, no. 1[1909]:13–14).

After 1900, Carpenter entered the wage economy as the keeper of the Dryad Point lighthouse just north of Bella Bella. The job paid one dollar a day (*MB* 2, no. 4[1905]:821). He looked upon Large as a fellow government man and colleague,[8] and considered seeking a white wife (*MB* 6, no. 1[1909]:13-14).

Carpenter would have been about twenty years old at the time of the great smallpox epidemic and so had seen the Heiltsuk population fall from about twenty thousand to about two hundred people. (Men of his generation recalled a period when all they did was dig graves for those who had died.)[9] He seems to have been very successful in adapting to the changes that took place during his lifetime.

Captain Carpenter was Richard (Dick) Carpenter, Du'ḵḻwayella.[10] He died at the age of ninety in March 1931 (Streich 1983; Beavis n.d.).

Large's collection included two paint stones that Carpenter used to mix his pigments (NS 23119, 23164), a painted kerfed chest with a lid (No. 34), and a feast bowl in the shape of a beaver (No. 42). These traditional objects may have been made for Heiltsuk use. They follow Heiltsuk artistic conventions. Huge bowls such as No. 42 were used in feasts and came in sets of four to represent "the divisions of the supernatural beings of the undersea, sky, land, and forest," according to Hawthorn (1967:178). Two animal-shaped feast bowls from Bella Bella that are now in the CMC (CMC VII-EE-37–38) were used by Chief Moody (Humchitt; see p. 73) at the feast marking his becoming head chief. The chest made by Carpenter (No. 34) is approximately the same size as Kwakwa̱ka̱'wakw boxes that were used to store "bits of costume and other paraphernalia employed in all the dances owned by the individuals, and hence theoretically the dances themselves with their appurtenant names" (Curtis 1915:130).[11]

Large's note that these objects are the work of Carpenter is useful for the attribution of other Heiltsuk works of the same period. Holm commented that

Captain Carpenter's chest is another of those very significant pieces which help make sense out of the attribution of Northwest Coast painting. . . . His work bears such close resemblances in style and detail to other . . . examples . . . that we feel fairly confident in isolating a "Bella Bella" painting style for the last half of the nineteenth century.[12]

A number of artifacts can be tentatively assigned to Carpenter because of their association with the keeper of the Dryad Point lighthouse: two paddles obtained from the lighthouse keeper at Dryad Point (RBCM 15832–15833), and a chief's settee (Fig. 26) photographed in 1900 at the Bella Bella lighthouse which had Carpenter's name on it when it was collected (RBCM 1856). As mentioned previously (p. 43), a similar settee, or chief's seat, was commissioned from "the most renowned wood carver among the Bella Bella" by J. Adrian Jacobsen when he was collecting for the Berlin museum in 1881 (MfV IVA 2475–2477; Macnair, Hoover, and Neary 1980:149). This carver is thought to have been Carpenter and both settees have been attributed to him. Both, however, are much more elaborately carved and painted than the painted chest (No. 34) and a plaque in the R. W. Large Memorial Hospital at Waglisla, both known to be Carpenter's work. Simple boxes such as a child's coffin collected at Bella Bella by F. Jacobsen in 1893 (RBCM 221) and the wooden spoons that are common in collections from Bella Bella (e.g., RBCM 16336–16337) are closer to Carpenter's known style, which is characterized by loosely drawn, freehand elements— thin, sinuous formlines, tulip-shaped U-forms, irregular single hatching—evenly distributed over an open field.

Carpenter's style, then, appears to become less complex and less structured toward the end of his life. This may indicate a changing aesthetic or it may be the result of practical considerations. An increased production of works for sale to an undemanding public, for example, could mean less time was spent on each piece. A different style might also indicate another hand. Carpenter's son, Fred, worked at boat building with his father and may have helped him with art works as well. The artist's great-grandson said that Carpenter suffered in later life from an inherited illness and speculated that the illness may have affected some of his technical abilities, resulting in looser and simpler compositions.[13]

FIG. 26. *This chief's settee was seen at the Bella Bella lighthouse in 1900. Captain Carpenter's name was written on it. Courtesy Royal British Columbia Museum, Victoria. CPN 1856.*

Kerfed Chest with Lid. See Catalogue, No. 34.

ENOCH (D. 1904)

Large's letters from the mission and other historical and ethnographic sources yield a surprising amount of information about the lives of Chief Robert Bell and Captain Carpenter and their place in Heiltsuk history and society. This information is surprising in that indigenous artists have been regarded by many ethnologists and art historians as anonymous craftspeople whose production had very little to do with the personal situation of the artist, expressing rather the ethos of the culture as a whole. Obviously, both personal and cultural aspects are involved, as they are in the arts of other, more documented, cultures, and the common assumption that "primitive" societies did not really have true art or artists (as Westerners define them) may have been as much the result of lack of information as of theoretical constructs.[14]

Cradle. See Catalogue, No. 11.

Enoch, who made the cradle in Large's collection (No. 11), is more the stereotypical aboriginal craftsman in that he contributed only one object to the collection and in that almost nothing is known about him from ethnographic and historical sources. Along with other Bella Bella people, he contributed money to the mission in 1887 (Barner n.d.). He died in 1904 and is buried at Bella Bella Grave Island I. His memorial also commemorates a woman named Lily Steve who died in 1905 at the age of twenty-five (Streich 1983). The fact that he had only one English name might indicate that he was born in the first half of the nineteenth century before Christian nomenclature was common and that he had not been baptized. It is likely that Enoch was elderly when he died in 1904.

Enoch's cradle (which would have been particularly interesting to Large, whose first child, Richard Geddes, was born in 1901) is constructed with care. The decorative and structural design details suggest that it was made to be functional and that its maker had made such things before. There is a similarly constructed cradle from Bella Bella in the Smithsonian Institution (NMNH 20556).[15]

GENERAL DICK (OLD DICK, 1822–1902?)

Like Enoch, General Dick has no recorded English surname or Heiltsuk name and is identified by Large as the maker of only one object, a painted paddle (No. 25). He was, however, the source of five carved wooden figures (Nos. 15–17, 29, 47). It is possible that he was more active as a carver than this incomplete documentation indicates, for similar paddles in other collections may also be his work, such as a paddle collected by Reverend Raley of Kitamaat (UBCMOA A1598), and two paddles collected at Bella Bella in 1899 (CMC VII-EE-16–17). I found no record of a "General Dick" in the archives and published literature, but there are several "Dicks" and some if not all of them may be the same person. Captain Richard Carpenter's nickname was Dick; "Dick" and "Dick Williams" contributed money to the Bella Bella church construction fund in 1890/91 (Barner n.d.); "Old Dick" was recorded as "a carver of curios" at Bella Bella in 1901 (Henderson 1901); and Large photographed "Dick Jakeswallis" whom he identified merely as "an old timer" from Bella Bella (see Fig. 27 and Appendix C).

Old Dick is commemorated on a Story Point burial ground memorial (Streich 1983),[16] and at the same site is a monument for Dick, who died in 1902, aged eighty years. Large described Old Dick as a "noted wood-carver and money-saver" (*MB* 6, no. 1[1909]:17). Surely he would have sought work by this carver for his collection, so it is at least likely that General Dick was indeed Old Dick, and the maker, as well as the source, of the five carved figures in Large's collection.

Large's predecessor, Dr. Jackson, said that Old Dick was haunted by the past, having played a key role in a notorious ambush of the Oweekeno by the Heiltsuk at a place in Schooner Passage, Rivers Inlet, called Slaughter Illahie. The Oweekeno were attacked there while travelling to a potlatch to which they had been formally invited, according to Jackson, by Old Dick (*MB* 6, no. 1[1909]:17). (Old Dick had been acting as the à̓élkv, an official who invited people to potlatches on behalf of the chief [see Harkin 1988:30].) The incident is recounted by Boas in *Bella Bella Texts*:

> Long ago a ᵋwī̓k·l̥enoxᵘ [Oweekeno] killed Hai'madzalas, chief of the Ō'yalitx [ʹUyalitx̌v]. Then the Bella Bella talked about it (and resolved) that they would now take revenge on the ᵋwī̓k·l̥enoxᵘ .... The tribes who were going to make war made ready to go to Rivers Inlet.... In the morning they started for the place Qwā'q̄ūmē [Slaughter Illahie]. Ahead of them were those who pretended to invite (the ᵋwī̓k·l̥enoxᵘ).... At night they came to the head of Rivers Inlet.

FIG. 27. *Dick Jakeswallis, a Heiltsuk elder. Photograph by R. W. Large, from "Souvenir of Bella Bella, B.C." Courtesy Royal British Columbia Museum, Victoria. PN 16462.*

That was the time when those who pretended to invite them blew their sacred whistles. Now they were asked [by the Oweekeno] to come out of their canoes. They stepped out of the canoes and arrived in the house of Wā'k·as [the Oweekeno chief]. Now this was the reason why they danced. . . . Now it was morning. Then they made ready. . . . Now said the head man of the inviters, "Let us try to get to Qwā'qūmē that we may eat before evening." . . . Now the inviters arrived at Qwā'qūmē with those whom they had invited. The warriors were ready behind the bushes.

In the ambush, seventeen Oweekeno chiefs were killed and four chiefs and thirty-two women and children were taken as slaves (Poutlass 1908). The Oweekeno chief Wā'k·as was spared and in gratitude gave his name as well as "the big river at Rivers Inlet and a place for getting provisions on the big lake" to the Heiltsuk leader (Boas 1928:133–35). This event, which took place about 1848 (Walbran 1909:368–69), was one of the last incidents of intertribal revenge, which were common before government gunboats, Indian agents, and missionaries set about replacing native with English law (Duff 1964:44; McIlwraith 1948, 2:377).

It is understandable that Old Dick would have been haunted by the past, for, if he was indeed born in 1822, he would have witnessed events such as the building of Fort McLoughlin, the smallpox epidemic, and the coming of the missionaries, all of which radically altered Heiltsuk society. His role at 'Qvaqvəmmi and his money-saving propensity no doubt indicate that Dick had been, and perhaps still was, an active potlatcher.

Large's description of five carved figures from General Dick is as vague as the name he gives their owner. Large calls the small carving of a doglike animal and a frog (No. 29) a "key ring," but it is difficult to see how the object would serve such a function. A similar carving (UBCMOA A131) has been described by Hawthorn as "probably the handle of an implement" (1967:365). The carving may represent Heiltsuk Bear and Frog crests, or it may illustrate a story.[17] The odd relationship of the animals (the frog hangs upside down on the chest of the "bear" which stands upright on its hind legs) is reminiscent of other whimsical or grotesque Heiltsuk carvings (e.g., CMC VII-EE-2–10) and this little carving may have been made as an amusing novelty. Small carved figures were also used in Heiltsuk ceremonies such as the Returned from Heaven (dhuẁláx̌a) dances given in connection with major potlatches, when the visiting chiefs were asked to remove the spirits, represented by wooden figurines, from the bodies of the novices (Drucker 1940:218).

The functions of the four "rough carved human figure[s]" (Nos. 15–17, 47) are also mysterious. They seem to be three different types of objects. Nos. 15 and 16 are small painted cedar figures representing men sitting with raised knees, bent elbows, and large hands raised to chin level. The more detailed carving, No. 16, has a distinctly protruding stomach. Although the hair that was nailed onto the head of this figure has worn away, the carvings must have been new when Large acquired them from General Dick. What they were intended to represent is not clear. A seated bear similar in size and posture is thought to have been carved for the tourist trade (RBCM 16343), but General Dick's figures are also reminiscent of grave effigy figures, which are often quite small,[18] and of full-sized Kwakwa̱ka'wakw potlatch figures with protruding stomachs that signified the wealth of the chief.

Carved Figures. See Catalogue, Nos. 15–16.

A larger, unpainted cedar carving, No. 17, has a waxy patina and signs of wear that suggest exposure to the elements.[19] The naturalistically proportioned figure stands with slightly bent arms as if its hands were in its pants pockets. The peaked cap and the incised line around the neck, which may indicate a jacket, suggest a uniform such as that worn by the members of the Bella Bella Cornet Band. A figure in a similar pose with what appears to be a similar hat formed the entrance pole of a house at Kimsquit in the 1880s,[20] and there was a carved figure of a man in a cap above the door of Chief Clelemen's house at Bella Coola.[21] At Bella Bella, visitors arriving by boat were surprised by a naturalistic figure of a member of the concert band holding a cornet, which stood on the top balcony of the fire and recreation hall. It had been carved by "one of our Indians," wrote Large, and often fooled new-comers with its realism (*MB* 6, no. 1[1909]:9). No. 17 is probably a similar architectural carving of a contemporary person.

The fourth figure, No. 47, is a ceremonial puppet with articulated arms. From the tattered condition of its green woollen clothing, it appears to be quite old. It was certainly made for ceremonial use. White cotton fringes at the neck and shoulders suggest the red cedar-bark paraphernalia of the Winter Ceremonials. This is a Túxvʔit puppet, associated with the female War Spirit dancer. A similar puppet (Fig. 28) collected by F. Jacobsen at Bella Bella (RBCM 100) is called a MontLemgyita figure and associated with the Túxvʔit, a Winter Dance that was usually performed by a woman.[22] The ceremonial puppet collected from General Dick, like the works of all of the artists discussed here, testifies to the survival of artistic and cultural traditions in turn-of-the-century Bella Bella.

Fig. 28. *Ceremonial puppet collected by Fillip Jacobsen at Bella Bella in 1893. Courtesy Royal British Columbia Museum, Victoria. CPN 100.*

Daniel Houstie (1880–1912)

In the case of Daniel Houstie, attributions have been made on the basis of stylistic analysis rather than on what is known about the artist.

Daniel Houstie died in 1912, when, if he is the same Daniel Houstie who was baptized (at the age of two years) in December 1882, he was thirty-two years old.[23] His youth may account for the scarcity of his work in other Bella Bella collections.[24] Daniel was a relative of Chief Tom Housty, an "old timer, loving old customs" (*MB* 5, no. 4[1909]:690), who was an active participant in feasts and potlatches and the manager of the Bella Bella sawmill, a position given to him in recognition of his high status.[25] The Houstie, or Housty, family (the name is spelled both ways at Bella Bella) was originally from Fort Rupert, but was living at Bella Bella by 1881 when they contributed a relatively large amount of money to the building of the schoolhouse (Barner n.d.). Like many Bella Bella people, they appear to have moved to the village about 1880 when the mission was established, and to have supported new institutions such as the school and sawmill while continuing to practise Heiltsuk traditions. Daniel Houstie's knowledge of traditional Heiltsuk culture is evident in the replicas of traditional objects that he made for Large. They illustrate the culture of his father's generation—those who were born before the smallpox epidemic and the amalgamation of the Heiltsuk groups.

With the possible exception of a carved walking stick (No. 61), Large described the objects made by Houstie as things that were no longer in use at Bella Bella at the turn of the century. However, like the dance mask (No. 57), which the missionary connected with the Interior Indians, they can be associated with known Heiltsuk cultural practices or with specific dances of the Shaman's (čaíqa) or Returned from Heaven (dhuw̓láx̌a) series.

The "old time halibut hook" (No. 71), which is made from a flat, V-shaped piece of bone (possibly, as Large claimed, the scapula of a mountain sheep), is carved with a profile face and inlaid with abalone. A bone barb is bound with cedar root to the bottom arm of the hook and the top arm is wrapped with the same material to allow for the attachment of a cedar line. This hook and its mate (No. 77) appear to be decorative rather than functional objects, but the presence of the cedar-root wrapping and the bone barb indicates that they are faithful to an original model.

The "carved whaling paddle" (No. 26), painted with a formline design in black and brown, is the rounded shape common to the central coast (Boas 1909:445), but its association with whaling is unclear. Drucker (1950:172) noted that the whale was not hunted in the area. Canoes were being replaced by sail and gasoline boats in Large's time, and this paddle, like the one made by General Dick (No. 25), has not been used.[26] Decorated paddles, like painted boxes, seem to have been part of the repertory of Bella Bella artists who carved for the tourist and artifact markets at the turn of the century.

The "carved stick used to keep in position the pad used to produce the flattening of infant's head" (No. 12) was an anachronism in turn-of-the-century Waglisla. Until the custom ceased in the nineteenth century, the people of the central coast, with the exception of the Haisla, had practised the Cowichan type of head deformation which produced a slight flattening of the forehead (Drucker 1950:191; Olson 1935, 1949:72). A pad of cedar bark was pressed to the infant's head to flatten it (Boas 1909:459; Curtis 1915:53). I have found only one reference to the use of a stick in the process. In his Bella Bella Notes, Boas mentions that "they press the heads of boys and girls with flat bundles of underbrush on forehead," and says that a stick, "beautifully carved" in the case of a noble child, was placed "on the child's chest" to keep part of the arrangement in place (Boas 1923:282). Unfortunately, details of the stick's function are unclear. Houstie's stick is carved to represent a whale with an eagle on its back, both Heiltsuk crest animals. There is a cylinder in the mouth of the whale and a notch at the tail end, presumably for attachment to some sort of strap arrangement that kept the head pad of a noble child in position.

No. 61, a "carved stick," is an elaborately carved cane or talking stick made from hardwood and inlaid with abalone. At the top a long-snouted wolflike being holds in its teeth a small skeleton, and in its concave paws a stylized skull with potlatch rings on its head. It stands on the head of a figure that has feather patterns incised on its arms and legs, and therefore must represent a bird in human form. This dramatic carving was published as a "ceremonial staff" (ROM 1976:11); its complex design and specific Man-eater and transformation imagery imply that it had a place in Heiltsuk ritual. The cannibal and skeletal motifs recall aspects of the Cannibal (tánís) dance of the Winter Ceremony in which Báxvbakválánusiwa, the Cannibal-at-the-North-End-of-the-World, is personified by the dancer who eats (or pretends to eat) a corpse. As well, the skull held by the wolflike monster in the carving is reminiscent of skulls that are incorporated into some tánís dance costumes. Transformation, bird, and skeletal motifs encode shamanic concepts of death, flight, disembodiment, and rebirth that are ritually expressed in the Shaman's (cáíqa) ceremonies. The tánís dance is the highest-ranked dance of the cáíqa series.

No. 66, a whistle made of thinly carved cedar bound with root, appears to be part of a set of eight reedless whistles in the 1906 collection (the others are No. 70, which is six whistles, and NS 28221).[27] A longer but similar whistle that is lightly incised with a

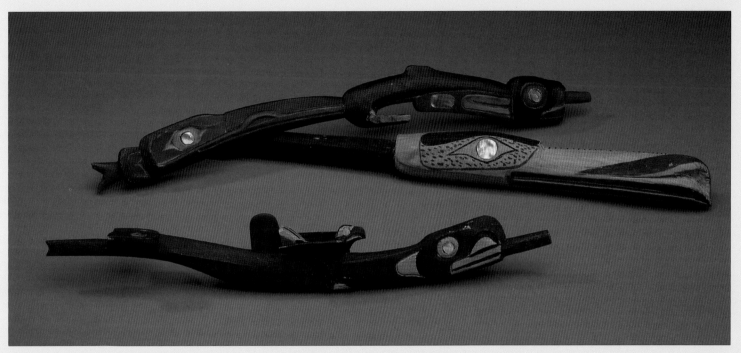

Carved Sticks. See Catalogue, Nos. 12–14.

simple formline design (No. 67) and No. 66 were collected from (but perhaps not made by) Houstie. These are also ceremonial objects—the whistles were the voices of the spirits in the Winter Dances and were used in both the Shaman's (ċaíqa) and Returned from Heaven (dhuẁláẍa) series. Olson (1954:246) reports that ċaíqa series tánís and Akḷlaʼaḷʼem dancers used whistles, while dhuẁláẍa dancers used a reedless tube, which vibrated.[28]

With the exception of the worn and damaged whistle (No. 67), the objects collected from Houstie appear to have been newly made. They support the premise that Large was buying, and perhaps commissioning, replicas of secular and ceremonial objects that illustrated traditional life at Bella Bella.

The most distinctive objects in Large's undocumented 1906 collection are a group of brown-and-black painted cedar boxes, implements, and what appear to be replicas of ceremonial objects (there are thirteen objects in this group). Because of their stylistic and iconographic similarity to the objects that Large documented as Houstie's production, these may also be the work of Daniel Houstie. The paddle made by Houstie (No. 26) exemplifies the artist's style and use of motifs; it was the starting point for an analysis of design elements, which suggests that these pieces were all made by him (see Appendix D).

In brief, Houstie's style is characterized by minimal colour and bold volumetric forms that extend into the corners of the design field. His use of two colours, black and an ochrelike brown, would have been consistent with "old-style" objects and evokes the period before the introduction (by the Hudson's Bay Company) of Chinese vermilion, when native artists had "no good red, only brown like iron rust" (Holm 1965:26). Houstie tends to outline the edge of the field, to use bold, compass-drawn circles and large, complex salmon-trout's-heads (standardized ovoid forms containing mouth-and-eye designs),[29] and to separate adjacent forms with narrow borders; these devices produce a centralized, concentric design. The rectangular ovoids and the squared U-shapes are precisely and evenly rendered. With the strong black formlines, which contrast with the delicate lines and the thin, regular hatchings they enclose, these elements give Houstie's paintings a forceful clarity. His carvings have the same minimal colour and graphic strength.

The objects that can be attributed to Houstie fall into three categories: boxes that illustrate early cooking methods, carved sticks that apparently illustrate an ancient head-flattening technique, and ceremonial objects that illustrate aspects of specific Heiltsuk Winter Dances recorded by ethnographers such as Olson and Drucker.

The black-and-brown painted boxes illustrate old methods of food production and storage. Before Western cooking techniques and containers were adopted, water-tight kerfed boxes were used for water and food storage and for cooking. Many foods were boiled or simmered in liquid-filled boxes. Wooden ladles were used to transfer water from storage boxes to cooking boxes and tongs were used to lift hot stones from the fire and place them in the cooking box to heat the cooking liquid. When the water reached the desired temperature, the food was added (see Stewart 1984:84 for a diagram of the process). The water box (No. 39) and the dipper (No. 38) collected by Large are a set, as are the cooking box (No. 37) and the tongs (No. 109).[30] The killer-whale box (No. 41) may be a replica of a food-storage box.

Such domestic utensils had been replaced by European metal containers in the nineteenth century, but there are other indications that these were not intended for use. The cooking tongs are made from a single piece of split wood, which is not reinforced as it would be if the tongs had really been intended to manipulate "hot stones for cooking," and they are elaborately painted, unlike the tongs and boxes used in daily food preparation (Jacknis 1974:18). The Bella Bella water box and dipper that James Swan collected from the Hudson's Bay Company in Victoria in 1875 (NMNH 20568 A–B), although painted differently, are almost identical in form to Large's box and dipper (Nos. 38–39). Swan identified his artifacts as "imitation[s] of old relics," and no doubt Large's were imitations as well. All the boxes are nevertheless kerfed and pegged, and their expert construction and clear formline designs attest to the continuation of nineteenth-century Heiltsuk box-making technology at Bella Bella.

The "Indian cradle support" (No. 14) matches the head-shaping implement carved by Houstie and described earlier (No. 12). It is a similarly carved stick in the shape of a whale and a long-beaked bird, probably a raven. Both sticks show two Heiltsuk crest animals (Whale and Eagle, and Whale and Raven), perhaps the crests of the child, and the construction is the same. The similarity of type and execution suggests that both of these objects were made by Houstie. Another stick (No. 13) is also described as an "Indian cradle support" but is similar only in length. It is a straight piece of wood in the shape of a bird's head with a short handle. How these sticks might function as cradle supports (or, as No. 12 is described, as head-flattening implements) is not clear.[31]

Six black-and-brown painted ceremonial objects and a mask with moveable eyes are stylistically related to the domestic articles attributed here to Houstie and, like them, seem to be replicas of old Heiltsuk artifacts. Other than associating them with a dance or war, Large did not explain how these objects were used, but ethnographic literature reveals that they have specific applications in Winter Dances.

Four of these six objects feature skulls. The "dance drinking box" (No. 48), the most complex artifact in the Large Collection, is a kerfed box on four legs. Four separate carvings are attached to the top of the box: a large, skull-like head inserted like a plug in a hole near the front of the top; two animals, probably land otters, sitting in the centre of the top with their snouts projecting upward on each side; and a skull-like face nailed onto the back of the box. Holes are drilled down through the snouts of the otters and the box top, and hollow sticks extend down through the holes and into the box. Kelp tubes may have been inserted through the animals' snouts into the box to act as straws. This elaborate object may have been associated with the third dance of the Returned from Heaven (dhuẇláx̌a) series, the Land Otter (WúalaL) dance, in which a dancer is possessed by the power of the land otter (Olson 1954:248). As well, there are two drinking dances in which such a container may have been used: the Urinating (Ha'gwagweh) dance, the fourth of the dhuẇláx̌a series, in which the dancer, who has returned from heaven possessed by a spirit, appears to drink gallons of water and urinate continuously as he dances around the house (Olson 1954:248), and the Healing Water (Heilikstaxsta) dance, one of the Shaman's (c̓aíqa) series, in which the dancer consumes healing water (Stevenson n.d., p. 72). The latter is the most likely association; the otters have red cedar bark, a symbol of the c̓aíqa series, around their necks.

The "cedar dance hat" (No. 55) is a hybrid of native and non-native forms: a carved, wooden, skull-like head and four wooden animal legs are attached to a European-style brimmed hat made of woven cedar bark. Like the dance drinking box, the hat is in the shape of a four-legged creature with skull-like heads front and back. The crown has a skull-like head painted on the back and ribs painted on each side. The brim is also painted, with eyes on the front, a profile mouth-and-eye on each side, and two stripes at the back to indicate the tail of the creature. The carved wooden head attached to the front of the crown is wrapped with red cedar bark, indicating that the hat was for a Winter Dance of the Shaman's (c̓aíqa) series—perhaps the fourth-ranked Skull (K̓lo'minuahslax) dance, in which the performer wears a mask or headdress of skulls (a prerogative associated with the Cannibal Spirit). Drucker's statement that in the Ghost dance (Lū̓ɫaɫ), another in the c̓aíqa series, the dancer wore a human skull bound to the top of his head (1940:208–9) agrees with Boas' information that the Ghost dancer ("who comes from Bella Bella") wore carved skulls on a red cedar-bark headband and four yellow cedar skulls around his neck (1930:110).

The large dance whistle (No. 69) takes the shape of a long, skull-like head with an open mouth from which the voice of the whistle sounds. At one time a bellows of what

Ceremonial Hat. See Catalogue, No. 55.

appears to be fish skin was attached at the bottom of the whistle with string and cedar root. Skin was also tied on top of the head. According to Boas (1897:651–53), the whistles used to imitate the cries of the Olala' spirit (the dance headdress of which represented a corpse) were carved and painted to represent the head of a corpse, and some were attached to bellows so that the whistles could be sounded by the arm movement of the dancer. The Olala' is part of the Ghost dance (Lūɫaɫ) (Drucker 1940:208–10).

The skull and ladle (No. 50) are undocumented, but included here because of stylistic similarities. Although catalogued separately, they fit together to form a single object. The ladle, which ends in a carved bear's head, relates to the man-eating habits of the Cannibal (tánís) dancer, and the carving on the handle may be associated with the Cannibal bear of the Kwakwaka'wakw. While nothing similar to the "dance drinking box" and the "cedar dance hat" exists in the other Bella Bella collections I have studied, the skull-and-ladle is a typical turn-of-the-century Bella Bella artifact. Two similar ladles in other museums were collected around the same time: BM 05.588.7297, before 1905, and DAM 1942.251/QBB-3-G, in 1896/97. The Brooklyn ladle (Fig. 29) is more finely carved than No. 50 but is virtually identical in shape and has a similar bear's head on the handle. The much smaller Denver ladle, which has a plain handle and is not as detailed as the Brooklyn example, was collected by a woman missionary at Bella Bella (see p. 47).

Two objects are associated with war, a "war spear" (No. 65) and a "painted war club" (No. 63). The spear is a long shaft of hardwood terminating in an incised bone blade, which Large described as "carved whale rib point." The point or blade protrudes from the mouth of a long-beaked bird, which has the same form and painted detail as the bird's head on the cooking tongs (No. 109). Below the feathered head and neck of the bird, the representations on the spear are a seated beaver, a wolf holding a small figure in its paws, and a seated figure whose feathered "hat" could be the tail of the bird. The war club has a grey pecked stone inserted in a short wooden shaft. The stone is painted to represent the beak of a bird, the body of which is incised and painted on the shaft. The club is much simpler than the spear and not as finely carved.

Both club and spear are ceremonial weapons. The Kwakwaka'wakw Fool (Nulamal) dancers carried lances or war clubs, many of which were carved and painted to represent Raven and used to threaten the offenders of the hamatsa or Cannibal Spirit (Boas

FIG. 29. *Ladle and wooden skull collected by C. F. Newcombe at Bella Bella and sold to the Brooklyn Museum in 1905. Courtesy Brooklyn Museum.*
BM 05.588.7297.

1897:476). Ceremonial harpoons were also used to "spear copper like a whale" at Kwakwaka'wakw marriage ceremonies (Hawthorn 1967:164). Among the Bella Bella, the Finding-a-supernatural-treasure (dhúgválá) dance, the first-ranked of the Returned from Heaven (dhuẃláx̌a) series, featured a dancer who carried a lance from which a row of carved heads was suspended (Drucker 1940:211). The ˇX̌íx̌ís dancer called Spearing-in-a-canoe has a great lance. "These lances are supposed to be the weapons used in capturing the spirits displayed in the potlatch. They are not shown in the dance during the potlatch itself; only the spirits are displayed" (Drucker 1940:211). The War dancer (Wawinalal, or UwinalaL) carried a club decorated with a crest belonging to the dancer (Drucker 1940:205; Olson 1954:248).

The "dance mask" (No. 60), the only mask in the 1906 collection, has similar characteristics to the mask known to be made by Houstie (No. 57). It is a heavy mask with exaggerated features, a sharply hooked nose, a wide rectangular mouth with protruding lips, a small pointed chin, heavy cheek ridges, and heavy brows over deeply set eyes with round white pupils. Both masks are painted red and green on black with rough hatching, and both have applied hair and moustaches. Both relate to a series of Heiltsuk grotesque masks in museum collections, and No. 60 is particularly comparable with AMNH 16/4736 (collected by George Hunt in 1899), NMAI 5/9833, and McM 1984.5, none of which has moveable eyes.

No. 60, however, like the mask that Large collected from Solomon (No. 58), has eyes that open and shut. The eyes are pivoted wooden ovals and were attached to the top of the inside of the mask with pieces of rubber. Strings were attached to the ovals with metal loops so that the wearer could pull the strings to make the eyes close, and release them to make the eyes snap open. The white pupils in the black and red orbs, bordered with long eyelashes of coarse hair, would suddenly appear. The effect must have been dramatic. Several grotesque Heiltsuk masks with moveable eyes were collected from Bella Bella about the same time: NMAI 9751, collected by Emmons in 1906; FMNH 19938, collected by Newcombe in 1905; and NMAI 2182, collected by Crosby in 1906.

According to Olson (1954:242), the seventh-ranked dance of the Shaman's (c̓aíqa) series is the Sleep Causing (Kḷya´LkyaLamas) dance, in which the dancer projects the spirit that causes sleep into the audience. Harkin (1988:52) calls this dance the maqax̣ súklaxi (clearing of the throat) and explains that "the dancer blows on his hands, thus 'throwing' sleep into a person." Boas describes the Tsimshian version of the same dance, in which the owner of the spirit wears a mask with eyes that roll open and shut (1897:655–56). The Sleeping Spirit dance was owned by Chief Robert Bell, who danced

Ceremonial Box. See Catalogue, No. 48.

it when Chief Moody Humchitt's father was married. All the audience was put to sleep except for two or three chiefs (Olson 1935, 1949:34).

On the evidence of the literature, the ceremonial objects attributed here to Daniel Houstie can be associated with specific dances in the Winter Dance cycles and even, in one case, with the owner of the prerogative and possible commissioner of the work. Although the objects are sometimes unique in museum collections (for instance, No. 48, the "dance drinking box," and No. 55, the "cedar dance hat"), it is not likely that they were inventions of the artist. Rather, they are probably replicas or adaptations of actual ritual paraphernalia used by the Heiltsuk and associated groups.

Large named five individuals who were making objects at Bella Bella in the first decade of the twentieth century. His collection of their work with its documentation opens several avenues for the study of Heiltsuk art history: analysis of the development of Heiltsuk art through time, understanding of the specific context of the collected art, study of the lives of the artists and the effects of their personal situations on their production, identification of each artist's work through stylistic analysis, and the possibility of further attributions to an artist whose style, dates, and village are known. This study has shown that the work of Bell and Carpenter can be better understood through the study of their lives and social situations, and that stylistic analysis of Houstie's work leads to the identification of other works by him. Personal information given by Large, rather than analysis of the objects, is the basis of the suggestion that General Dick may be the carver Old Dick. And although little is known about Enoch, the setting for his work has been established.

It is clear from these examples that Large's information about the artists as individuals illuminates the context and meaning of turn-of-the-century art from Bella Bella and that missionary sources do indeed contain useful information for the study of First Nations art history.

Notes

1. The artistic importance of the Heiltsuk has been noted by McIlwraith (1948, 1:39–40), Holm (1981:178), and Macnair, Hoover, and Neary (1980:37).

2. See also Henderson (1901). Chief Bell's position as officer of the Bella Bella Cornet Band may, like that of Chief Tom Housty as head of the Bella Bella sawmill, have been an honorary one.

3. Chief Moody Humchitt succeeded Bell as head chief. The name 'Qa'aít was passed to Bertie Humchitt (Olson 1935, 1949:28).

4. There is a memorial to Chief Bell in Waglisla village, and another at Bella Bella Grave Island II (Streich 1983).

5. This was probably the occasion remembered by Mary Vickers when Chief Moody Humchitt (Waúyala), Bell's successor, invited other tribes to Bella Bella and gave away money (Vickers 1985).

6. Photography was one of Large's enthusiasms. He photographed the buildings, boats, and people of Bella Bella, and carried his camera with him on his travels. Some of his pictures of Bella Bella and other places (such as a whaling station on the west coast of Vancouver Island) were featured in the *Missionary Bulletin* (e.g., *MB* 3, no. 1[1906]:109, 114; *MB* 5, no. 1[1908]:13; *MB* 5, no. 4[1909]:688, 691, 700.) The pamphlet, *Souvenir of Bella Bella, B.C.* (Large n.d.), reproduces Large's photographs of the following Bella Bella people and scenes: Mr. and Mrs. James Star (Starr), Mr. and Mrs. William Brown, Dick Jakeswallis, Eli Wallace and his sister, a group of four Humchitt children, the Bella Bella band, Jacob White's launch, Fred Carpenter's schooner, Fred Anderson's house, the Bella Bella church and school, the interior of the church, the mission house, the fire hall, the hospital, the hospital staff, the cottage for tuberculosis patients, the Rivers Inlet hospital, the Dryad Point lighthouse, a street in Bella Bella, part of the village showing the mission property, the Bella Bella sawmill, two women from Kimsquit in front of a rack of drying herring spawn, and grave houses near Old Town and Waglisla.

7. The name Captain may derive from Carpenter's association with boats, or from his high status in Heiltsuk society (cf. King George of Kimsquit and General Dick of Bella Bella).

8. Large betrayed his feelings of superiority when he wrote that he was taken aback by Carpenter's familiarity (*MB* 2, no. 4[1905]:822).

9. Cyril Carpenter, interview, July 1986. The drastic decline in the Heiltsuk population can be seen by comparing Tolmie's 1834 tally of the Heiltsuk with the DIA's population statistics for 1889 (Tolmie 1963:320; DIA 1890:486). As Harkin points out (1988:156), if these figures are correct the Heiltsuk population was reduced by 85 per cent in fifty-five years.

10. Richard Carpenter (Du'k̓ḻwayella) was also known at Bella Bella as Mxsáqv (Rainbow), and Wúx̌vúas. Pam Brown has researched Du'k̓ḻwayella's life and work (Brown n.d.). Examples of his paintings were included in the 1993 UBCMOA exhibition "The Transforming Image," curated by Karen Duffek, Bill McLennan, and Lyle Wilson (catalogue forthcoming, University of British Columbia Press).

11. Carpenter's kerfed chest (No. 34) is 34.6 x 30.8 x 47.8 cm. The one described by Curtis was approximately 35.5 x 35.5 x 50.8 cm.

12. Bill Holm, letter to the author, 5 February 1986.

13. Cyril Carpenter, interview, July 1986.

14. In Western culture, art is conceived of as a discrete category of decorative or illustrational objects without practical function, and artists as specialized, individual, creative producers. Art and artists play very different roles in First Nations cultures: what we call art is not a discrete category but permeates all aspects of secular and ceremonial life, and the maker of the object is secondary to the person who owns the right to commission and display it. As a result of these differences, there has been considerable debate concerning the classification of ethnographic objects as art. For further discussion of the topic, see M'Closkey (1985), Vastokas (1987), Townsend-Gault (1988), and Phillips (1989).

15. A cradle collected at Bella Bella in 1893 (RBCM 344) is shaped and constructed differently, having a slatted wood platform inside.

16. Also commemorated on this memorial is Isabella Hope Humchitt, 1903–5 (Streich 1983).

17. Another carving from Bella Bella of a bear with a frog on its chest is RBCM 233.

18. Effigy figures on the grave of a Bella Bella chief are shown in a Maynard photograph of 1884 or 1888 (RBCM PN 10073; Richard Maynard was a Victoria-based photographer who made several journeys along the coast in the 1880s). A grave effigy figure from Kitamaat (UBCMOA 358) is 29.7 cm high.

19. Bill Holm has suggested that this figure may be unfinished (letter to the author, 5 February 1986).

20. AMNH photograph 39988/44308.

21. Photograph by Harlan I. Smith, reproduced in McIlwraith (1948, vol. 1, fig. 24).

22. According to Boas (1897:492) the name of the puppet of the Kwakwa̱ka'wakw Tuxw'id dancer was nō'nLEmg·ila (making foolish).

23. Pole Island memorials give the dates of Daniel Housty's death as 15 November and 30 November 1912, and Daniel Houstie's death as 30 December 1912 (Streich 1983). Large's collection notes imply that the name Houstie, or Housty, means stone hammer.

24. A carved "chief's stick" (RBCM 2312), which is similar to No. 61, is one of the few objects in museum collections that can be attributed to Daniel Houstie on stylistic grounds. It is made of polished yew wood carved in the form of a human figure above a lizardlike animal and a whale. Dr. C. F. Newcombe collected it at Bella Coola in 1913 but noted that it had been made at Bella Bella.

25. The actual managing of the sawmill was done by someone more interested in European-style business. The 1881 census lists Housty (Tom Houstie ?) as thirty-three years old.

26. An almost identical paddle is illustrated in Holm (1965:84).

27. Four of these whistles are the same as Houstie's, one is squared at one end (ROM 28218, No. 70), and one is an "invisible" whistle (ROM 28220, No. 70). NS 28221 was traded to the National Museum of Australia in 1907. It is possible that these whistles came in sets. F. Jacobsen collected nine assorted whistles at Bella Bella in 1893 (e.g., RBCM 128); he associated them with a Summer Dance, that is, with the Returned from Heaven (dhuẃláx̌a) series.

28. McIlwraith (1948, 1:13) observed that the horns were used in the Shaman's (c̓aíqa) dances and the flat whistles in the Returned from Heaven (dhuẃláx̌a) series, while Drucker noted: "the whistles used in the dluwalaxa differ in form from those of the shaman's series; from descriptions they seem to have been trumpetlike affairs. Natives refer to them in English as 'horns' to distinguish them" (1940:205).

29. See Holm (1965:34).

30. The cooking stone (NS 23149) that Large obtained from Willie West and sent to Toronto in 1901 would also fit into this group.

31. Bill Holm has pointed out that this stick (No. 13) resembles a dance wand (letter to the author, 5 February 1986).

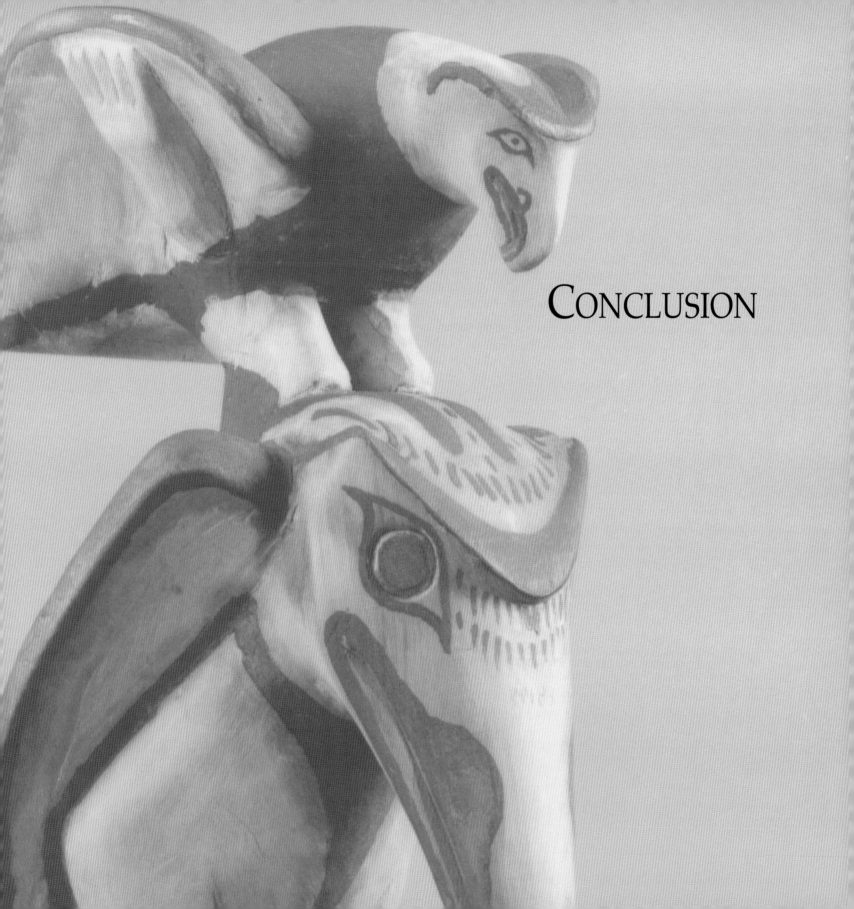

CONCLUSION

Between about 1880 and 1920, during the great period of museum anthropology, representatives of museums and their agents made extensive collections of First Nations artifacts to illustrate a way of life that they believed was destined to disappear under the onslaught of European culture. The men of science who assembled the collections presented their material and data in the ethnographic present, even though many of the tools and objects they collected had been, or were in the process of being, replaced or displaced by foreign objects and ideas. Perhaps because they spent so little time in the villages where they gathered their artifacts, the collectors also represented the material they collected as anonymous products of primitive peoples; only rarely are specific people and places identified as sources of objects.

On the Northwest Coast, the museum age of anthropology coincided with another period—the age of missions. The Bella Bella mission was begun in 1880, and by 1920 the Methodist Church was well established in the community. A similar chronology applies to other coastal missions. The missionaries were active in the artifact-collecting that characterized the period, but their point of view was different from that of the museum agents—it was personal and individual rather than scientific and general. Their collections were responses to particular circumstances; they were unplanned rather than premeditated programs of cultural representation. The missionaries' involvement in, and promotion of, the progress of their villages prevented them from using the artificial, ethnographic present tense, which ignored the changes that had taken place since the arrival of the Europeans. At the same time they documented, at least in outline, the cultural history of the peoples among whom they worked. Specific information about a specific community and time were important to the missionary, but were often ignored by the museum collector.

Large lived among the Heiltsuk at Bella Bella for twelve years and was an active collector both for the Ontario Provincial Museum and for the American Museum of Natural History. In his notes on the artifacts he collected and in his published letters to the supporters of the mission, Large presented the personal and specific documentation that is crucial for the understanding of the community of Bella Bella between 1898 and 1910, when the relocation of the village was paralleled by radical social change. Because Large combined the somewhat opposed approaches of the museum professional and the missionary, and because the Heiltsuk people were actively involved in creating the collection, the ROM's Large Collection is a remarkable record of Bella Bella and is particularly valuable as a historical document.

The Large Collection came not from a traditional native community of the nineteenth century but from a new, model Methodist village. The people used European tools, worked for wages in the fishing and other industries, dressed in European-style clothes, lived in single-family dwellings, learned English, and practiced Christianity. Yet, despite the changes in the community, modified Heiltsuk ceremonial traditions and social structure were maintained.

Large, because he lived in the village and knew the people well, was able to present his collection as the product of a group of individuals. He was influenced by the prevailing evolutionist ideas of his time, and he was aware of the ethnological importance of the objects and stories that he collected, but he did not see the people of Bella Bella as unchanging, anonymous primitives. As the resident minister and doctor, he was in a position to record personalized, specific information. He is the only observer to have documented the Heiltsuk of Bella Bella in the first decade of this century and the only one to be interested in the day-to-day life and concerns of the people. He did not present them as static, but as living, changing, modern individuals. His collection was in many ways a response to Heiltsuk concerns. This is what makes his collection so important as a record of the community.

Because of Large's unique perspective, five Bella Bella artists are known by name. It is possible to recognize their works and to attribute other, undocumented, work to specific individuals. Regional and personal styles can be recognized within a turn-of-the-century Bella Bella style. The Large Collection shows that, even though the objects came from a modernized community, traditional Heiltsuk content survived. It is recognizable in replicas of traditional implements and ceremonial objects, which the Heiltsuk made available to Large, and some of which may have been commissioned by Large for the collection.

It has been said that the missionary record is "of incalculable value to the Northwest Coast" (Lillard 1984:19). But because the missionaries opposed so many aboriginal traditions and worked to change native society, their writings and collections have often been overlooked as ethnographic sources. While this study does not sanction missionary attempts to eradicate First Nations culture, it does illustrate the value of a missionary doctor's collection. The ROM's R. W. Large Collection is an important record of the art and history of Bella Bella.

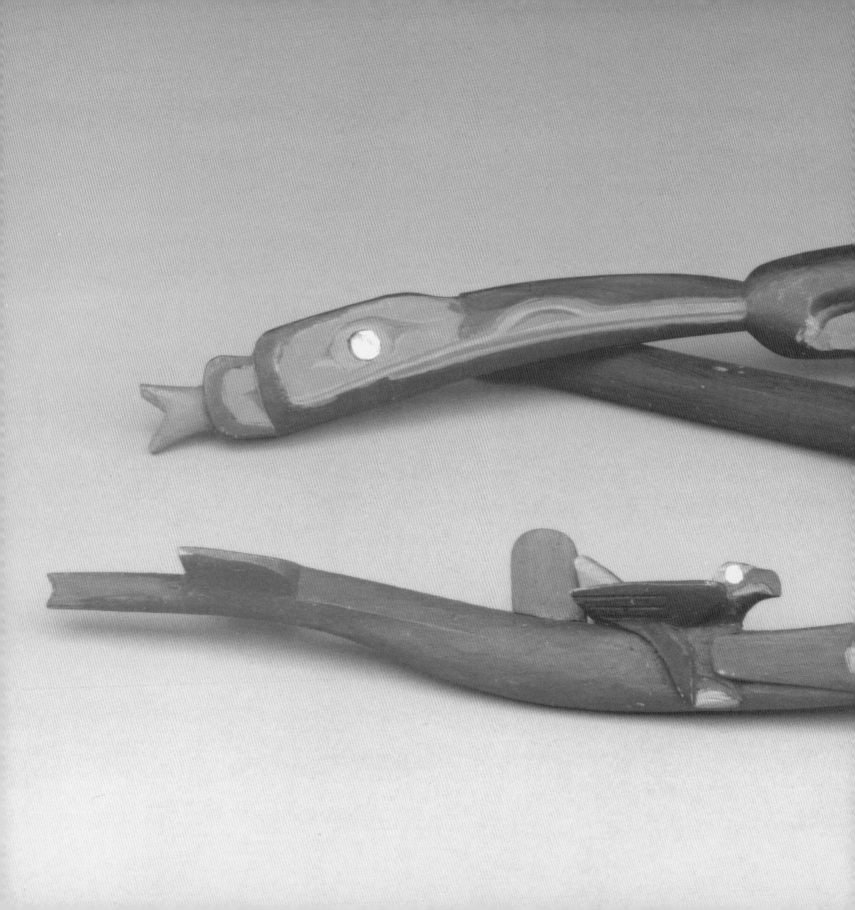

APPENDICES

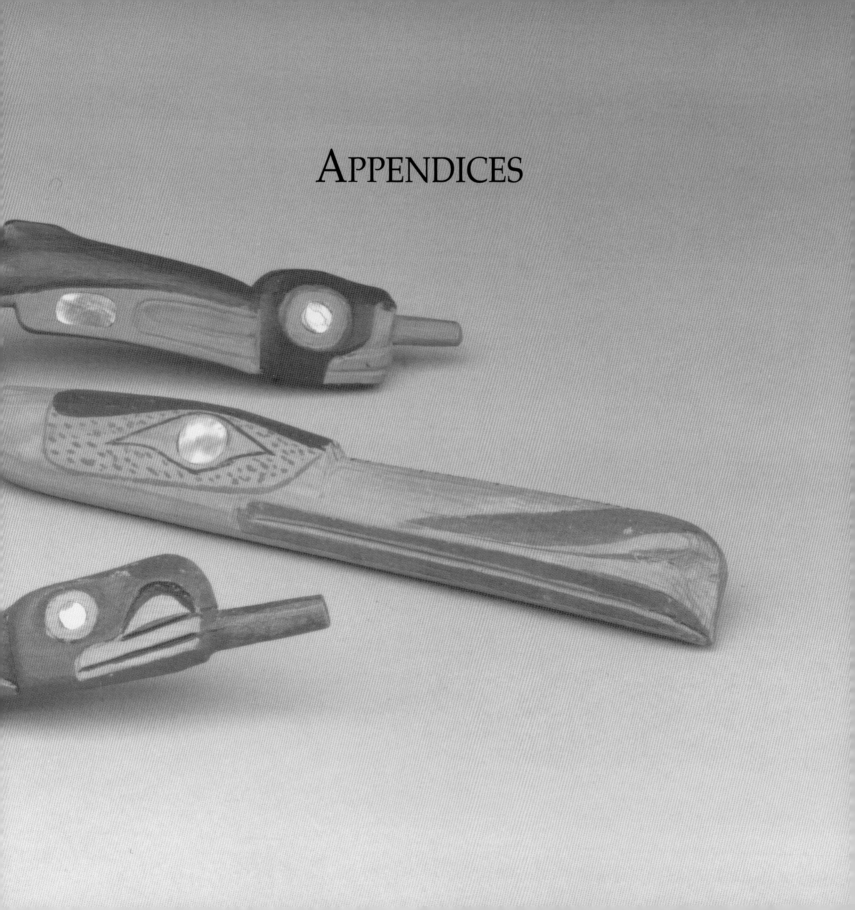

Appendix A: Methodist Missionaries at Bella Bella, 1880–1914

Compiled from information given in Crosby 1914, McKervill 1964, *MB, MO.*

16 May 1880: William Henry Pierce, native teacher and evangelist, sent from the Methodist base. At this time, Reverend Thomas Crosby was the Chairman of the Western Conference of the Methodist Church, based at Port Simpson.

22 October 1880–1884: Charles M. Tate, first minister at Bella Bella

6 August 1884–1886: W. B. Cuyler, died at Bella Bella of tuberculosis

1886–1887: James Calvert

1887–1888: Cornelius Bryant

1889–1891: R. B. Beavis

1892–1893: George F. Hopkins

June 1893–1895: R. B. Beavis

1895–1896: No permanent resident missionary; Miss Henrietta Reinhardt (also Reinhart), schoolteacher; Mr. Brett, temporary missionary

1897: Dr. J. A. Jackson, first medical missionary (retired because of ill health, but lived at Bella Bella until at least 1901)

December 1898–December 1910: Dr. Richard Whitfield Large

November 1906–June 1907: Dr. W. Raynor, filling in while Large was on furlough

1911–1912: Dr. C. C. Schlichter, became ill with diabetes;

Dr. A. F. Leper, died at Bella Bella, July 1912

1912: Dr. G. M. Hanna, temporary doctor; Dr. A. E. Best, temporary doctor

Summer 1912: Dr. George Darby, temporary doctor

1914: Arrival of Dr. George Darby, permanent doctor and minister

Appendix B: Dr. Richard Whitfield Large: Chronology

Compiled from information given in Crosby 1914, R. G. Large 1968, *MB, MO.*

February 1873: Born at Orangeville, Ontario; son of a Methodist minister, Reverend Richard Large

1890: Graduated from Weston High School, Toronto

1891: One year at the University of Toronto

1892–1893: Schoolteacher in Ontario

1893–1897: Attended Trinity Medical School, Toronto

1897–1898: Residency in surgery at Toronto General Hospital

July 1898: Worked at the Japanese hospital, Steveston, Fraser River

October 1898: Passed Medical Board of British Columbia examinations, Victoria

December 1898: Arrived at Bella Bella ('Qélc)

1899: Ordained for special purposes at Nanaimo

May 1899: Married Isabella M. Geddes of Toronto, at Vancouver

Spring 1899: Visited Steveston, Fraser River

Summer 1899: First summer at Rivers Inlet Hospital, a summer facility built at Wannock Cannery in 1897 by Thomas Crosby and Dr. A. E. Bolton

1900: Officiated at opening of new church at China Hat (Klemtu)

June 1900: Visited Goose Island during the fur seal hunt; treated over forty children who had fallen ill there

1901: Birth of first son, Richard Geddes; moved to the new mission house built for him by the Heiltsuk at Waglisla (New Bella Bella)

1902: Received into full conference of the Methodist Church

Spring 1902: Trip to Toronto

27 October 1902: Opened new hospital at Waglisla

1903: Birth of second son, Gordon; opened Heiltsuk–built day school at Waglisla

1904: Toured coastal communities for smallpox vaccination and treatment

Summer 1904: Rivers Inlet Hospital at Wannock Cannery destroyed by fire

1905–1906: Built new hospital at Green's Cannery, Rivers Inlet

December 1906–June 1907: On furlough in Toronto and U.S.A.

1907: Small isolation hospital built for tuberculosis patients at Waglisla

3 January 1909: Dedication of new church at Waglisla

December 1910: Left Waglisla

January 1911: Became superintendent of Port Simpson Hospital

20 August 1920: Died at Prince Rupert General Hospital, aged 47; buried at Port Simpson

APPENDIX C: CONTRIBUTORS TO THE LARGE COLLECTION

Information in this appendix is from Streich 1983, Canada Census 1881, DIA *Annual Reports* and Henderson's B.C. Directories for the years indicated, and Barner n.d., as well as other works cited.

Large named twenty-five contributors to his 1901 collection, among them five artists (Chief Robert Bell, Captain Carpenter, Enoch, General Dick, and Daniel Houstie). This appendix draws on Large's letters and other archives to present information about the contributors. Most were born before the smallpox epidemic of the 1860s and the amalgamation of the Heiltsuk at Bella Bella, and had lived through the great social upheaval of the late nineteenth century. For the most part, they were supporters of the church, the school, the band, and other new institutions, but were at the same time important chiefs, shamans, and upholders of Heiltsuk traditions.

Unlike many artifact collectors and anthropologists, Large had a personal and sustained relationship with the community that supplied his artifacts, and his collection shows Bella Bella art and artifacts as the products and property of individuals.

CHIEF ROBERT BELL
(1859–1904)

MAKER of No. 35, Indian cedar box; No. 62, war club; No. 40, box
SOURCE of No. 68, Indian dance whistle
1881 CENSUS: Robert Bell was not listed; the head chief of Bella Bella was Humtchit [Humchitt] and the second chief was Waukosh
C. 1890: Baptized by Reverend Beavis with the

name John Milton (?) (Beavis n.d.)
DIA 1897–1899: First chiefs at Bella Bella were Boston Humpsit [Humchitt] and Kittee; second chiefs were Charley Tihe, Housty, Nu-nu-cus [Núṅukvas], and Carpenter
B.C. DIRECTORIES: 1901, Chief of tribe, Robert Bell; 1903, Robert Bell & Co. Indian General Store

Robert Bell (see Ch. 5), a Raven, was probably from the village of ʼQábá. He held the ʼQvúqvaẏaítx̌v chiefly name ʼQaʼaít. The ʼQvúqvaẏaítx̌v were the last Heiltsuk group to move into Bella Bella. They left their village after it was destroyed by fire in the 1890s.

CALISTOCK
(b. 1849?)

SOURCE of NS 23101, stone hammer (Housʼte)
1881 CENSUS: Kalisbock, aged 32; Jacob Kalistock, aged 9
1882: Subscription to schoolhouse bell, two dollars

R. G. Large (1968:57), son of the missionary, remembered Calistock:

> Many of the older people had gone barefoot for years and the splayed and misshapen feet were a problem when it came to shoes. I remember watching my father trace out on brown paper a particularly large pair belonging to Job Calestock, so that shoes could be made for him in Vancouver.

According to Franz Boas (1932:137), Job Galastock's (Calistock's) father's mother's mother was a daughter of Gwinō', a Raven man from the Tsimshian town of G.ēʼlanEg.īʼ. Calistock was one of those who helped Boas in the fall of 1923 and contributed the following stories to *Bella Bella Tales*: "Raven and Squirrel," "Raven and Glebe," "Raven and the Invisible Ones," "Raven is Killed," "MEnē'q.iLis," "ĂwīʼLḷīdExᵘ," and "The Wolves" (Boas 1928:19–21, 25, 66–67, 141). It is clear that

Calistock was a Bella Bella elder and historian.

CAPTAIN CARPENTER
(1841–1931)

MAKER of No. 34, Indian cedar box; No. 42, food box, representing Beaver
USER of NS 23119, stone used for paint
SOURCE of NS 23164, stone used for painting
1881 CENSUS: Carpenter aged 35, native carpenter
DIA 1897: Carpenter was a second chief of Bella Bella
1900: Became keeper of the Dryad Point Light (*MB* 2, no. 4[1905]:821–22)
HEILTSUK NAMES: Duʼkḷwayella, Wúx̌vùas

Richard (Dick) Carpenter, one of the five Bella Bella artists named by Large (see Ch. 5; Fig. 26), was a well-known canoe and boat builder as well as the lighthouse keeper. In addition to the canoes for the American Museum of Natural History and the Fisheries Exhibition in London, he built a large canoe at Sagar Lake. When it was half finished, he paid a barrel of rum to the men of Bella Bella to help him get it to the beach. According to Olson (1935; 1949:10), the completed canoe was given to the (Tsimshian) chief of Kitkatla, who gave it to Queen Victoria.

GENERAL DICK
(Old Dick, 1822–1902?)

MAKER of No. 25, canoe paddle
SOURCE of No. 29, key ring; No. 15, rough carved human figure; No. 16, rough carved human figure; No. 17, rough carved human figure; No. 47, rough carved human figure
1881: Subscription to bell and paint for schoolhouse, fifty cents
B.C. DIRECTORIES: 1901, Old Indian Dick, carver of curios; 1905, Dick Douglas, Indian General Store

I suspect that General Dick is Old Dick, the carver of curios. However, there is a photograph taken by Large of Dick Jakeswallis (see Fig. 27), captioned "an old timer at Bella Bella" (R. W. Large n.d. ; *MB* 6, no. 3[1910]:517), and it is possible that both Old Dick and General Dick (see Ch. 5) are other names for this Dick Jakeswallis (Zíxsíwális), a respected elder, the father-in-law of Chief Humchitt, and the grandfather of Captain Carpenter's daughter-in-law. Alternatively, the photograph could be of the man known only as Dick, who died in 1902, but most of Large's Bella Bella photographs were taken after that date. It is also possible that General Dick is another name for Captian Richard (Dick) Carpenter, but I think this is unlikely because Large distinguished between the two artists in his catalogue list, and the objects assigned to each are stylistically dissimilar. Another possibility is that Captian Carpenter and Dick Jakeswallis are the same person, although, to my knowledge, Richard Carpenter did not hold the title Zixsiwalis. It is known that Old Dick's widow married the man who received Reverend Crosby when he first came to Bella Bella, William Brown (*MB* 6, no. 1[1909]:17–18).

ARTHUR EBBSTONE
(Bella Bella Jack, 1846–1903)

SOURCE of NS 23104, spinning disc
1881 CENSUS: Arthur Ebstom, aged 34; Maria, aged 30
1881: Baptized, aged about 35 years, also his wife, Marie, aged about 30 years, and their daughter, Minnie (Beavis n.d.)
1881: Subscribed to bell and paint for schoolhouse, two dollars
1882: Subscribed to bell for schoolhouse, three dollars
B.C. DIRECTORY: 1892, Arthur Erbstem, fisherman

Arthur Ebbstone (see Ch. 3) was also known as Bella Bella Jack (Crosby called him Ebstone Jack). About 1880 he worked on a steamer handling coal and also travelled to Puget Sound for seasonal work picking hops. While passing through Victoria, he was converted to Christianity after hearing the preaching of Reverend Pollard at the Pandora Street Methodist Church mission hall for Indians. The story of his conversion was told often by Bella

Bella missionaries (e.g., Tate 1916, 1917; Crosby 1914:143–44). "Since coming to Bella Bella," wrote R. W. Large,

> I have found Arthur still seeking to lead the people to Christ. . . . Few lived as faithfully as Arthur, a simple, warm hearted, unlearned Indian. . . . He was always poor, but a few days before he died he gave me $4.50—all the money he had I think—to send to a Bella Coola man to pay for some potatoes purchased but not paid for. [*MB* 1, no. 4(1904):418]

Ebbstone "lived a consistent and Christian life, and for many years was the efficient watchman of Bella Bella" (Beavis n.d.). He died 22 October 1903.

ENOCH
(d. 1904)

MAKER of No. 11, old time Indian cradle (see Ch. 5)

REVEREND J. EDGAR
(George Edgar), China Hat

SOURCE of NS 23126, stone axe, probably a whetstone (Klah-qua-bah'-la); NS 23130, stone paint pot

George (not J.) Edgar, a Tsimshian from Hartley Bay, was sent by Crosby to China Hat (Klemtu) on Swindle Island in 1897 to establish a school and mission. The mixed ˇXíx̌ís and Tsimshian village had fifteen houses, a church, two trade stores kept by Indians, and a population of 120 in 1900 (*MO* 20, no. 2[1901]:35).

FIREMAN

SOURCE of No. 118, stone hammer (Hous-'te)

There was a firehall at Bella Bella, and the name "Fireman" may have referred to a member of the Bella Bella volunteer firefighting brigade. But it may also have referred to the office of Fireman, which was a traditional Heiltsuk ceremonial prerogative. The tenth potlatch listed by

Olson (1954:236) is the Fireman potlatch:

> With the open fire it is a fairly common occurrence that the roof planks catch fire at the edge of the smoke hole. If this happens during a masked dance, only one man, who has the title Xo'lalas, is permitted to leave the house to put out the fire. No one else may move during the dance. If the Xo'lalas puts out the fire, he must give a potlatch when the dance is finished. . . . With the reduced number of people in the tribe these offices may be held by children, the present holder having filled the post since he was a mere lad. The marks of office are a bearskin cape and a cedar neck ring.

MR. HARRIS
(b. 1833, 1842, or 1846; d. 1902 or 1906)

SOURCE of NS 23163, stone axe (Klah-qua-bah'-la)
1881 CENSUS: Mr. Harris, aged 48
1881: Baptism of Robert, son of Mr. and Mrs. Harris (Beavis n.d.)

PAUL GEORGE
Kimsquit

SOURCE of No. 27, carved eagle
DIA 1899: Chiefs at Kimsquit: King George and Captain John; population of the village: 78

Paul George was probably related to King George, one of the two old chiefs who governed Kimsquit. Although the Kimsquit chiefs petitioned the government for a teacher (they asked for a white man with a wife and children), they did not want a missionary, but later, in 1904, Reverend J. C. Spencer was allowed to build a small church in the village (*MB* 8, no. 1[1905]: 119–20; *MB* 2, no. 2[1904]:302–34; see Ch. 4).

DANIEL HOUSTIE
(1880?–1912)

MAKER of No. 61, carved walking stick; Nos. 71, 77, old time halibut hook and sinker; No. 12, carved stick to keep in position the

pad used to produce the flattening of infant's head; No. 26, carved whaling paddle; No. 57, dance mask used by Interior or Stick Indians
SOURCE of No. 66, dance whistle; No. 67, dance whistle
1881 CENSUS: Housty, aged 33
1881: Housty and wife, subscription to school-house, six dollars
1882: Housty, subscription to schoolhouse bell, eight dollars and fifty cents
DECEMBER 1882: Death of Housty's child
DIA 1897: Housty was a second chief
B.C. DIRECTORY: 1905, Tom Housty, Manager of Bella Bella sawmill

The name is spelled both Houstie and Housty. Daniel Houstie (see Ch. 5 and Appendix D) may have been a relative of Chief Tom Housty, a high-ranking chief at Bella Bella who continued to uphold Heiltsuk traditions. After he attended a tombstone (memorial) feast at China Hat (Klemtu), Chief Housty reciprocated with a similar feast at Bella Bella; Large did not approve: "Time was lost [and] money squandered on feasting and lavishly overpaying the visitors to outdo them" (*MB* 5, no. 4[1909]:690–92).

HERBERT HUMCHIL
(Bertie Humchitt?, 1881–1974)
SOURCE of No. 98, chief's horn spoon
1913: Bertie Humchitt was the leader of the Bella Bella Cornet Band.

Herbert Humchil (Humchitt) may have been Bertie Humchitt, the son of Bob Humchitt and Alice Starr, who held the title ʼQaʼaít after Chief Robert Bell (Olson 1935; 1949:28). The Humchitts were, and still are, important Bella Bella chiefs.

TIMOTHY HUNT
(b. 1860 or 1867; d. 1922)
SOURCE of No. 32, O'wekeno (Oweekeno) walking stick (see Ch. 4)
1882: Mr. and Mrs. Hunt, subscription to schoolhouse bell, two dollars
PHOTOGRAPH: A gravestone on Pole Island in

memory of Timothy Hunt is engraved with a whale with two dorsal fins, on each of which sits a raven with outstretched wings (HCEC photograph).

BOB LAWSON
(b. 1858; d. before 1909)
SOURCE of No. 99, chief's horn spoon; No. 95, shell pendant, abalone
1881 CENSUS: Robert Lawson, aged 23; Emily, aged 22

Lawson was for many years the watchman of Bella Bella (Beavis n.d.). He died before 1909, when Reverend C. M. Tate made a return visit to the village to dedicate the Bella Bella church (Tate n.d.).

CHIEF NOONEYUAS
(1835–1904)
SOURCE of No. 100, spoon
1881 CENSUS: Noonaquos, aged 46, Hunter; Mary
DIA 1897: Nu-nu-cus was a second chief
PHOTOGRAPH: Chief Noon-i-quas and his wife in their canoe, going out to meet the steamship *Barbara Boscowitz* in the harbour (Fig. 22).
HEILTSUK SPELLING: Núṅukvas

At his baptism, Núṅukvas took the name Arthur Wellington (Beavis n.d.). His death in 1904 was reported in the quarterly newsletter, *Na-Na-Kwa; or, Dawn on the Northwest Coast*, published by Reverend Raley at Kitamaat. "Old Noonikass died in May," wrote Raley (1904b). "He was a very industrious man and made a living by fishing and drying spawn of herring. We purchased from him the fish eggs for the [Kitamaat Girls'] Home every year" (see Fig. 18).

OLIVER
(Alert Bay)
MAKER of No. 86, silver brooch; No. 87, bracelet; No. 88, eagle brooch

J. QUANOOTME
(d. 1903?)
SOURCE of No. 84, cedar playing disc
HEILTSUK NAME: ʼKvánúthmi

JOHNNY REID
(1850–1925)
SOURCE of NS 23132, stone hammer (Hous-'te)

DR. SAM
(1821–1906?)
SOURCE of NS 23122, stone playing disc; No. 31, walking stick; No. 33, crude walking stick

Dr. Sam (see Ch. 4), who was called KļeʼbxEla (Boas 1923:264) or Kʼilhālaʼ (thistle dance), was nōʼłtsēʼstał, a healer who was able to suck balls (bullets?) out of wounds (Boas 1923:264). When Sam performed, he wore only a dancing apron and carried two rattles. On one occasion, he called for a bearskin blanket to wear. When he put the robe over his shoulders, he could not remove it, even though it was not held on. (The apron, bearskin, and rattle constituted the traditional costume worn by Northwest Coast shamans in healing rituals.) Dr. Sam, assisted by an old man shaman, sucked the sickness out of Moses Knight when he was twelve years old and was paid ten dollars (Boas 1923:263–64).

OLD SANDY
(d. 1908)
SOURCE of No. 78, stone halibut sinker; NS 23128, stone axe (Klah-qua-bahʼ-la)
1881: Subscription for schoolhouse, two dollars
1882: Subscription for schoolhouse bell, fifty cents

Large recounts the story of Old Sandy's evil box (mestachie box), its discovery, and the opening of it at a public meeting (*MB* 5, no. 4[1909]: 701–2). Sandy died suddenly of heart disease in the summer of 1908 (see Ch. 4).

SOLOMON
SOURCE of No. 58, mask, Stick, Sinash (or Interior Indian); No. 59, mask, Stick, Sinash (or Interior Indian)

FRANK WEST

SOURCE of NS 23148, playing disc
1913: Member of the Bella Bella Cornet Band

Frank West worked as a trapper. He was adopted by Willie West, who may have been his uncle.

WILLIE WEST
(1864–1944?)

SOURCE of NS 23149 stone, used by the Indians in cooking seaweed
1881 CENSUS: William West, aged 17
1881: Subscription to schoolhouse, one dollar and fifty cents; Betsy West, three dollars
1913: Member of the Bella Bella Cornet Band
PHOTOGRAPH: Willie West's house (HCEC photograph)

Willie West, who worked as a drag seiner, helped Drucker in the 1930s (Drucker Papers, p. 99). An incident recounted by Franz Boas about West's wife is notable as an illustration of the continuation of aboriginal beliefs and powers among Christian Heiltsuk. West's wife was a twin, and twins were thought to have a special relationship with salmon. Once, Mrs. West was out in a canoe and could not make headway against the wind. She threw off her blanket, took some salt, blew it four times out of her mouth, and patted her chest. Immediately, a large salmon jumped in front of the canoe. The canoe shook, and then went on easily (Boas 1923:283).

ALFRED WILSON
(1865–1935)

SOURCE of No. 83, stone playing disc; No. 1, Hyda basket (see Ch. 4)

CHARLES WINDSOR
(1858–1938)

SOURCE of No. 94, bear's tooth pendant; NS 23103, small stone axe; NS 23105, playing disc
1881 CENSUS: Charles Windsor, aged 23
1882: Subscription to schoolhouse bell, one dollar and fifty cents
B.C. DIRECTORIES: 1892, 1899, Charles Windsor, fisherman

Along with Moses Knight, Charles Windsor often took services for Reverend Beavis, and functioned as a translator for the missionary (Beavis n.d.). He worked with Boas in the fall of 1923 and recorded the following stories which were published in *Bella Bella Tales*: "Raven and Eagle," "Tslǔˈmqălǎqs," "The Eagle Clan of the La'tstsa," and "Qlasa'u" (Boas 1928:14, 17, 65–66, 160).

JIM WISE
(1827–1907)

Wise is not mentioned in Large's catalogue, but may have been the source of NS 27966, a doctor's floating stone, because Large reported that Jim Wise showed him how the floating stone trick was performed (see p. 80).

APPENDIX D: WORKS BY DANIEL HOUSTIE AND ASSOCIATED OBJECTS

A small group of replicas of early Heiltsuk domestic articles from Large's 1906 collection are all very similar in style. They include a pair of wooden tongs "for hot stones for cooking" carved with a birdlike head at one end (No. 109), and three bentwood boxes identified by Large as a cooking box (No. 37), a dipper (No. 38), and a water box (No. 39). All are painted with black and brown designs and appear to have been new when Large acquired them.

Stylistically similar to the tongs is a small carved stick in the shape of a bird's head (No. 13) called "Indian cradle support." It is one of two sticks from the 1906 group so identified. The other (No. 14) is in the form of a whale and a bird, possibly Raven. It is curved and has a notched projection at one end and a small wooden cylinder at the other. This stick has the same form and stylistic characteristics as an object from the 1901 collection, "carved stick used to keep in position the pad used to produce the flattening of infant's head" (No. 12), which is in the shape of an eagle riding on the back of a whale. Large identified the carver of

No. 12 as Daniel Houstie.

Houstie is also named as the maker of a painted paddle (No. 25), a dramatic dance mask (No. 57), an intricately carved "walking stick," probably a speaker's staff (No. 61), and a bone halibut hook (No. 71). The distinctive black and brown design on the paddle exhibits design elements also seen on the water and cooking boxes.

The same hand can be detected in the designs on a group of ceremonial objects (probably newly made replicas) in the 1906 collection. Large identified them as a dance drinking box (No. 48), a dance hat (No. 55), a painted war club (No. 63), a war spear (No. 65), and a dance whistle (No. 69). A carved ladle with a wooden, skull-like head in the bowl (No. 50) can also be included in this group. Although this object has no documentation at all, the skull/ladle is a Heiltsuk object type and this one is very similar to the ceremonial objects in Large's 1906 collection.

I believe that all of these objects were made by Daniel Houstie. The attribution is based on detailed formal analysis of the objects mentioned. Rather than describe all the design elements and their relationships in the text, I have put them in chart form here. (Only objects with formline designs are in the chart. The dance mask, No. 57, made by Houstie, and a similar dance mask, No. 60, probably also made by Houstie, are not included in the design analysis because they are sculptural and do not have the same design elements as the objects with two-dimensional formline patterns.) An "x" indicates the presence of the design element. The objects made by and attributed to Houstie are listed numerically by catalogue number below. (For more information about Daniel Houstie, see Ch. 5 and Appendix C.)

No. 12, carved stick used to keep in position the pad used to produce the flattening of infant's head, made by Daniel Houstie
Nos. 13–14, two carved sticks, "Indian cradle supports"
No. 26, carved whaling paddle, made by Daniel Houstie
No. 37, cedar cooking box

Works by Daniel Houstie and Associated Objects: Design Analysis

Design Elements	Made by Houstie				Here Attributed to Houstie													
Catalogue Number	12	25	61	71	13	14	37	38	39	41	48	50	55	63	65	69	77	109
domestic/maritime technology	X	X		X	X	X	X	X	X	X							X	X
ceremonial			X								X	X	X	X	X	X		
brown & black on natural cedar	X	X			X	X	X	X	X	X	X	X	X	X	X	X		X
thin swelling formlines tapering at junctions		X					X	X	X	X	X	X	X					
squared forms comprise design that fills the available space		X					X	X	X	X						X		
inner ovoids separated from formlines by narrow border		X					X	X	X	X					X			
freehand hatching ////		X					X	X	X	X		X			X			
freehand hatching XXX							X	X	X							X		
freehand hatching \\\\		X					X		X	X								
black hatching in brown outlines and/or brown in black		X					X	X	X	X								
long squared ovoids		X	X				X	X	X	X								
long tapered eye with squared oval pupil		X					X		X	X								
short downturned eye with large round pupil		X						X			X		X					
square teeth indicated by thin lines		X	X		X		X	X	X	X	X		X				X	
sickle shapes at joints of claws or limbs							X				X							
arched, rounded eyebrows			X		X						X			X	X	X		
hair indicated by short irregular strokes			X								X	X		X	X	X	X	
black or brown "mask"											X	X		X	X	X		
concentric circle in top half of circular element		X					X	X	X	X			X					
outline around perimeter of design		X					X	X	X	X								
painted							X	X	X	X								
carved and painted	X	X			X	X					X	X	X	X	X	X		X
carved, not painted			X	X												X		
large round abalone pupil in short downturned eye			X	X	X									X	X	X	X	X
oval abalone inlay			X									X		X	X			
rounded teeth			X									X			X			
flat inverted T-shaped nose			X												X			
straight lips that do not meet at corners			X												X			
attached cedar and/or carved elements			X								X	X	X	X	X	X	X	
salmon-trout's-head motif		X					X			X								
face within circle motif							X		X	X								
skull motif			X								X	X	X			X		
profile head with downturned toothy mouth and round eye		X							X				X					
long-nosed bird with dotted eye area															X			X
snub-nosed whale with round eyes	X				X					X								

No. 38, wooden dipper

No. 39, water box

No. 41, box (not documented as part of the Large Collection)

No. 48, dance drinking box

No. 50, skull/ladle (not documented as part of the Large Collection)

No. 55, cedar dance hat

No. 57, dance mask, made by Daniel Houstie (not in chart)

No. 60, dance mask (not in chart)

No. 61, carved walking stick, made by Daniel Houstie

No. 63, painted war club

No. 65, war spear, carved whale-rib point

No. 69, large dance whistle

No. 71, old time halibut hook, made by Daniel Houstie (hooks are made from scapula of mountain sheep)

No. 77, not documented as part of the Large Collection, identical to No. 71

No. 109, tongs for hot stones for cooking

APPENDIX E: OBJECTS FROM OTHER COMMUNITIES (1901 COLLECTION)

The Large Collection contains some objects that originated in communities other than Bella Bella. Large may have collected them from Heiltsuk people, from visitors to Bella Bella, or on his own travels.

ALERT BAY

No. 86, silver brooch made by Oliver

No. 87, bracelet made by Oliver

No. 88, eagle brooch made by Oliver

CHINA HAT (KLEMTU)

NS 23126, stone axe, probably a whetstone (Klah-qua-bah'-la) from Reverend J. (George) Edgar

NS 23130, stone paint pot from Reverend J. (George) Edgar

FORT RUPERT

No. 20, model totem pole

No. 21, model totem pole

No. 6, woman's cedar-root hat with painting representing an eagle

No. 126, cedar-bark canoe bailer

No. 53, dance headdress used by Fort Rupert people

No. 54, dance neck ornament used by Fort Rupert people

No. 90, silver earrings

No. 91, child's silver earrings

FRASER RIVER

No. 89, silver brooch (sockeye salmon)

GOOSE ISLAND

NS 23106, stone hammer

NS 23181, stone hammer (Houstie)

KIMSQUIT

No. 27, carved eagle from Paul George

APPENDIX F: PURCHASE PRICES, 1906 COLLECTION (NS 27847–27977)

The prices paid by the Ontario Provincial Museum for Large's second (1906) shipment of artifacts from Bella Bella are an indication of the relative values of native artifacts in the first decade of this century. The information here is compiled from the inventory/price list that accompanied Large's second shipment (NS file). Prices are analysed in Chapter 3.

$0.25

1 war club handle (No. 111)

1 basket (No. 4)

$0.50

1 yew wood box, old model (No. 44)

1 painted clam shell (No. 128)

1 basket (No. 3)

4 gambling sticks, bone (No. 82)

1 bone chisel (NS 27906)

2 sealbone gamblers (NS 27908–27909)

1 bird from dance mask (No. 49)

1 box (probably No. 40)

1 doctor's floating stone (NS 27966)

$0.75

1 big spoon, plain (No. 105)

$1.00

1 small stone axe on handle (NS 27858)

2 stone axes with handle as used in getting cedar boards from tree (No. 121, NS 27860)

1 bone implement for removing inner bark from hemlock (No. 110)

1 wooden dipper (No. 38)

1 copper rattle (No. 51)

1 small extension basket (No. 2)

1 stone charm (NS 27967)

1 stick pin (No. 93)

1 whalebone bark beater (No. 114)

$1.25

2 carved sticks, Indian cradle supports (Nos. 13–14)

$1.50

1 small cedar mat (No. 8)

3 small Coppers (No. 96)

$2.00

1 silver brooch (NS 27885)

2 copper head ornaments (No. 56)

2 bone disks (Nos. 112–113)

$2.50

5 halibut fish hooks (No. 73)

10 stone fragments (NS 27968–27977)

$3.00

1 cedar cooking box, with tongs for hot stones (Nos. 37, 109)

1 scalloped-edge dance implement (No. 46)

1 dance mask (No. 60)

1 water box (No. 39)

1 pair earrings (NS 27887)

1 stone knife (NS 27901)

$4.00

2 cylindrical stones used as hammers to hit
    wedges (NS 27931–27932)
1 cedar dance hat (No. 55)

$5.00

1 painted war club (No. 63)
1 large dance whistle (No. 69)
1 slate totem (smaller) (No. 23)
1 slate knife (carved) (No. 45)
1 dance drinking box with three figures on top
    (No. 48)
1 large food box (No. 43)
6 assorted horn spoons (Nos. 101–103, NS
    27888–27889, 27892)

$6.50

1 slate totem (No. 22)
2 large silver bracelets (No. 92, NS
    27884/906.2.1–2)

$8.00

2 copper bracelets, one of them native copper
    (No. 85, NS 27913)

$10.00

1 Indian carved box, used for dance masks, etc.
    (No. 36)
1 high crown dance hat (No. 57)
7 gambling discs, assorted sizes (NS
    27924–27930)
10 assorted stone axes (NS 27933–27942)
1 carved cane (No. 64)

$11.50

23 gambling stones (NS 27943–27965)

$12.00

3 carved stone hammers, flat, for driving stakes
    in river (there are four, not three, hammers
    listed on the Normal School accession list:
    Nos. 122–123; NS 27916, 27918)
4 stone warclubs and 1 carved stone halibut
    sinker (Nos. 79, 124; NS 27919–27920, 27922)

$20.00

1 war spear with carved whale-rib point (No.
    65)

APPENDIX G: TOOLS, FISHING GEAR, AND GAMING PIECES, BY TYPE

More than half of the objects (57 per cent) that
R. W. Large sent to the Ontario Provincial
Museum from Bella Bella tools, fishing gear,
and gambling paraphernalia that were no
longer used in turn-of-the-century Bella Bella.
They illustrated the old ways and represent the
kinds of artifacts that the OPM was actively
soliciting in Large's time.

TOOLS

32 stone axes or chisels
21 stone hammers and hammer fragments
11 stone fragments
4 bark beaters
4 paint stones and paint pot
3 bone chisels
3 spinning discs
2 shell and stone knives and fragments
1 canoe bailer
1 canoe awl
1 cooking stone
1 stone mortar
1 cradle stick
Total: 85 (30 per cent of total collection)

FISHING GEAR

14 fish hooks
5 sinkers
4 pile drivers
1 leister spear
1 net dryer
1 fish club
Total: 26 (9 per cent of total collection)

GAMING PIECES

50 playing or gaming discs and stones (17.5 per
    cent of total collection)

APPENDIX H: OBJECTS NOT EXAMINED

The objects collected by R. W. Large at Bella Bella
were sold to the Ontario Provincial Museum
when it was housed in the Toronto Normal
School (see Ch. 1, n. 1). They were given Normal
School (NS) accession numbers. Subsequently,
they were divided between the departments of
New World Archaeology and Ethnology at the
Royal Ontario Museum. These departments now
form the Department of Anthropology. Only
those objects now in ROM Ethnology were available for this study, but since it is important to
realize the scope of the whole collection, the rest
of the objects are listed here, arranged by type.
(For a complete numerical listing of the objects
sent by Large from Bella Bella, see Appendix J,
"Concordance.") Most are undecorated stone
and bone tools and are now in the ROM's
Archaeology collections. Some objects were traded to museums in Australia and Haiti and a few
that have been loaned out for displays and
exhibits were unavailable for this study.

BASKETRY

1. NS 28196 Cedar-bark mat (unavailable)
2. NS 28198 Cedar-bark mat (exchanged with
    National Museum of Australia, Sydney,
    1907)
3. NS 28201 Cedar-bark mat (exchanged with
    National Museum of Australia, Sydney,
    1907)
4. NS 28203 Basket (birch-bark) (unavailable)

CARVINGS

5. NS 23152 Stick used to suspend cradle upon
    (unavailable)
6. NS 28256 Eagle's head (carved in Baryte
    heavy spar) (unavailable)

CEREMONIAL OBJECTS

7. NS 27966 Doctor's floating stone
8. NS 27967 Stone charm
9. NS 28204 Headdress (cedar bark)
    (exchanged with National Museum of
    Australia, Sydney, 1907)
10. NS 28205 Ceremonial wand (exchanged

with National Museum of Australia, Sydney, 1907)

11. NS 28221 Dance whistle (exchanged with National Museum of Australia, Sydney, 1907)

12. NS 28222 Dance clapper (exchanged with National Museum of Australia, Sydney, 1907)

Fishing Gear

13. NS 23171 Halibut sinker. Finding spot: Bella Bella

14. NS 28207 Halibut sinker (exchanged with National Museum of Australia, Sydney, 1907)

15. NS 28208 Halibut sinker

16. NS 28210 Old-time halibut hook (exchanged with National Museum of Australia, Sydney, 1907)

17. NS 28211 Halibut hook (exchanged with National Museum of Australia, Sydney, 1907)

18. NS 28213 Cod hook (exchanged with National Museum of Australia, Sydney, 1907)

Gaming Pieces

19. NS 23105 Playing disc. Source: Chas. Windsor, Bella Bella

20. NS 23122 Stone playing disc. Source: Dr. Sam, Bella Bella

21. NS 23148 Playing disc. Source: Frank West, Bella Bella

22. NS 27908 Sealbone gambler (a note in the NS accession list reads: "27908 numbered incorrectly 28247"; because these items were not available for study, it is not clear whether there is another object 28247; see no. 62 below)

23. NS 27909 Sealbone gambler

24–30. NS 27924–27930 7 gambling discs

31. NS 27943 Gambling stone

32. NS 27944 Gambling stone (exchanged with Musée d'Ethnologie d'Haiti, July 1944)

33–53. NS 27945–27965 21 gambling stones

54–58. NS 28225–28229 5 gambling stones

59. NS 28230 Gambling disc

60–61. NS 28231–28232 2 gambling discs

(exchanged with National Museum of Australia, Sydney, 1907)

62. NS 28247 Gambling disc (this may be the same object as no. 22 above)

Jewellery

63. NS 27884 Large silver bracelet (ROM 906.2.2) (unavailable)

64. NS 27885 Silver brooch (unavailable)

65. NS 27887 Pair of earrings (unavailable)

66. NS 27913 Copper bracelet (unavailable)

Spoons

67. NS 27888 Horn spoon (unavailable)

68. NS 27889 Horn spoon (exchanged with Musée d'Ethnologie d'Haiti, July 1944)

69. NS 27892 Horn spoon (unavailable)

Stone Hammers and Clubs

70. NS 23101 Stone hammer (Hous-'te). Source: Calistock, Bella Bella

71. NS 23106 Stone hammer. Finding spot: Goose Island

72. NS 23131 Stone hammer (Hous-'te). Finding spot: Bella Bella

73. NS 23132 Stone hammer (Hous-'te). Source: Johnny Reid, Bella Bella

74. NS 23178 Stone war club. Finding spot: Bella Bella

75–76. NS 23179–23180 2 stone hammers (Houstie). Finding spot: Bella Bella

77. NS 23181 Stone hammer (Houstie). Finding spot: Goose Island

78–81. NS 23182–23185 4 stone hammer fragments. Finding spot: Bella Bella

82. NS 27916 Pile driver

83. NS 27918 Pile driver

84. NS 27919 Stone war club

85. NS 27920 Stone war club

86. NS 27922 Stone war club

87–88. NS 27931–27932 2 cylindrical stones, used as hammers

Stone and Bone Axes and Chisels

89. NS 23103 Small stone axe. Source: Chas. Windsor, Bella Bella

90. NS 23121 Stone axe (Klah-qua-bah'-la). Finding spot: Bella Bella

91. NS 23126 Stone axe, probably from a whetstone (Klah-qua-bah'-la). Source: Rev. Edgar, China Hat

92. NS 23128 Stone axe (Klah-qua-bah'-la). Source: Old Sandy, Bella Bella

93. NS 23163 Stone axe (Klah-qua-bah'-la). Source: Mr. Harris, Bella Bella

94. NS 23166 Stone axe (Klah-qua-bah'-la). Source: Bella Bella (exchanged with Musée d'Ethnologie d'Haiti, July 1944)

95–97. NS 23167–23169 3 stone axes (Klah-qua-bah'-la). Finding spot: Bella Bella

98. NS 27858 Small stone axe

99. NS 27860 Stone axe

100–109. NS 27933–27942 10 stone axes

110–118. NS 28236–28244 9 stone axes or chisels

119. NS 27906 Bone chisel

120. NS 28248 Bone chisel

Painting Tools

121. NS 23119 Stone used for paint by Capt. Carpenter, Bella Bella

122. NS 23130 Stone paint pot. Source: Rev. Edgar, China Hat

123. NS 23164 Stone used for painting. Source: Capt. Carpenter, Bella Bella

124. NS 28245 Paint stone

Miscellaneous Tools

125. NS 23104 Spinning disc. Source: Arthur Ebbstone, Bella Bella

126. NS 27901 Stone knife

127. NS 23149 Stone used by Indians in cooking seaweed; after oolichan oil is added, the heated stone is put in. Source: Willie West, Bella Bella

Pipe

128. NS 28249 Small pipe. Finding spot: Bexley Township (labelled Innisfil Township). This object is apparently from Ontario and was sold to the OPM by Large in 1904. For some unknown reason it is numbered in sequence with the Bella Bella artifacts and so is included here.

129–133. NS 28250–28254 5 sea-lion teeth
134. NS 28255 Wolf's or dog's left underjaw, showing muted fracture

FRAGMENTS

135. NS 23134 Stone fragment. Finding spot: Bella Bella
136–145. NS 27968–27977 10 stone fragments
146. NS 28235 Fragment of stone hunting knife

APPENDIX I: SOME HEILTSUK WORDS

This appendix is an alphabetical listing of some of the Heiltsuk names of people, places, and ceremonies found in the text. Unless otherwise indicated, orthography and definitions are based on Rath (1981).

ak!la'a!'em According to Olson, a dance of the **ċaíqa** series.

ȧélkv Inviter; an official who formally invites people to a potlach.

aLasiml According to Drucker, a Stick Indian spirit represented in a dance. A variation of **áthsemx**, people living in the woods.

Báxvbakváláṅusiwa Cannibal spirit, or the supernatural power by which the **tánís** dancer is possessed. Given by Boas as **Baxᵘbakwalanuxᵘsi'weᵋ**, the Cannibal-at-the-North-End-of-the-World.

ċaíqa Shaman; true shamans; dancers in the Shaman's series of the Winter Ceremonial.

da'sgyu Olson's spelling of **dásigiú**, bad shamans or workers of evil magic.

dlĩala Used by Drucker to mean a major potlach. A variation of **dhiála**, to invite

people from another village to a potlatch.

dlugwola According to Drucker, Finding a Supernatural Treasure dance. **Dhúgvála** is a dance performed to obtain the right to use one's supernatural power.

dhuẇláẋa (To move) down again; Returned from Heaven series, the second of the Winter Ceremonials. Also called **mitla**.

Du'ḳļwayella One of the Heiltsuk names of Captain Richard Carpenter, a Bella Bella artist, lighthouse keeper, and **'Uyalitẋv** chief. Among Carpenter's other Heiltsuk names were **Mxsáqv**, which can be translated as rainbow, and **Wúẋvúas** (see Ch. 5 and Appendix C).

Haémzit A chiefly name of the **'Uyalitẋv**. Humpshet and Humpsit are two of the anglicizations of the name, which is now commonly written Humchitt.

hailíka In shamanic healing, to cure someone by removing bad medicine; in the Winter Ceremonial, to remove powers of spiritual possession.

hailĩkila Ceremonial healers. Drucker's spelling of **hailíḱinuẋv**, a shamanic healer who removes bad medicine or a ritualist who removes the supernatural spirit that possesses a dancer. Olson gives **he'likuXu** for good shamans or healers. See also **heilikstaxsta**.

hámáċa Another name for **tánís** (Cannibal) dance or dancer

heilikstaxsta Healing water dance, according to Stevenson. A variation of **hailíka**, to cure someone in shamanic healing by removing bad medicine and, in the Winter Ceremonial, to remove powers of spiritual possession. See also **hailĩkila**.

Houstie Heiltsuk family name, also spelled Housty. That R. W. Large gave Hous-'te as the word for stone hammer implies that the name is related to the term for sledge hammer, **ẋúċ**, connoting great power and force. Daniel Houstie was one of the five Bella Bella artists named by Large (see Ch. 5 and Appendix C).

'Isda Elcho Harbour village

'Isdaítẋv People or person from **'Isda**. Members of this Heiltsuk-speaking group now live at Waglisla.

ḳļo'minuahslax Drucker's spelling of the Heiltsuk term for Skull dance. **Ẋúǧvemṁálás** means skull.

ḳļya'LkyaLamas According to Olson, a Sleep-causing dance. Olson also gives **ḳļytlis'naulauks** as the Sleep dance. **'Ḱálha** means to sleep; **ḱáḷlá** (plural, **ḱáḱeḷllá**), to anaesthetize, to put to sleep with anaesthetic. See also **maqaẋ súklaxi**.

lũłał According to Drucker, the Ghost dance. **Lúlha** means haunted, or bothered by a ghost. Someone made a ghost dancer, or having become partially paralysed, is **lúlhlákv**. See also **olala'**.

maqaẋ súklaxi Harkin gives this as a name for Sleep-causing dance, with its literal meaning of clearing of the throat. Rath gives to clear the throat as **haẏélẋut**. See also **ḳļya'LkyaLamas**.

mestachie box belonging to medicine man. **'Iẋsáċi** means container for medicine.

náẇálakv Supernatural power; someone or something having, resulting from, or exposed to supernatural power.

Núṅukvas Heiltsuk chiefly name. The man who held the name during Large's tenure took the Christian name Arthur Wellington.

olala' According to Boas, part of the Ghost dance. See **lū̵ła̵ł**.

pḵvs Wild Man of the Woods, a supernatural creature. See No. 57.

'Qábá Kokyet, a village on Yeo Island.

'Qa'aít Heiltsuk chiefly name. Also spelled Kaiete and Kahyi't by early observers.

'Qélc Old Bella Bella or Old Town at McLoughlin Bay, Campbell Island. Can be translated as having kelp. The English name Bella Bella perhaps derives from **pelbala** meaning having a thin and flat end or point, as in a point of land.

'Qvúqvaí Koqui, a village at Gale Creek. (The name means calm water.)

'Qvúqvaẏaítx̌v Calm water people; people or person from **'Qvúqvaí**. Members of this Heiltsuk-speaking group now live at Waglisla.

tánís Cannibal dancer; Cannibal ceremony, the first-ranked dance of the **ċaíqa** series of the Winter Ceremonial. Also called **hámáċa**.

túxv'it A ceremonial puppet. See No. 47.

Uẇigalitx̌v People or person from Calvert Island.

uwinalal War dancer, according to Olson. Drucker spelled it **uwinalaL**. Both words are variations of **wáwínalalh**, war dance.

'Uyalitx̌v Seaward people, people or person living seaward. (**'Uya** means seaward.) Members of this Heiltsuk-speaking group now live at Waglisla.

Uẇíthitx̌v People of the inlet, landward people, people or person from Roscoe Inlet. (**Uẇíthálá** means landward.) Members of this Heiltsuk-speaking group now live at Waglisla.

Wáglísla New Bella Bella; Waglisla, on Campbell Island. The name denotes a spreading stream, part of a beach that is flooded by a river, a river delta, or the running of river water over a part of the beach.

Waúyala A chiefly name of the **'Qvúqvaẏaítx̌v**.

wúalaL According to Olson, the Land otter dance. Harkin gives **ulala** as the lowest-ranked in the Shaman's series of dances. The word for land otter is **ḱvlá**.

x̌ámála Orphan class, people without status in Heiltsuk society

˘X̌íx̌ís Down river people, people from the north, or Heiltsuk people or person from Kynock who now live at Klemtu (**Lhemdu**, sometimes called China Hat), a village on Swindle Island.

Yáláthi Goose Island, an island in Milbanke Sound seaward of Bella Bella which was the site of an annual fur seal hunt and is still an important Heiltsuk camp.

Yáláthitx̌v People or person from Goose Island. The **Yáláthitx̌v**, a Heiltsuk-speaking group once living on **Yáláthi** and neighbouring seaward islands, were wiped out by the epidemics that followed contact with Europeans.

Zíxsíwális Heiltsuk chiefly name. Dick Jakeswallis was an "oldtimer at Bella Bella" during R. W. Large's tenure. Also transliterated as Sillsiwallis and Dji'ksi-walis (see Ch. 5 and Appendix C under "General Dick").

APPENDIX J: CONCORDANCE

This concordance lists all the Normal School accession numbers for the three shipments of artifacts sent from Bella Bella by R. W. Large. Each item discussed in this Catalogue is cross-referenced by its catalogue number (No.) and now carries the prefix "ROM" instead of "NS"; the items not discussed in the Catalogue are listed by type in Appendix H, "Objects Not Examined," and cross-referenced by the numbers assigned to them in Appendix H (H).

NS 23101–23193

Accessioned
1 January 1902
(92 items; there was
no object for 23107)

23101 H 70
23102 No. 94
23103 H 89
23104 H 125
23105 H 19
23106 H 71
23107 (no object)
23108 No. 106
23109 No. 98
23110 No. 99
23111 No. 66
23112 No. 107
23113 No. 34
23114 No. 35
23115 No. 28
23116 No. 86
23117 No. 87
23118 No. 88
23119 H 121
23120 No. 95
23121 H 90
23122 H 20
23123 No. 83
23124 No. 84
23125 No. 29
23126 H 91
23127 No. 1
23128 H 92
23129 No. 78
23130 H 122
23131 H 72
23132 H 73
23133 No. 118
23134 H 135
23135 No. 57
23136 No. 58
23137 No. 59
23138 No. 67
23139 No. 27
23140 No. 25

23141 No. 31
23142 No. 32
23143 No. 61
23144 No. 62
23145 No. 71
23146 No. 20
23147 No. 42
23148 H 21
23149 H 127
23150 No. 11
23151 No. 12
23152 H 5
23153 No. 26
23154 No. 21
23155 No. 68
23156 No. 6
23157 No. 33
23158 No. 126
23159 No. 108
23160 No. 80
23161 No. 53
23162 No. 54
23163 H 93
23164 H 123
23165 No. 127
23166 H 94
23167 H 95
23168 H 96
23169 H 97
23170 No. 10
23171 H 13
23172 No. 119
23173 No. 89
23174 No. 90
23175 No. 91
23176 No. 100
23177 No. 104
23178 H 74
23179 H 75
23180 H 76
23181 H 77
23182 H 78
23183 H 79
23184 H 80
23185 H 81
23186 No. 120

23187 No. 72
23188 No. 18
   (ROM 963x149)
23189 No. 19
   (ROM 966x84.160)
23190 No. 15
23191 No. 16
23192 No. 17
23193 No. 47

NS 27847–27977

Accessioned
8 November 1906
(131 items)

27847 No. 36
27848 No. 37
27849 No. 109
27850 No. 73
27851 No. 73
27852 No. 73
27853 No. 73
27854 No. 73
27855 No. 13
27856 No. 14
27857 No. 105
27858 H 98
27859 No. 121
27860 H 99
27861 No. 110
27862 No. 38
27863 No. 111
27864 No. 44
27865 No. 51
27866 No. 63
27867 No. 69
27868 No. 22
27869 No. 23
27870 No. 45
27871 No. 46
27872 No. 128
27873 No. 2
27874 No. 48
27875 No. 60
27876 No. 3
27877 No. 4

27878 No. 55
27879 No. 7
27880 No. 43
27881 No. 39
27882 No. 64
27883 No. 92
27884 H 63
27885 H 64
27886 No. 93
27887 H 65
27888 H 67
27889 H 68
27890 No. 101
27891 No. 102
27892 H 69
27893 No. 103
27894 No. 96
27895 No. 96
27896 No. 96
27897 No. 56
27898 No. 56
27899 No. 112
27900 No. 113
27901 H 126
27902 No. 82
27903 No. 82
27904 No. 82
27905 No. 82
27906 H 119
27907 No. 114
27908 H 22
27909 H 23
27910 No. 49
27911 No. 65
27912 No. 8
27913 H 66
27914 No. 85
27915 No. 122
27916 H 82
27917 No. 123
27918 H 83
27919 H 84
27920 H 85
27921 No. 124
27922 H 86
27923 No. 79

27924 H 24
27925 H 25
27926 H 26
27927 H 27
27928 H 28
27929 H 29
27930 H 30
27931 H 87
27932 H 88
27933 H 100
27934 H 101
27935 H 102
27936 H 103
27937 H 104
27938 H 105
27939 H 106
27940 H 107
27941 H 108
27942 H 109
27943 H 31
27944 H 32
27945 H 33
27946 H 34
27947 H 35
27948 H 36
27949 H 37
27950 H 38
27951 H 39
27952 H 40
27953 H 41
27954 H 42
27955 H 43
27956 H 44
27957 H 45
27958 H 46
27959 H 47
27960 H 48
27961 H 49
27962 H 50
27963 H 51
27964 H 52
27965 H 53
27966 H 7
27967 H 8
27968 H 136
27969 H 137

27970 H 138
27971 H 139
27972 H 140
27973 H 141
27974 H 142
27975 H 143
27976 H 144
27977 H 145

NS 28196–28256, 28307

Accessioned 29
April 1907 (61 items)

28196 H 1
28197 No. 9
28198 H 2
28199 No. 24
28200 No. 81
28201 H 3
28202 No. 5
28203 H 4
28204 H 9
28205 H 10
28206 No. 125
28207 H 14
28208 H 15
28209 No. 74
28210 H 16
28211 H 17
28212 No. 75
28213 H 18
28214 No. 76
28215 No. 70
28216 No. 70
28217 No. 70
28218 No. 70
28219 No. 70
28220 No. 70
28221 H 11
28222 H 12
28223 No. 52
28224 No. 115
28225 H 54
28226 H 55
28227 H 56

28228 H 57
28229 H 58
28230 H 59
28231 H 60
28232 H 61
28233 No. 97
28234 No. 30
28235 H 146
28236 H 110
28237 H 111
28238 H 112
28239 H 113
28240 H 114
28241 H 115
28242 H 116
28243 H 117
28244 H 118
28245 H 124
28246 No. 116
28247 H 62 (same
   object as 27908)
28248 H 120
28249 H 128
28250 H 129
28251 H 130
28252 H 131
28253 H 132
28254 H 133
28255 H 134
28256 H 6
28307 No. 117

GROUPED WITH LARGE COLLECTION BY BLACK
(5 items)

ROM 912x16.A&B No. 40
ROM 950x76 No. 41
ROM 954x35 No. 50
ROM 956x16.1 No. 77
ROM 956x145.5 No. 50

CATALOGUE

Catalogue of the R. W. Large Collection in the Ethnology Collections of the Department of Anthropology, Royal Ontario Museum

O bjects listed in the original Normal School catalogue accession list of the Large Collection, but not discussed in this Catalogue, are listed in Appendix H, "Objects Not Examined." For a complete numerical list of all objects sent by R. W. Large from Bella Bella to the Normal School/Ontario Provincial Museum, see Appendix J, "Concordance." Descriptions of materials are made on the basis of visual analysis only. Large's descriptions are in quotation marks.

Five objects with no provenance data (Nos. 40–41, 50, 77; ROM "x" numbers) are included in this Catalogue because they are so similar in execution, material, scale, and design to the objects collected by R. W. Large that I believe they are part of his collection.

Four unlabelled objects in ROM Ethnology that cannot be positively identified as part of the Large Collection are not included here. The objects are a round stone, which may be the one described in the NS accession list as "stone used by Indians in cooking seaweed; after oolican oil is added, the heated stone is put in" (NS 23149); two plain wooden spoons (possibly NS 27888 and NS 27892); and a damaged, rolled-up cedar mat (possibly NS 28196).

Information about the people whom Large identified as sources or makers of the objects in his collection is found in Appendix C.

BASKETRY: BASKETS, HATS, MATS, BAG

1. Basket, ROM 23127

Cylindrical Haida basket of natural-coloured spruce root with four dark brown horizontal bands and a raised diamond pattern in the rim.

Accessioned 1 January 1902 as NS 23127, "Hyda basket." Collected from Alfred Wilson, Bella Bella.

Size unknown (at the time of writing, this basket was on display at the ROM).

Natural and dyed spruce root, woven. Diamond pattern in rim made by intersecting diagonal rows of three-strand twining stitches.

CONDITION
Dark colour may imply age.

COMMENTS
The shape and design are typically Haida.

Associated Objects: No. 83, stone playing disc, also collected from Wilson; Nos. 2–5, NS 28201, baskets.

2. Telescoping Basket, ROM 27873

Small tubular basket in two parts, one of which fits inside the other. The outer basket has a knob on top and is decorated with double rows of raised stitching. The inner basket has a striped pattern and a loop of string at the bottom for a handle.

Accessioned 6 November 1906 as NS 27873, "small extension basket." Sold to the OPM for $1.

Outer basket, 13.7 cm high x diam. 8.2 cm; inner basket, 14.5 cm high x diam. 6.4 cm

Woven spruce root, braided twine. Top has three rows of double diagonal twists over wrapped twining (Z-twist); bottom has flat striped pattern (S-twist).

CONDITION
Appears old; top has blackened sides; colour is dark overall.

COMMENTS
There is nothing inside the basket to indicate its function, but baskets such as this were used as shot pouches and as containers for eagle down—eagle down was a symbol of peace and had ceremonial uses, particularly in the Returned from Heaven (dhuẇláx̌a) dance series.

Associated Objects: Nos. 1, 3–5, NS 28201, baskets.

3. Basket, ROM 27876

(See also p. 69)

A small, checkerwork basket with brown and black striped pattern and a handle. "Mrs. Large" written twice on the bottom.

Accessioned 6 November 1906 as NS 27876, "[one of] two baskets." Sold to the OPM for 25 or 50 cents.

No. 3 (centre), No. 4 (left), No. 5

11 cm high x 16.2 cm long x 13.2 cm wide

Woven, undyed, black, and brown split cedar. Striped pattern of three strands each of brown and black created with coloured wefts woven through undyed warp strands. Top rim and handle made of natural strands twisted over a core. Bottom plain checkerwork, each strand split to form two warps on the sides.

CONDITION
Handle is broken.

COMMENTS
This basket was probably made for Mrs. Large.

Associated Objects: Nos. 1–2, 4–5, NS 28201, baskets.

4. Basket, ROM 27877
(See also p. 69)
Flat, openwork basket with elaborate rim pattern.

Accessioned 6 November 1906 as NS 27877, "[one of] two baskets." Sold to the OPM for 25 or 50 cents.

26 cm high x 30.9 cm long x 10.5 cm wide

Woven cedar root. Diagonal warp strands cross at each row of horizontal wefts on sides. Checkerwork bottom with three rows of openwork. Rim pattern strengthened by strands wrapped around core.

CONDITION
Brittle; bottom bent out of shape.

COMMENTS
Boas (1909:390–91) identifies flat, openwork baskets with diagonal warp strands as spoon baskets. Stewart (1984:130) illustrates a similar bag that was used to carry wedges used to split planks from logs or from living trees.

Associated Objects: Nos. 1–3, 5, NS 28201, baskets.

5. Basket, ROM 28202
(See also p. 69)
Large rectangular basket with striped pattern and row of openwork below rolled rim. The basket has a flat bottom and flexible sides.

Purchased October 1906 and catalogued 29 April 1907 as NS 28202, "cedar bark basket."

16.8 cm high x 21.9 cm long x 8.5 cm wide

Plain and dyed (black/brown) cedar bark in checkerboard weave on sides of basket. Plain checkerboard bottom. Row of crossed warps creates openwork band below rolled rim. Body of basket has seven stripes made with three rows of plain cedar bark alternating with two of dyed.

CONDITION
Good.

COMMENTS
This is a common utility basket.

Associated Objects: Nos. 1–4, NS 28201, baskets.

6. Hat, ROM 23156
Coarsely woven northern-style hat with high crown and inner rim. The hat is painted to represent a bird; its eyes and a noselike shape are on the sides of the crown, and its beak, feet, feathers, and tail are distributed around the brim. On the top is a cross of four teardrop shapes. Inside the brim, "$5.00" is written in green paint.

Accessioned 1 January 1902 as NS 23156, "woman's hat, made from cedar rootlets, painting representing an eagle." Finding spot: Fort Rupert.

20 cm high x diam. 38 cm

Woven cedar root with a zig-zag pattern of slip-stitch twining on the brim. Red thread wound around the inner rim. Painted green, red, and black.

CONDITION
Looks new.

COMMENTS
Heiltsuk chiefly lineages arranged marriage alliances, which were often formalities rather than personal unions, to obtain wealth and prestige. A generous bride-price was paid by the groom's family and after a year the bride could be

redeemed, or bought out, when her lineage returned the bride-price with interest. The bride was then free to marry formally and to be bought out again to increase her property and status (see Olson 1955:334). According to Curtis (1915:131), a woman who had been married and bought out four times had the honourable title ó'ma, and "she alone [was] permitted to wear a painted hat." Drucker (1950:260) says the best woven hats were made by the Bella Bella and Haida, and George Darby did collect a very similar hat at Bella Bella (UBCMOA A1129). On Haida hats, according to Holm (1981:187–88; 1983a:48), the pattern at the crown is the signature of the painter.

Associated Objects: No. 126, canoe bailer, Nos. 90–91, earrings, collected from Fort Rupert. Nos. 52–54, head and neck rings, said to have been used by Fort Rupert Indians. Similar hats with similar designs: UBCMOA A3843 (Haida), UBCMOA A4089 (Haida).

Published: ROM 1976:7, "woman's hat."

7. Hat with Four Rings, ROM 27879
(Colour photo, p. 72)
Small, coarsely woven hat with four "potlatch" rings. Brownish red stripe painted on the edge of each ring, and a formline design, probably representing a bird, drawn with brownish red and black paint on the brim. The hat does not have an inner headband.

Accessioned 6 November 1906 as NS 27879, "high crown dance hat." Sold to the OPM for $10.

28.9 cm high x diam. 32.5 cm

Coarsely woven cedar bark with diagonal pattern on brim. Brownish red and black painted design. Four rings tied on with leather thong.

CONDITION
Looks new.

COMMENTS
Drucker (1950:189) did not find these high-crowned ceremonial hats at Bella Bella and believed that they were worn only by the Oweekeno and Haisla, but in fact this type of hat was worn by all the peoples of the northern and central Northwest Coast. The basketry cylinders are called "potlatch rings," because a common ethnological explanation of them was that each stood for a potlatch given by the owner. As Holm (1983a:47) says, "this is too simple an explanation, but at least we can be certain that [the rings'] presence indicates chiefly status." Reverend Raley collected a Bella Bella "Lamenget," or ceremonial hat (possibly UBCMOA A1465, which is smaller and older than No. 7) made of woven cedar bark with four rings; he believed that each ring represented "certain standing and was won by those holding high rank and won by endurance tests" (Matthews 1934:32). A totem pole that Reverend Raley collected from the "Humchitt tribe" of Bella Bella (UBCMOA A6543) was said to show "the famous Lanemget, or magic hat" (Matthews 1934:27). Barbeau also uses the word: he refers to the ringed hat as the "Lanemhait crest" (1950, I:399).

Associated Objects: No. 6, painted woven hat; No. 55, woven dance hat.

Published: ROM 1976:18, "potlatch hat."

8. Mat, ROM 27912
(Colour detail, p. 68)
Small mat with a diagonal checkerwork pattern of seven horizontal bands.

Accessioned 6 November 1906 as NS 27912, "small cedar mat." Sold to the OPM for $1.50.

121.2 cm long x 71.8 cm wide

Woven cedar bark. Diagonal plaiting with bands of twilled weave. Horizontal bands are 17.5 cm apart and stop about 4 or 5 cm from the sides.

CONDITION
Broken along former fold line.

COMMENTS
Mats were used to line walls, to cover canoes so that they would not dry out, and for bedding and seating. The sitting mat was about 180 x 60 cm and was doubled over for use (Boas 1909:389). Mat-making was one of the aboriginal arts encouraged by the missionaries (at the Kitamaat mission's fall fair, prizes were awarded for the best cedar-bark mats woven in the traditional manner [Raley 1904a].)

Associated Objects: No. 9, NS 28196, NS 28198, NS 28201, cedar-bark mats.

9. Mat, ROM 28197
(Colour detail, p. 68)
Woven cedar-bark mat with a diagonal stepped pattern, bordered by two black stripes on each side.

Purchased October 1906 and catalogued 29 April 1907 as NS 28197, "cedar bark mat."

160 cm long x 87 cm wide

Woven natural and dyed (black) cedar bark. Pattern of twelve diagonal rows alternating vertical and horizontal bands of black, banded on each side with two black stripes which intersect at the corners to form squares. A band of warmer-coloured bark, 6 cm wide, extends along each side, 6.5 cm from the edge.

CONDITION
Good.

COMMENTS
See No. 8.

Associated Objects: No. 8, NS 28196, NS 28198, NS 28201, cedar-bark mats.

10. Frog-Shaped Bag,
ROM 23170/902.2.8
(See also p. 68)
A flat, woven cedar-bark bag in the shape of a frog, with articulated wooden arms, legs, and head attached. The frog's wide, hinged mouth is the opening of the bag and is lined with cloth printed in a paisley pattern. A strip of cloth is attached to the back of the head as a handle.

Accessioned 1 January 1902 as NS 23170, "slipper case, representing frog, made by Bella Bella woman."

55 cm long x 45 cm wide x 9 cm high

Diagonally woven checkerwork cedar-bark bag. Cedar limbs painted light green; cedar head painted light green with red and black details. The articulated jaw of the frog is supported by a wire wrapped with striped red flannel and is held together by string looped around the opening through metal eyelets. Opening is cloth-lined. Handle is white wool, sewn to the bag.

CONDITION
Good.

COMMENTS
This bag is made of traditional materials arranged in a novel form. It was probably made for the tourist trade or for Large's collection. The articulated arms and head of the bag are reminiscent of traditional puppets used in the Winter Ceremonies.

Associated Objects: None.

Published: Drucker 1965, fig. 20, "Bella Bella frog bag"; ROM 1976:6, "frog bag"; Black 1989:277, pl. 18.

CARVINGS: CRADLE AND CRADLE STICKS, FIGURES, HOUSE POSTS, MODEL POLES, PADDLES, PLAQUE, SMALL CARVINGS, WALKING STICKS

11. Cradle, ROM 23150
(See also p. 114)
Plank cradle with a high, notched, backward-sloping headboard, slightly flared sides, and low foot panel with a wide, shallow notch. The top third of the side and foot panels is decorated with a red-orange band textured with incised lines. Below this border on each side is the profile head of a long-beaked bird and what are probably wing designs. The headboard design is a face with eyes formed by salmon-trout's-head design motifs. The foot panel is plain. Although crudely executed, the painting exhibits the thin, swelling formlines characteristic of Bella Bella painting at the turn of the century. On the inside of each side, three parallel slanting ridges have been cut to allow the wood to bend. Loops of coarse twine are attached to each side. Inside the cradle a twill blanket was sewn into the wood at the edges with cedar root.

Accessioned 1 January 1902 as NS 23150, "old time Indian cradle, made by Enoch." Collected at Bella Bella.

79 cm long x 23.4 cm wide x 24.9 cm high

Cedar with black and red-orange paint, coarse S-twist twine, wool twill blanket material sewn into the cradle with cedar root.

CONDITION
The blanket that lined the inside has been worn or cut away.

COMMENTS

Perhaps this cradle was made for Large's first child, who was born in 1901. Boas (1909:348, 458–59) describes the manufacture of Kwakwaka'wakw plank cradles and the bedding used in them.

Associated Objects: NS 23152, "stick used to suspend cradle upon." A cradle from Kitamaat (UBCMOA A6519), collected by Reverend Raley, has low, rounded end panels and irregular sides; another Bella Bella cradle (NMNH 20556) has the same basic shape, construction, and decoration as No. 11.

Published: Black 1989:283, pl. 26.

12. Carved Stick, ROM 23151
(See also p. 121)

A curved stick carved in the shape of an eagle riding on the back of a whale. At one end the stick is notched; at the other a cylinder projects from the mouth of the whale.

Accessioned 1 January 1902 as NS 23151, "carved stick used to keep

in position the pad used to produce the flattening of infant's head, made by Daniel Houstie." Collected at Bella Bella.

28.1 cm long x 4 cm wide x 3 cm thick

Carved cedar painted black and brown. Abalone discs inlaid in eyes and in whale's tail.

CONDITION
Good; looks new.

COMMENTS

The central coast tribes used soft cedar-bark pads and bandages to shape infants' foreheads; a flat forehead was considered ideally beautiful (McIlwraith 1948, 1:702–3; Drucker 1950:191; Boas 1909:459; Olson 1935, 1949:72). Only Boas (1923:282) mentions the use of sticks in the process. According to his source, Moses Knight, the sticks of noble children were "beautifully carved" and were placed on the chest. Details of the arrangement are not clear. Eagle and Whale are probably the child's crests.

Associated Objects: Nos. 13–14, similar carved sticks, accessioned as "Indian cradle supports."

Published: Black 1989:281, pl. 22.

13. Carved Stick, ROM 27855
(See also p. 121)

Straight stick, carved in the shape of a bird's head, with a short handle.

Accessioned 6 November 1906 as NS 27855, "[one of] two carved sticks 'Indian cradle supports.'" Sold to the OPM for $1.25 (for the two).

31.6 cm long x 3.2 cm wide x 2.3 cm thick

Carved cedar, black and brown paint, abalone inlay in eyes.

CONDITION
No signs of wear; but one piece of abalone inlay missing.

COMMENTS

The function of this stick is not clear. It is similar in shape to a singer's baton, and may have been

mislabelled by Large (Bill Holm, letter to the author, February 1986). In style and execution it resembles No. 109 (tongs); stylistic analysis suggests that both items were made by Daniel Houstie (see Appendix D).

Associated Objects: Nos. 12, 14, carved sticks. See No. 37 for a list of black and brown painted cedar objects. See Appendix D for objects made by Daniel Houstie.

14. Carved Stick, ROM 27856
(See also p. 121)

Curved stick carved in the shape of a whale and a long-beaked bird, possibly a raven. A small round projection extends from the mouth of the whale and there is a forked projection behind the raven's head.

Accessioned 6 November 1906 as NS 27856, "[one of] two carved sticks 'Indian cradle supports.'" Sold to the OPM for $1.25 (for the two).

31.6 cm long x 2.9 cm wide x 1.8 cm thick

No. 12 (bottom), No. 13 (centre), No. 14

Carved hardwood, painted red and black, abalone inlay in eyes.

CONDITION
Right fin is broken, but there are no signs of wear.

COMMENTS
Raven, which is probably the bird represented on this stick, and Whale are Heiltsuk crests. The stick is the same in form as No. 12, identified by Large as a "carved stick used to keep in position the pad used to produce the flattening of infant's head, made by Daniel Houstie," and was probably also made by Houstie (see Appendix D). How these sticks would have been used with the pads that deformed an infant's head is not clear. By Large's time head-shaping was no longer practised, so these sticks were anachronisms and were probably made for Large to illustrate an "old time" custom.

Associated Objects: Nos. 12–13, carved sticks.

15. Carved Figure, ROM 23190
(Colour photo, p. 117)
Roughly carved and painted figure with upraised arms and large, four-fingered hands. Black V-neck shirt is painted on. Eyes and brows are painted black; hands, ears, nostrils, and mouth painted red; head and legs are natural wood. Head is flat on top and painted with irregular stripes on the back to indicate hair.

Accessioned 1 January 1902 as NS 23190, "rough carved human figure." Collected from General Dick, Bella Bella.

32.5 cm high x 9 cm wide x 8.5 cm thick

Carved cedar, red and black paint. Moveable forearms attached with nails. Figure is truncated just above the knees with a straight saw cut. Painting incomplete on back of figure.

CONDITION
Looks new.

COMMENTS
The function of this figure is unknown. It resembles puppetlike figures used in Winter Dance performances. A carving of a bear with an upside down frog on its chest (RBCM 233), which is similar in execution and scale, is included in an RBCM display of Northwest Coast pieces made for the tourist trade.

Associated Objects: Nos. 16–17, No. 29 ("key ring"), figures collected from General Dick; No. 25, paddle, made by General Dick.

16. Carved Figure, ROM 23191
(Colour photo, p. 117)
Roughly carved and painted figure with raised arms and large, four-fingered hands curved above a protruding stomach, sitting in a squatting position with knees bent. "Mask" over the eyes, T-shaped design on cheeks; mouth, nostrils, ears, and feet painted red. Eyes, brows, fringed moustache, short V-necked shirt, and legs (pants) painted black. Body painted with red and black stripes.

Accessioned 1 January 1902 as NS 23191, "rough carved human figure." Collected from General Dick, Bella Bella.

30 cm high x 11.8 cm wide x 12.7 cm thick

Carved cedar, red and black paint. Remains of soft, fuzzy brown hair on head. Hair nailed to forehead; arms attached with nails. Painting incomplete on back of figure.

CONDITION
Hair has worn away, but otherwise figure looks new.

COMMENTS
Although this figure may have been made for the tourist trade, it resembles the doll-like puppets used in Winter Dance performances as well as larger potlatch figures representing chiefs or their speakers. Potlatch figures often had bulging stomachs, which indicated the wealth and largesse of the chief.

Associated Objects: See No. 15.

Published: Black 1989:285, pl. 27.

17. Carved Figure, ROM 23192
Standing figure in a peaked cap, arms at sides with elbows bent as if the hands were in the pockets of the pants. The bottom flares into a small base that has two pegs in the bottom. A line incised around the neck may indicate a jacket.

Accessioned 1 January 1902 as NS 23192, "rough carved human figure." Collected from General Dick, Bella Bella.

54.5 cm high x 17 cm wide x 12 cm thick

No. 15 (left), No.16

Carved, unpainted cedar. Waxy, honey-coloured patina. Adze marks visible.

CONDITION
Wood has raised grain and appears weathered, particularly on front of figure. Nose and peak of cap broken off, base worn at sides.

COMMENTS
The pegs at the bottom indicate that this figure once stood in some sort of base. The figure appears to be wearing a uniform, and may represent a member of the Bella Bella Cornet Band. A life-sized polychromed figure of a band member stood on the upper balcony of the Bella Bella fire hall and often surprised newcomers with its realism. Figures in peaked caps and European dress decorated at least two other structures on the central Northwest Coast—at Kimsquit such a figure was the entrance pole of a house (AMNH negs. 39988, 44308), and at Bella

Coola the house of Chief Clelemen had a smaller figure over the front door (AMNH neg. 46086). Figure carvings were also memorials, so this may have been a grave figure.

Associated Objects: See No. 15.

18. House Post, ROM 23188 or 23189/963x149
Post that supported one of the main beams of a house at 'Qélc (Old Bella Bella), carved to represent a bear holding a human child between its raised paws. Small profile faces are carved in the ears of the bear. A deep rectangular notch between the bear's ears received one of the two main lateral beams of the house. (The beams were rectangular in cross-section.)

Accessioned 1 January 1902 as NS 23188 or 23189, one of two "house posts." Collected at Bella Bella.

367.5 cm high

Carved cedar with remains of brown-red and black paint; adze marks visible.

CONDITION
Wood darkened from exposure; paint faded and worn. The post is now in two pieces: the head has been sawn from the body.

COMMENTS
The carving illustrates the bear-mother myth (see pp.94–96; Boas 1932:67–69). This post stood at the southeast corner of a house in

front of the church at 'Qélc, identified (possibly by Franz Boas) in the AMNH files as "house 1." The post that once supported the northeast corner of this house (AMNH 16/8379, Fig. 23) shows the bear mother holding a cub rather than a human child. Together the poles illustrate the human-animal correspondence emphasized in the bear-mother story. The other two posts, No. 19 and AMNH 16/8380 (Fig. 24), are carved in the form of killer whales. Large bought the two AMNH posts for Boas in 1900 for twenty dollars. "The owners were

in need of money," he wrote to Boas (26 November 1900) "[and] I had to pay for the posts at once" (AMNH 1900).

The two bear-mother posts were photographed at 'Qélc in August 1897 (AMNH negs. 42852, 42854), in 1901 by Newcombe (RBCM PN 143, PN 482), and by Winter and Pond (Alaska State Library PCA 87-1350). The photographs show a roofless, dilapidated house that was used to store large dugout canoes and European-style boats.

Associated Objects: Other house posts from Bella Bella: BM 11.696.1–11.696.4, collected in 1911 by C. F. Newcombe.

Published: ROM 1976:24, "Bear Mother house post."

19. House Post, ROM 23188 or 23189/966x84.160
Post that supported one of the main beams of a house at 'Qélc (Old Bella Bella), carved to represent a killer whale, the body of which is bent double with the head and tail at the bottom. The large dorsal fin rising from the curved back of the whale has a rectangular notch that supported one of the two main lateral beams of the house. Small profile faces are carved in the dorsal fin of the whale, and full faces in the fins at the sides of the head.

Accessioned 1 January 1902 as NS 23188 or 23189, one of two "house

posts." Collected at Bella Bella.

296.5 cm high

Carved cedar, brown-red, white, and black paint. Adze marks visible.

CONDITION
Wood darkened from exposure; paint faded and worn.

COMMENTS
This post supported the southwest corner of a house that stood in front of the church at 'Qélc, identified (possibly by Boas) in the AMNH files as "house 1." It stood directly behind the bear-mother post at the southeast corner, No. 18. A corresponding whale post (northwest corner, AMNH 16/8380, Fig. 24), was sold along the with the bear-mother post (northeast corner) by Large to Boas in 1900 for twenty dollars (see No. 18). The whale posts stood at the back of the house, and

because the land sloped up from the beach, they are shorter than the bear-mother posts.

The posts from this house appear to be the ones drawn by Moses Knight for Drucker (1940:209) to show "posts and screen of a potlatch house (Istetx ['Isdaítx̌v] Bella Bella)." Knight related that "these killerwhale posts are used for the potlatch following a performance of the dluwulaxa [dhuẃláx̌a] society." The screen that separated the dancers and their paraphernalia from the audience extended between the posts. Those drawn by Knight face inward, towards the centre of the house, whereas the ROM and AMNH posts faced towards the sides.

A similar killer-whale post was collected somewhere on the Northwest Coast between about 1900 and 1905 by an employee of the Alaska Steamship Company, who repainted it and set it up on his property on Bainbridge Island, Washington (Fig. 23). The post was washed away and destroyed in a storm. Viola Garfield obtained a photograph of it from the man's daughter, Mrs. Alfred F. Woolsey (Garfield 1949; University of Washington Libraries, Special Collections Division, neg. no. 18/48; see Black 1992).

Killer whale (Blackfish) was probably a crest of the owner of the house. According to Olson, "totem poles gave crests of a man and could be acquired from both father and mother" (1935, 1949:55–59); Olson recorded that

Chief Moody's father was Blackfish-Bear, and that the name Woyilah [Waúyala] is both a Blackfish and a Bear name.

Photographs of the ROM and AMNH whale posts were taken while the house was still standing at 'Qélc, although roofless and dilapidated, in August 1897 (AMNH negs. 42853, 42855), in 1901 (Newcombe photographs, RBCM PN 143, PN 482), and by Winter and Pond (Alaska State Library PCA 87-1350).

Associated Objects: See No. 18.

Published: ROM 1976:21, "Salmon house post."

20. Model Totem Pole, ROM 23146
(See also p. 44)
A large model pole with a vertical frieze of figures on a tapered plank backboard. At the bottom is a shallow shelf and rectangular wooden plug that would have allowed the pole to stand in the ground or in some sort of base. The back is flat and undecorated. The figures on the pole are as follows (top to bottom): a bird, two fish (probably whales with small dorsal fins), a bird, an octopus or devil fish with eaglelike beak, a killer whale with a seal on its back (an inverted humanlike face is the whale's blowhole), an upside-down human figure with black moustache joined by the tongue to a doglike animal (probably a land otter), a wolf, and a small standing figure with upraised arms. The

figures interlock: the tail of the otter is in the mouth of the killer whale; the tongue of the otter is in the mouth of the inverted man; and the wolf bites the head of the standing man at the base of the pole.

Accessioned 1 January 1902 as NS

23146, "small totem pole (Kwakiutl Indian)." Finding spot: Fort Rupert.

105.5 cm high x 13.9 cm wide x 7.5 cm thick

Carved and polychromed wood. Figures painted with red and silver paint and graphite. White backboard with blue scallops along the edge. The projecting bird is attached to the pole with a long metal spike that fits into a hole at the top.

CONDITION
Good.

COMMENTS
The style of the pole is consistent with the Fort Rupert provenance, but a similar pole in the British Museum (1905.7-21.2), with figures arranged against a flat white background, came from Bella Coola. The Bella Coola pole is reproduced in Coe (1976, fig. 329) with the following caption:

> Wooden painted openwork totem pole/house pole model, probably used on the front of a house or for a potlatch pole. Since these models were specimen carvings for sale, liberties would be taken with their forms, not allowable in the originals.

Associated Objects: No. 21, model pole. For other objects from Fort Rupert, see Appendix E.

21. Model Totem Pole, ROM 23154

(See also p. 44)
A large wooden model pole with a vertical frieze of figures arranged on a tapered plank background, on which parts of the figures' bodies, such as claws and fins, are painted. A shallow shelf and a carved rectangular plug at the bottom would have allowed the pole to stand in the ground or in some sort of base. The back is flat and undecorated. The figures on the pole are as follows (top to bottom): a bird, an upside-down head with cross-hatched appendages; a squatting figure holding on to the tail of a bird, which faces downward; a winged face; a whale facing downward with a small figure on its back holding on to its tail; a fish in the mouth of the whale; a bird; and the head of a sculpin with hornlike ears.

Accessioned 1 January 1902 as NS 23154, "carved wooden totem pole." Finding spot: Fort Rupert.

132.1 cm high x 17.6 cm wide x 12.7 cm thick

Carved wood, painted with graphite, red, green, yellow, and blue obtained from bluing. (The paint has the quality of poster paint.) The projecting bird at the top is attached with two long metal spikes that fit into holes in the pole.

CONDITION
Good.

COMMENTS

See No. 20.

Associated Objects: No. 20, model totem pole. For other objects from Fort Rupert, see Appendix E.

22. Model Totem Pole, ROM 27868

Small argillite model pole with flat back and half-round base. Figures are as follows (top to bottom): an animal (frog?) with a stippled head, squatting with its arms around knees; a bear; and a beaver holding a stick. On its head the beaver has four potlatch rings, which are between the legs of the bear.

Accessioned 6 November 1906 as NS 27868, "[one of] two small slate totems." Sold to the OPM for $5.

24.9 cm high x 5 cm wide x 4.5 cm thick

Carved argillite.

CONDITION
Good.

COMMENTS
This pole is Haida. It may (like No. 1, the Haida basket collected from Alfred Wilson) have been collected at Bella Bella, or Large may have purchased it during his travels on the coast.

Associated Objects: No. 23, argillite pole.

23. Model Totem Pole, ROM 27869
Small argillite model pole with flat back and half-round base. Figures are as follows (top to bottom): a human wearing a hat and holding a paddle, a killer whale facing downward with its tail bent over its back and its dorsal fin to one

No. 22 (left), No. 23

side, a bear, and a frog.

Accessioned 6 November 1906 as NS 27869, "[one of] two small slate totems." Sold to the OPM for $6.50.

29.2 cm high x 6 cm wide x 3.9 cm thick

Carved argillite.

CONDITION
Good.

COMMENTS
This finely carved Haida pole has a slight ridge running down the centre of the paddle, whale, and frog. See No. 22.

Associated Objects: No. 22, argillite pole.

24. Model Totem Pole, ROM 28199

(Colour photo, p. 52)
Small model pole depicting the following (top to bottom): an eagle, a raven, a bear holding a small human face in its paws and flanked by two Coppers with painted faces and ribs, and a whale's head. The pole is straight and flat at the back of the Coppers, the bear, and the whale. The mouth of the whale is truncated by a straight saw cut at the bottom of the pole. The eagle and the raven are carved in the round, with the eagle perched naturalistically on the raven's shoulders.

Purchased October 1906 and catalogued 29 April 1907 as NS 28199, "totem pole."

41.3 cm high x 12.6 cm wide x 13.3 cm thick

Predominantly carved natural cedar; red and black painted details.
CONDITION

Looks new.

COMMENTS
This pole was made for the tourist trade. In size and style it is unlike more typical Bella Bella model poles, such as NMNH 74743–74747 collected by James Swan in 1884, and UBCMOA A6543 collected by Reverend Raley, both of which are thin columns of intertwined figures.

Associated Objects: Nos. 20–21, model poles from Fort Rupert; Nos. 22–23, Haida argillite poles.

Published: ROM postcard.

25. Paddle, ROM 23140
(Colour photo, p. 57)
Wooden paddle with rounded, tapering blade and red and black formline designs on natural wood.

Accessioned 1 January 1902 as NS 23140, "canoe paddle, made by General Dick." Collected at Bella Bella.

146 cm long x 13.6 cm wide

Carved wood, red and black paint.

CONDITION
Looks new.

COMMENTS
Holm (1983a) describes a stylistically similar paddle in a private collection as an example of ultra-primary painting, with both the ultraprimary and the primary

designs in black, and the secondary patterns in red. He also says that "the paddle, with its long, elliptical blade, lack of shoulders at the base of the blade, and convex-sided shaft is typically Bella Bella" (Holm 1983a:93).

Associated Objects: No. 26, paddle made by Daniel Houstie. Paddles with similar designs, possibly also by General Dick, are UBCMOA A1598, collected by Reverend Raley of Kitamaat; CMC VII-EE-16 and VII-EE-17, collected at Bella Bella before 1899. Other objects collected from Dick: Nos. 15–17, 29, 47, carvings.

26. Paddle, ROM 23153
(Colour photo, p. 57)
Paddle with rounded blade. Formline design on natural wood, with shallow carving. Two small profile heads incised and painted on the transverse handle.

Accessioned 1 January 1902 as NS 23153, "carved whaling paddle, made by D. Houstie." Collected at Bella Bella.

133 cm long x 13.8 cm wide

Carved cedar, black and brown paint.

CONDITION
Good; looks new.

COMMENTS
The elliptical shape of the paddle is typically Bella Bella (see No. 25).

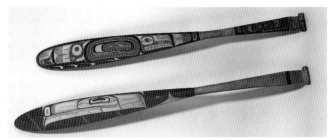

No. 25 (bottom), No. 26

It was probably made for sale, because "paddles made for actual canoe use were never carved; the blades thinned by carving would almost surely break if used" (Holm 1983a:93). The description "whaling paddle" may be misleading, because Drucker (1950:172) says the whale was not hunted in the area. Because Large identified Houstie as the maker, this paddle is an important source of information about the style of this artist.

Associated Objects: No. 25, paddle made by General Dick. Paddles from Kitamaat (UBCMOA A1492) and Bella Bella (RBCM 2056) exhibit similar decoration, and an almost identical paddle was published by Holm (1965:84).

Published: Black 1989:288, pl. 29.

27. Circular Plaque with Carved Eagle's Head, ROM 23139/902.2.7
(Colour photo, p. 88)
Wooden disc with the carved head and neck of an eagle attached. The bird's head is unpainted and has a dark patina. The long eyes below heavy brows are inlaid with

abalone; the neck is carved with three rows of feathers. The head and neck project from the body of the bird which is painted inside a deeply incised oval. Around the body oval are painted the wings, legs, and tail of the bird. The back of the plaque is unpainted and shows distinct, regular adze marks.

Accessioned 1 January 1902 as NS 23139, "carved eagle." Collected from Paul George, Kimsquit.

61 cm high x 59.3 cm wide x 19.5 cm thick
Carved and painted cedar with

abalone inlay. Gritty silver-blue and black paint. Head and neck of eagle affixed to disc with three nails.

CONDITION
Appears weathered; paint has run, particularly on the left side, and there are insect holes on the right side.

COMMENTS
One of the two hereditary chiefs of Kimsquit was called King George. The carving style appears to be typical of the area between Bella Coola and Bella Bella, and the form is probably taken from the carved and painted crests found on grave houses in this area. An RBCM photograph (PN 4582; see Fig. 20) of "Bella Coola Indians dead houses, Dean Channel," illustrates a similar motif.

Associated Objects: UBCMOA A1363 (Fig. 19) "shield" collected by George Darby at Bella Bella.

Published: ROM 1959, fig. A65, "circular plaque representing an eagle, date and tribe unknown"; Walker Art Center 1972, no. 198a; Haberland 1979:75; Black 1989:283, pl. 25 and cover.

28. Small Wooden Hand, ROM 23115
A simple carving of a stylized wrist and curled hand with four fingers.

Accessioned 1 January 1902 as NS

23115, "small key ring." Collected at Bella Bella.

4.5 cm long x 2.7 cm wide x 2.7 cm thick

Unpainted wood.

CONDITION
No signs of wear or exposure.

COMMENTS
The function of this object is not clear.

Associated Objects: No. 29, a carving obtained from General Dick, is also described by Large as a "key ring."

29. Small Carving, ROM 23125

A small wooden carving of a standing bear or dog with an upside-down frog hanging below its chin. Because the animal's toes curl under, the carving does not stand upright. The wood has a dark patina.

Accessioned l January 1902 as NS

23125, "key ring." Collected from General Dick, Bella Bella.

14.2 cm high x 3.5 cm wide x 7 cm thick

Carved hardwood, perhaps stained.

CONDITION
The dark colour of the wood makes it hard to judge the age of this carving.

COMMENTS
Large's description of this object as a "key ring" is puzzling. A similar small carving from Bella Bella (UBCMOA A131) is "probably the handle of an implement" accord-

ing to Hawthorn (1967:365). There is a record of small wooden carvings having been used in Haisla Returned from Heaven (dhuẁláx̌a), or mitla series of dances in connection with major potlatches. Visiting chiefs were requested to dance and remove the spirits, in the form of wooden figurines, from the novices (Drucker 1940:218). The style of this carving is typically Heiltsuk and its similarity to a larger carving from Bella Bella (RBCM 233) suggests that the subject is typically Heiltsuk as well. The RBCM carving, which was made for the tourist trade, shows a bear with a frog on its chest. The whimsical nature of the carving is characteristic of much Bella Bella work, for example, a group of polychromed figures and wooden rattles in the Canadian Museum of Civilization (CMC VII-EE-2–VII-EE-10, CMC VII-EE-18–VII-EE-22).

Associated Objects: Nos. 15–17, 47, carved figures collected from General Dick; No. 25, paddle made by General Dick. No. 28, carving of a small hand, was also entered in the NS catalogue as a "key ring."

30. Small Carved Stone, ROM 28234
Curved stone carved to represent a seal, with head, face, and flippers indicated.

Purchased October 1906 and catalogued 29 April 1907 as NS 28234, "stone seal."
4.9 cm long x 2 cm wide x 2 cm

thick

Carved stone.

CONDITION
Good; some marks could have been caused by abrasion.

COMMENTS
The carving, although minimal, is expressively naturalistic. This object may be a scratching stone or small creaser. The shape of the stone suggests that it was meant to be held between the thumb and index finger.

Associated Objects: This object is unique; other small ornaments in the Large Collection are perforated.

31. Walking Stick, ROM 23141
A T-shaped stick, the handle of which is roughly carved in the shape of a bird or fish. The shaft is thin and not quite straight. The wood has a glossy patina.

Accessioned 1 January 1902 as NS 23141, "walking stick." Collected from Dr. Sam, Bella Bella.

93.5 cm long x 12.2 cm wide x 2.6 cm thick

Roughly carved wood.
CONDITION

Looks worn.

COMMENTS
Walking sticks like this one were used by First Nations people and were not necessarily made for sale. Olson (1935, 1949:56) records that one of the Rivers Inlet families owned a walking stick with rattles of deer hooves or eagle beaks at the top, and many late nineteenth-century photographs of the Northwest Coast show native people with walking sticks.

Associated Objects: NS 23122, stone disc, No. 33, walking stick, collected from Dr. Sam; Nos. 32, 61, walking sticks.

32. Walking Stick, ROM 23142
An L-shaped wooden stick, the handle of which is roughly carved in the shape of a grotesque head with a long nose or beak and exaggerated mouth. The shaft is thin and curved. The wood has not been treated.

Accessioned 1 January 1902 as NS 23142, "O'wekeno walking stick." Collected from Timothy Hunt, Bella Bella.

82.7 cm long x 10.4 cm wide x 2.8 cm thick

Carved, untreated wood.

CONDITION
Looks old and worn; wood is dry and cracked; eight burn marks about half-way down one side of

shaft.

Alan Hoover of the RBCM has suggested that the carving on this stick reflects an Oweekeno stylistic tradition that is also evident in grotesque masks (e.g., No. 57, AMNH E/962) from both Rivers Inlet and Bella Bella (pers. comm., 1986). The carved handle of another walking or talking stick from Bella Bella (NMNH H89101)—a grotesque head with hooked nose and tubular

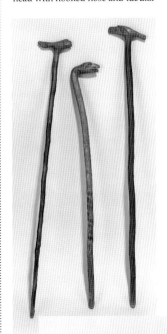

No. 31 (left), No. 32, No. 33

nostrils—resembles central Northwest Coast Cannibal bird masks.

Associated Objects: Nos. 31, 33, 61, walking sticks.

33. Walking Stick, ROM 23157
Crude cane made from a T-shaped stick. The handle is carved to represent the head of a bird, possibly an eagle, with a blunt or sharply curved beak. The bird's tail comes out of the head at the back.

Accessioned 1 January 1902 as NS 23157, "crude walking stick." Collected from Dr. Sam, Bella Bella.

95 cm long x 13.6 cm wide x 2.5 cm thick

Carved wood with a black patina.

CONDITION
Patina may indicate that the stick is old.

COMMENTS
See No. 31.

Associated Objects: See No. 31.

CONTAINERS: BOXES, FEAST BOWLS, BENT BOWL

34. Kerfed Chest with Lid,
ROM 23113.
(See also p. 113)
Chest with lid, painted on each side with traditional designs. The painting follows northern Northwest Coast artistic conventions for the decoration of bent wood chests, with complex formline designs representing the front and back of an animal on the long sides, and nearly identical profile birds on the sides. The lid is painted red-brown.

Accessioned 1 January 1902 as NS 23113, "Indian cedar box made by Capt. Carpenter." Collected at Bella Bella.

34.6 cm high x 47.8 cm long x 30.8 cm wide

Cedar; black and red-brown paint. The chest is finely crafted; the sides are made from a single steamed and bent plank in the traditional fashion. The side seam is joined and the bottom is attached with pegs.

CONDITION
The paint appears to have faded; otherwise, the box appears to be new.

COMMENTS

Because Large identified Captain Carpenter as the maker, this box is a source of information about the style of this important Bella Bella artist.

Associated Objects: No. 42, feast bowl made by Carpenter; NS 23119, NS 23164, two paint stones used by Carpenter. Among the other objects that are thought to be by this artist are a plaque in the R. W. Large Memorial Hospital at Waglisla; a chief's seat (RBCM 1856, Fig. 26) and two paddles (RBCM 15832, 15833); and a bent bowl collected at Bella Bella by George Darby (UBCMOA A1722). Research continues to assign works to Captain Carpenter on the basis of style. See, for example, the book based on a 1993 UBCMOA exhibit, "The Transforming Image," forthcoming from University of British Columbia Press.

35. Kerfed Box with Lid, ROM 23114

A crudely made, small bent box with a plank lid. The back and front of an animal are shown on the longer sides of the box, and simple ovoid shapes decorate the shorter sides.

Accessioned 1 January 1902 as NS 23114, "Indian cedar box made by Chief Robt. Bell." Collected at Bella Bella.

21.5 cm high x 20.5 cm long x 18.7 cm wide

Cedar, red and black paint. Bottom and sides nailed together.

CONDITION

Appears to have been new when collected. The wood has split at one corner because of the stress put on it during fabrication.

COMMENTS

Although the box is roughly made and painted, the basic structure of the design, if not its execution, follows the conventions of box decoration.

Associated Objects: No. 62, club or talking stick, made by Bell; No. 40, box, probably made by Bell; No. 68, whistle collected from Bell.

36. Kerfed Chest with Lid, ROM 27847

Lidded chest, deeply and precisely carved on front and back with traditional formline designs. On one side is a being with raised human hands, squared ears above the eyes, and claws at the sides of the head; on the other is a being with raised claws rather than human hands, and fin or wing details at the sides of the head. On the ends

are complex tripartite painted designs of the type found on the bent boxes of the northern Northwest Coast.

Accessioned 6 November 1906 as NS 27847 "Indian carved box, for dance masks." Sold to the OPM for $10.

44.5 cm high x 88.5 cm long x 54.5 cm wide

Cedar with remains of red-brown and black paint, which was probably originally red, blue, and black. The box was made from four separate planks, each side cut with tenons, sewn together with cedar root or withe, and pegged with wooden pegs. The base has a shallow depression carved in the inside and a groove around the edge to receive the sides. Roughly adzed on the inside. In the formlines above the eyes on front and back are two holes for the lashing that would have held the heavy lid in place. There are metal staples in the top, in one end, and in

the side with human hands.

CONDITION

An old chest. Worn and discoloured with signs of exposure; the surface is almost uniformly black. The paint on the sides is faint and worn; one side is very dark. The lid is damaged on one side.

COMMENTS

Large's description, "for dance masks," is probably correct. Chests like this were used to store ceremonial regalia, but they were also used as coffins, and the condition of this box suggests that it may have come from a grave site. Similar chests were used by the peoples of the entire northern Northwest Coast.

Associated Objects: Bella Bella mortuary box (FMNH 19978), Bella Bella mortuary box collected by Dorsey in 1897 (FMNH 51988), Bella Bella coffin collected by Jacobsen in 1893 (RBCM 220).

37. Kerfed Box, ROM 27848

(Colour photo, p. 24)

A lidless, chest-shaped container with bold formline designs on four sides and bottom. A rounded stick "handle" is attached at the top centre of one long side. Each of the two longer sides of the box shows a bear's head framed by a brown circle. On one side the legs of the animal extend from the chin around the perimeter of the box to end in clawed feet at the top; on the opposite side the legs start above the head and follow the perimeter to the bottom. One of the shorter sides of the box has a salmon-trout's-head design; the opposite side has a similar motif that resembles the profile head of a raven. On the bottom is a complex design of two profile raven's heads inside a circle with tail feathers and claws above and below.

Accessioned 6 November 1906 as NS 27848, "cedar cooking box." Sold to the OPM along with "tongs for hot stones for cooking," No. 109, for $3.

45.5 cm high x 32.3 cm long x 24.5 cm wide

Cedar with black and brown painted design. Faint lines, possibly graphite, can still be seen outlining some of the forms. The sides are made from a single plank, kerfed and joined together with wooden pegs; the bottom is attached separately. The "handle" is bound on with cedar root or withe.

CONDITION

Looks new; green residue (glue?) at pegged joint. Cedar shavings inside the box.

COMMENTS

This box was probably made for Large to illustrate the "old time" method of cooking with hot stones. It is unlikely that authentic cooking boxes would have been so elaborately decorated. The design on the long sides of the box may represent the front and hind quarters of a bear in its den. The painter of this box also decorated No. 38 (dipper), No. 39 (water box), No. 48 (ceremonial box), and other black and brown painted cedar objects collected by Large. Stylistic analysis suggests that the artist is Daniel Houstie (see Appendix D).

Associated Objects: NS 23149, cooking stone. Black and brown painted cedar domestic utensils: Nos.

12–13, carved sticks; No. 109, cooking tongs; No. 38, dipper; No. 39, water box; No. 41, chest. Black and brown painted cedar ceremonial objects: No. 63, club; No. 69, whistle; No. 48, ceremonial box; No. 50, skull/ladle; No. 55, dance hat; No. 65, spear.

Published: Black 1989:288, pl. 30.

38. Dipper, ROM 27862

(Colour photo, p. 24)

A small kerfed box or bowl with a straight handle extending from the bottom, painted with formline designs on four sides and simple geometric patterns on bottom and handle. The box represents the body of an animal, perhaps a bear, with the handle as its tail. The stylized head design on the short side opposite the handle has round eyes below two large ear-like U-shapes and a wide toothy mouth. The other short side has a

simple, asymmetrical design consisting of a central circle with attached U-shapes. The long sides of the box, representing the animal's flanks, have identical profile head designs. On the bottom is a simple X-design.

Accessioned 6 November 1906 as NS 27862, "wooden dipper." Sold to the OPM for $1.

Bowl, 14.4 cm high x 14.8 cm long x 31 cm wide; handle, 20.5 cm long x 3.1 cm wide x 1 cm thick

Cedar, black and brown paint. The sides are made from a single piece of wood, bent and joined with wooden pegs. The bottom and handle are carved in one piece and pegged on.

CONDITION

Good; no signs of use or wear.

COMMENTS

This dipper was probably meant to accompany No. 39, water box. Stylistic analysis suggests that this dipper was made by Daniel Houstie (see Appendix D).

Associated Objects: James Swan collected a similar dipper and water box from Bella Bella in 1885 (NMNH 20568 A–B), which he described as a reproduction of an old artifact. See No. 37 for other black and brown painted objects in the Large Collection.

Published: Black 1989:288, pl. 30.

No. 37 (bottom left), No. 38 (centre), No. 39 (right), No. 41 (top left)

39. Kerfed Box, ROM 27881

(Colour photo, p. 24)

Kerfed box with transverse handle, painted with formline designs representing an animal, probably a bear. The front shows a face with large, toothy mouth, oval eyes, and triangular ears, surrounded by a black circle. There are U-shapes above and below the circle. The back has a similar design—a round-eyed face, divided mouth, and triangular ears surrounded by a black circle, with U-shapes above and below the central motif. The long sides have salmon-trout's-head designs with squared U-shapes below. In the upper left of each long side there is a distinctive profile head design with round eye and large, toothy mouth. The bottom of the box is plain. The upward-curving handle is painted with a central black band flanked on each side by two thin brown stripes.

Accessioned 6 November 1906 as NS 27881, "water box." Sold to the OPM for $3.

38.8 cm high x 28 cm long x 23.7 cm wide

Cedar; black and brown paint. A single piece of wood was steamed and bent to form three of the sides; fourth side and bottom attached with wooden pegs. The handle is a curved stick bound to each long side with twisted cedar-root cord.

CONDITION

Good; irregular stain on the inside

about three-quarters of the way up; burn marks inside.

COMMENTS

A new version of the traditional water bucket described by Boas (1909:422–23), Curtis (1915:15), Drucker (1950:184), and Stewart (1984:86). The design may represent a bear in its den. The profile face at the top left of each long side is similar to the design on the side of No. 55 (dance hat) and on the paddle by Daniel Houstie (No. 26). This motif is also found on carved chests from Bella Bella (e.g., FMNH 19978, CMC VII-EE-51). Stylistic analysis suggests that this bucket was made by Daniel Houstie (see Appendix D).

Associated Objects: See No. 38.

Published: Black 1989:288, pl. 30.

40. Kerfed Chest with Lid, ROM 912x16.A&B

A crudely made, small, painted bentwood chest with a plank lid. The back and front of an animal are shown on the sides of the chest. Simple ovoid shapes decorate the ends.

There is no accession data for this object. It is undoubtedly the box listed in the price list (NS file), but it is not in the NS catalogue list. It was part of Large's 1906 collection and was purchased by the OPM for 50 cents.

14 cm high x 26.1 cm long x 6.2 cm wide

Cedar; red and black paint. Bottom and sides nailed together. Lid has projecting lip around sides.

CONDITION

Although top is dirty, chest looks new.

COMMENTS

Although this box is roughly made and painted, the basic structure of the design, if not its execution, follows the conventions of chest decoration. It is so similar in form, execution, and scale to No. 35, a cedar box made by Chief Robert Bell, that it must have been made by the same hand.

Associated Objects: No. 35, kerfed box, No. 62, club or talking stick, made by Bell; No. 68, whistle collected from Bell.

41. Kerfed Chest, ROM 950x76

(Colour photo, p. 24)

A lidless chest with formline designs on four sides. The two longer sides each have an identical killer-whale design. The whale's body is bent into a U-shape, with the head, perforated dorsal fin, back, and tail of the animal each filling a corner. The blowhole and fins of the whale are also indicated. The shorter sides have profile head designs with ear and circle motifs in the upper corners. All four sides have a painted border around most of the design.

There is no accession data for this object.

21 cm high x 34.5 cm long x 26.4 cm wide

Cedar; black and brown paint. Steamed and bent plank, pegged together, bottom pegged on. Some preliminary drawing, probably graphite, can be seen. There are wooden plugs in the shorter sides.

CONDITION

Looks new.

COMMENTS

Because this box is so close in form and execution to the other black and brown painted cedar boxes in the collection, I believe it was collected at Bella Bella about 1906, probably by Large. Stylistic analysis suggests that it was made by Daniel Houstie (see Appendix D).

Associated Objects: See No. 37.

42. Feast Bowl, ROM 23147

Massive oval wooden bowl in the shape of a beaver. The animal's feet extend out from the base of the bowl at front and back. The front paws rest on a flat stick. The face of the beaver, its chin slightly raised, is carved in three dimensions and projects over the front paws. It is decorated with a simple red and black formline design. Above the animal's forehead a thick, flat rim extends around the top of the bowl, dipping slightly at the sides, and coming to a rounded point at the tail end, where a formline face is carved on the rim's flat upper surface.

Accessioned 1 January 1902 as NS 23147, "food box, representing beaver with stick in front paws, made by Capt. Carpenter." Collected at Bella Bella.

31 cm high x 183 cm long (at centre) x 71.4 cm wide (at centre)

Carved wood; red and black paint.

CONDITION

Condition and repairs indicate that the bowl is old. Wood has a dark patina and appears worn. Paint is worn and faded. There is a large crack in the face of the beaver just beside the nose on the right side and a crack at the bottom front under the chin. Both cracks were repaired before the bowl was collected: a large nail to reinforce the face and a piece of wood in the split under the chin. The rim is worn and dented. There is no trace of oil; the interior of the bowl is dry.

COMMENTS

Although as early as 1834 Niblack (1890:337) noted that "wash bowls are used as food receptacles, and are taking the place of the native wooden bowls," large wooden feast bowls were retained because of their ceremonial importance. Olson (1935, 1949:21) reported that two huge dishes in the shape of a wolf and a sea lion were given by the people of Bella Bella to the people of Hartley Bay when the latter attended a funeral potlatch at Bella Bella. Because they were given away at a funeral feast, the bowls would never be copied again at Bella Bella. According to Hawthorn (1967:178), great feast dishes were among the treasures brought by a bride and came in sets of four to represent the divisions of supernatural beings: undersea, sky, land, and forest.

Associated Objects: No. 43, feast bowl. Other feast bowls from Bella Bella: CMC VII-EE-37 and VII-EE-38, used by Chief Moody in 1890 at "the feast of the hereditary chief (crowning of the chief)"; FMNH 85078, collected by Newcombe in 1903. See No. 34 for other associated objects.

43. Feast Bowl, ROM 27880

Massive rectangular bowl with flaring sides and projecting rim. On the long sides the rim is flat and narrow. At each end or shorter side it widens to a triangular shape reminiscent of a Copper, with a slight central ridge. Formline faces, probably representing the head and tail of a bear, are carved in these projections of the rim. The larger face has eyebrows with bumps that represent ears, sharply carved eyes with round pupils, a round nose, a wide mouth, and claws beside the face. The smaller face, at the other end, has similar eyebrow treatment, a mouth with U-forms at each side, and no claws.

Accessioned 6 November 1906 as NS 27880, "large food box." Sold to the OPM for $5.

26.8 cm high x 165 cm long x 63 cm wide

Carved wood. The carving is shallow but sharp and precise.

CONDITION

Appears to be old; black patina. Inside is dry; edges are dented. A crack down the centre was reinforced before the bowl was collected.

COMMENTS

See No. 42. The formline carving on this bowl is in the style of the northern Northwest Coast. Heiltsuk art is often described as intermediary between the northern and southern coastal styles, exhibiting characteristics of each convention.

Associated Objects: See No. 42.

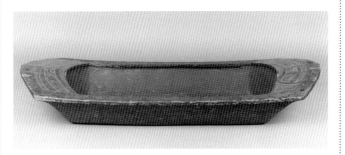

44. Bent Bowl, ROM 27864

An undecorated kerfed bowl with bulging sides.

Accessioned 6 November 1906 as NS 27864, "new wood box, old model." Sold to the OPM for 50 cents. The price list (NS file) records this object as "yew wood box, old model."

12.5 cm high x 28 cm long x 23.1 cm wide

Unpainted wood (yew?); roughly made. The sides are made from a single piece of wood—shaped, kerfed, steamed, and bent, with only one side seam, joined with nails. The bottom was made separately and nailed on; nails come through the bottom. Adze marks are visible.

CONDITION
As new.

COMMENTS
Unlike traditional bent-corner bowls, this bowl is roughly constructed and undecorated. It may have been made at Large's request to illustrate "old-time" technology and way of life.

Associated Objects: None.

CEREMONIAL OBJECTS: BATONS, CARVINGS, CLAPPER AND RATTLE, COSTUME, MASKS, STAFFS, WHISTLES

45. Stone Baton, ROM 27870
(Colour photo, p. 93)

Flat, knife-shaped object with a short handle with a knob at the end and a curved, leaf-shaped blade incised on both sides. Side one: a profile human head in a small-brimmed, conical hat projects above a vertically striped band with irregular concentric half circles at each end; below this, geometric patterns (concentric half circles and circles, single and cross-hatching) fill the remaining half of the blade. Side two: a profile wolf, the head of which resembles a Nuu-chah-nulth wolf mask with a large square snout with a half circle on top, a square eye, a long, straight mouth, and three curved hairs extending from the back of the head; the body has short legs and a long tail with radiating lines; in front of the head of the wolf is a T-shape on its side (i.e., a shape like the left side of an H).

Accessioned 6 November 1906 as NS 27870, "carved slate knife." Sold to the OPM for $5.

34.5 cm long x 12.5 cm wide x 1.5 cm thick

Carved grey stone, possibly slate, with some white-turquoise paint in the incised lines.

CONDITION
Paint appears to have worn away; tip is slightly chipped.

COMMENTS
The iconography on this artifact suggests a ceremonial connection, and it is probably a dance wand or baton. The vertically striped band below the profile head is topped with a row of cross-hatching, perhaps representing a cedar-bark neck ring with long fringes; the animal on the reverse is a masked Nuu-chah-nulth wolf dancer. The knifelike shape suggests a shamanic function: "Shamans also used wands or batons in their practice, some of which represented magical weapons with which they battled the malevolent powers opposing them" (Holm 1983a:94).

Associated Objects: No. 46, bone baton; NS 27901, stone knife.

46. Bone Baton, ROM 27871

Bone baton with a short handle, which has a knob at the end, and a slightly curved, knifelike blade with scallops along one edge. One side is incised with a crudely executed formline design of a profile head, perhaps a Cannibal bird. The scallops are the teeth of the creature.

Accessioned 6 November 1906 as NS 27871, "scalloped edge dance implement 'official sceptre'." Sold to the OPM for $3.

26.2 cm long x 4.4 cm wide x 1.5 cm thick

Bone (whalebone?), crudely carved and incised.

CONDITION
Bone looks old and worn. The unincised (flat) side is grey and polished; the incised side is porous.

COMMENTS
This is a dance wand or baton. According to Holm (1983a:94), "dancers gestured with wands in time to the dance song, responding to the words with appropriate movement." See also No. 45.

Associated Objects: No. 45, stone wand or baton.

47. Puppet, ROM 23193

Figure with moveable forearms, dressed in green wool shirt and pants; discoloured white cotton and navy wool fringes at neck and shoulders. The flat forearms end in carved hands, the palm of each pierced with a small hole to allow the arms to be manipulated by strings (arms will move horizontally only). The figure has a large round head, and holes around the hairline above the ears indicate that it once had hair. The figure does not have feet, but nail holes in the bottom of the legs suggest that it was once attached to a base.

Accessioned 1 January 1902 as NS 23193, "rough carved human figure." Collected from General Dick, Bella Bella.

68 cm high x 22 cm wide x l6 cm thick

Unpainted cedar, roughly carved; details such as pupils, teeth, and ears accentuated with graphite. Forearms are tied onto long, flat pieces of horn (?) screwed into the underside of the arms at the elbows. The horn is notched where the forearm is attached with white string and grey thread. The forearm pieces have half-circles cut out at the elbows to allow the arms to swing. The clothing is made of green wool, white cotton, and navy wool serge, sewn together with string and dark thread, and nailed onto the back of the puppet with iron and round-headed brass nails.

CONDITION
Appears to have been old when collected. Wood has a dark patina and raised grain; clothing is worn and very fragile.

COMMENTS
This figure is probably a Túxvʾit puppet, associated with the female war spirit dancer. For a discussion of its ceremonial context, see Boas 1897:501–9.

Associated Objects: See No. 15 for other objects collected from and made by General Dick. Other Túxvʾit puppets: UBCMOA A4514–A4515; RBCM 98, 100 (Fig. 28); Glenbow Museum AA352.

48. Ceremonial Box, ROM 27874/906.2.4 A&B
(See also p. 128)

A covered box on four legs with a large, skull-like head and two crouching animals inserted into holes in the top, and a flat oval face nailed to the top of the back panel. The neck of the skull-like head is inserted into a hole at the front of the top. Extending from the bases of the two animals are long, sloping, hollow sticks that fit into holes in the centre of the top. The animals' tubular snouts, which point up and extend beyond the sides of the box, are also hollow. The animals' short front and back legs rest on top of the box; their feet are painted on the top rather than carved. Although the top is fixed in position, the large head and the animals can be removed to access the inside. The sides of the box are painted with formline designs—split profile heads with clawed feet on the front and back, and a face with a wide, toothy mouth surrounded by a flattened circle on each side. The legs of the box wrap around each corner of the sides and have faces with large eyes and wide, toothy mouths painted on at the tops.

Accessioned 6 November 1906 as NS 27874, "dance drinking box." Sold to the OPM for $5.

51.2 cm high x 42.5 cm long x 37.5 cm wide

Carved cedar; black and brown paint. Animals and legs of box attached with wooden pegs. Flat head nailed on. Abalone inlay in eyes of attached heads and ani-

mals. Remains of black fur on both attached heads. Cedar bark around necks of animals.

CONDITION
Top is soiled, hair has worn away, and animals are missing three forelimbs.

COMMENTS
Both heads attached to this box suggest skulls. The designs on the sides of the box are also skull-like—a common Heiltsuk motif found on several objects collected in turn-of-the-century Bella Bella such as a dish and spoon collected in 1906 (NMAI 4670). The animals on top are probably land otters, powerful spirit helpers connected with death and transformation. Stylistic analysis suggests that this box was made by Daniel Houstie (see Appendix D).

Large's description of this object as a "dance drinking box" is probably correct, although no other artifact of this type has been found. The large head plugs a hole through which the box could be filled. Straws could be inserted through the snouts of the otters

and down into the box through their long attached sticks. The Oweekeno have at least two drinking dances: the Ha'gwagweh dancer, the fourth-ranked of the Returned from Heaven (dhuẃláx̌a) series, appeared to drink gallons and gallons of water and to urinate continuously as he circled the fire; the Healing Water dancer (Heilikstaxsta) was one of the Shaman's (c̓aíqa) society performers (Olson 1954:35; Stevenson n.d., p. 72). Land otters are connected with the Oweekeno Wua'LaL dancer, the third-ranked of the dhuẃláx̌a series, who was possessed by the spirits of these powerful animals (Olson 1954:33).

Associated Objects: Similar skull motifs are found on No. 69, dance whistle, No. 55, dance hat, and No. 50, skull/ladle. See No. 69 for other associated objects.

49. Small Wooden Bird, ROM 27910
(See also p. 80)
This small, simply carved, wooden bird with a shallow depression in

the top is a piece of a mask. The bird has a flat head, a thin, straight beak, a short tail, and an egg-shaped body with wings indicated.

Accessioned 6 November 1906 as NS 27910, "bird from dance mask." Sold to the OPM for 50 cents.

8 cm high x 17.4 cm long x 6 cm wide

Unpainted cedar. Small hole (diam. 9 cm) in bottom. Carving is very simple with little surface detail.

CONDITION
Edges are worn; wood looks old; black, glossy patina on neck.

COMMENTS
This small bird has the head and beak of a gull. It may have been originally attached to a Ḵumugwe' mask, such as UBCMOA A3634, which was collected from the Fort Rupert (Tsax̱is Band) Kwakwa̱ka'wakw but originated at Bella Bella. That mask is topped with a rotating starfish, on each arm of which sits a small wooden gull.

Associated Objects: cf. UBCMOA A3634, Ḵumugwe' mask.

50. Ladle, ROM 954x35, and Wooden Skull, ROM 956x145.5
(See also p. 49)
A large, wooden ladle (ROM 954x35) with a short handle that ends in a carved bear's head. The black head of the bear rises at right angles to the short handle and looks over the bowl, which has a hole drilled in the centre. The bear's head has a flat back, a projecting snout with drilled nostrils, and projecting brows over drilled eye holes. The outside of the ladle is painted with a form-line design that suggests the head of an animal or bird with round eye and long, toothy mouth or beak. The inside is painted with a simple formline design.

A carved wooden skull (ROM 956x145.5) with eyes of abalone inlay. Hair and a wide, straight mouth full of teeth are indicated by painted lines. A short cylindrical post at the base of the skull fits snugly into the hole in the ladle.

There is no accession data for this object.

Ladle, 44.7 cm long x 19.2 cm wide x 7.5 cm deep; skull, 24 cm high x 12 cm wide x 15 cm thick

Carved cedar; black and reddish brown paint. Abalone inlay in eyes; remains of hair or fur nailed on head.

CONDITION
Tip of ladle is split. Hair or fur has worn away.

COMMENTS
Although ladle and skull have separate accession numbers, they form a single artifact. This ladle is included in the collection because it is similar in form and execution to the black and brown painted cedar ceremonial objects collected by Large at Bella Bella, and stylistic analysis suggests that it was made by Daniel Houstie (see Appendix D).

The skull-ladle is a typical Bella Bella object. The Denver Art Museum has a miniature skull-ladle that was collected at Bella Bella in 1896/97, perhaps by the schoolteacher Miss Reinhardt (DAM 1942.251/QBB-3-G). A similar skull-ladle was collected in 1905 at Bella Bella (BM 05.588.297, Fig. 29). The ROM ladle was probably used, or is a copy of one that was used, in the Shaman's (c̓aíqa) ceremonies associated with the Cannibal (tánís) dancer. The bear suggests the Cannibal bear of the Kwakwa̲ka̲'wakw; the motif on the outside of the ladle may represent one of the Cannibal bird servants of Báxvbakválánusiwa, the Cannibal-at-the-North-End-of-the-World, whose spirit possesses the tánís initiate.

Associated Objects: Other black and brown painted ceremonial objects in the Large Collection: No. 63, club, No. 69, bellows whistle, No. 48, drinking box, No. 55, hat, No. 65, spear.

Published: Black 1989:281, pl. 23.

51. Rattle, ROM 27865
(See also p. 81)
A plain wooden disc with a straight handle that flares slightly towards the bottom. At the top an inverted triangle of folded sheet copper encloses small rattling objects, probably stones.

Accessioned 6 November 1906 as NS 27865, "copper rattle." Sold to the OPM for $1.

50.5 cm long x diam. 19 cm x 2.2 cm thick

Carved unpainted wood, sheet copper, noisemakers (stones?). The sheet of copper is bent over a wooden support. Disc, handle, and projection supporting the copper are carved from one piece of wood.

CONDITION
Wood is dry.

COMMENTS
The triangular projection alludes, both in shape and material, to the copper plaques (Coppers) that are symbols of wealth on the Northwest Coast. Rattles used in a Kwakwa̲ka̲'wakw child-naming ceremony were either made of copper or made in the shape of a Copper (Hawthorn 1967:148). Large's rattle is a much simpler version of a dance fan from Bella Bella collected by James Swan in 1877 (NMNH 20636), which consists of a disc painted with a form-line face, with two folded copper "ears," and two straight wooden handles. At the base of each "ear" is a tuft of white fur. Holes around the perimeter of the disc probably held red cedar bark. The use of these particular objects is not known, but, like all Northwest Coast rattles, they "belonged to the supernatural world [and their] use always implies the presence of supernatural power" (Holm 1983a:25).

Associated Objects: Triangular Bella

Bella rattle UBCMOA A1111, made from folded sheet copper, collected by George Darby.

52. Clapper, ROM 28223
Clapper with straight sides, rounded ends, and a short handle. Fish design incised on one side only.

Purchased October 1906 and catalogued 29 April 1907 as NS 28223, "dance clapper."

26.5 cm long x 4 cm wide x 3 cm thick

Carved and incised cedar; clapper section made in two pieces and bound together with pounded cedar bark. Inside hollowed out. Stained brownish red.

CONDITION
Good.

COMMENTS
According to Drucker (1940:211, 218), split-stick rattles were the instruments of the Returned from Heaven (dhuẁláx̌a) society dancers.

Associated Objects: NS 28222, dance clapper, exchanged with the National Museum of Australia in 1907.

53. Headdress, ROM 23161

A head ring made of ten tubes of tightly wound cedar bark alternating in rows of Z- and S-twist fibres; flat panels at front and back.

Accessioned 1 January 1902 as NS 23161, "dance headdress used by Fort Rupert Indians, B.C."

8.7 cm high x 17 cm wide x 23.2 cm deep; diam. approx. 20 cm

Cedar bark, twisted and sewn; lined with red cloth.

CONDITION
Lining cloth is worn.

COMMENTS
George Hunt collected cedar-bark rings (e.g., AMNH l6/4732–16/4735) at Bella Bella probably in 1897. Although many residents of Bella Bella no doubt kept their cedar-bark dance regalia, it is unlikely that they would have shown it to Large, who vocally opposed the continuation of aboriginal ceremonies. Cedar bark dyed red with alder bark symbolized the sacredness of Winter Ceremonies, particularly the Shaman's (c̓aíqa) series, thought to have originated with the Heiltsuk (Boas 1909:404, 1930:105; Holm 1983a:39).

Associated Objects: No. 54, cedar-bark neck ring. For a list of objects collected at Fort Rupert, see Appendix E.

54. Neck Ring, ROM 23162

Ring with symmetrical pattern of chevron braiding, bound cedar bark, S-twist bark fringes, and plain, beaten cedar-bark fringes.

Accessioned 1 January 1902 as NS 23162, "dance neck ornament used by Fort Rupert Indians, B.C."

43 cm high x 25 cm wide x 4 cm thick; circumference, exclusive of fringe, 114 cm

Dyed cedar bark bound with beige cotton thread and strips of black cotton cloth.

CONDITION
Good.

COMMENTS
Participants in the Shaman's (c̓aíqa) ceremonies might also wear elbow, wrist, knee, and ankle rings of red-dyed cedar bark. Each dance was distinguished by a dif-

ferent type of ring. This neck ring resembles that worn for the first level of the Kwakwa̱ka̱'wakw Xa'niats'amg·ilaku^u dancer (Boas 1897:453).

Associated Objects: No. 53, NS 28204, head rings. For a list of objects collected at Fort Rupert, see Appendix E.

55. Ceremonial Hat,
ROM 27878/906.2.5
(Colour photo, p. 125)

Hat with wide brim and shallow crown. A flat, oval, skull-like head is attached to the front of the crown. Shredded red cedar bark is wrapped around the back of the skull and lies on the hat's brim on either side of the skull-head. A pattern of curved lines painted on the sides of the crown represents the ribs of the skull-headed creature. On the back of the crown is painted a round-eyed face with a large, toothy mouth. Four flat, wooden legs are attached to the brim of the hat at the edges of the ribcage. The front legs are bent,

the back legs straight. Painted on the brim are, at the front, two eyes under the skull; at each side, a profile head with large eye and long toothy mouth; and at the back, stripes that represent the tail of the animal.

Accessioned 6 November 1906 as NS 27878, "cedar dance hat." Sold to the OPM for $4.

17.5 cm high x diam. 42.5 cm

Woven cedar bark in diagonal checkerwork pattern, with black painted design. Carved cedar additions painted black and reddish brown. Wooden legs attached to brim with white string. Skull-head has abalone discs inlaid in eyes and is wrapped with shredded cedar bark.

CONDITION
Looks new.

COMMENTS
The hat represents a creature with a skull-like head; Large's description of it as a "dance hat" is proba-

bly correct, although its condition suggests that it was not used. Stylistic analysis suggests that this hat was decorated by Daniel Houstie (see Appendix D). The paraphernalia of the Kwakwaka'wakw Ghost dance, which originated with the Heiltsuk, included a head ring with a split human skull attached. The Bella Bella Ghost dancer (lūɬaɬ) wore a human skull bound to the top of his head (Boas 1930:110, Drucker 1940:210).

Associated Objects: See Nos. 48, 69.

Published: ROM postcard.

56. Two Copper "Horns," ROM 27897–27898
Two narrow, triangular-shaped ornaments from a headdress, made of sheet copper, with rounded corners, each corner pierced with a small hole. The flat bases flare outward and the triangles slant backward, giving them a slightly S-shaped profile. They were made in the shape of bear claws or horns of a mountain goat in imitation of a shaman's crown.

Accessioned 6 November 1906 as "two copper head ornaments." Sold to the OPM for $2 (for the pair).

Each, 14.5 cm long x 3.8 cm wide

Cut, shaped, and polished pieces of sheet copper, each pierced with three small holes.

CONDITION
Good, but these horns or claws are fragments of a headdress.

COMMENTS
These copper ornaments from a dance headdress, probably belonging to a Healer (hailīkila), one of the ranked dancers in the Returned from Heaven (dhuẃláx̌a) series. Their pierced bases would have been sewn to a leather headband and the tops linked with braided sinew. A headdress collected by F. Jacobsen in 1893 (RBCM 84), has copper rays instead of bear claws or goat horns and is described as a Tsimshian shaman's crown.

Associated Objects: None.

57. Mask, ROM 23135/902.2.6
(Colour photo, p. 77)
A heavy mask with grotesque features—heavy brows, protruding hooked nose with flaring nostrils, grooved cheek ridges, rectangular mouth with thick squared lips, and sharp projecting chin. The mouth and eyes are bored through the wood and the back is roughly finished, as if it had been carved with an axe. There is a hole (diam. 1.75 cm), slanting inward, drilled under the left pupil.

Accessioned 1 January 1902 as NS 23135, "dance mask used by

Interior or Stick Indians, made by Daniel Houstie." Collected at Bella Bella.

29 cm high x 22 cm wide x 24.5 cm deep

Carved cedar, painted red, green, and white on black. Some remnants of dark hair or fur nailed on head and under nose. A rather tight leather harness with fur on one side is affixed to the back of the mask at the centre of the top and sides. The harness is machine-stitched; stitching is white on one side, black on the other.

CONDITION
Hair has worn away.

COMMENTS
The mask represents a pk̓vs (Wild Man of the Woods, the Kwakwaka'wakw Bukwús). According to Olson (1954:248), the seventh-ranked dance of the Returned from Heaven (dhuẃláx̌a) series was the Monster-in-human-

form dance (Pu'kus). This mask is typically Heiltsuk in style and was made by a Bella Bella carver, so Large's description of it as "used by Interior or Stick Indians" is misleading.

Associated Objects: Nos. 58–60, masks. For other objects made by Daniel Houstie, see Appendix D. Nos. 66–67, whistles collected from Houstie.

Published: ROM 1959, fig. A64, "dance mask, date and tribe unknown"; Drucker 1965, fig. 3, "Bella Bella mask"; ROM 1976:16, "Bookwus"; Black 1989:279, pl. 21; Hilton 1990:318, fig. 5b, "'Bukwus' by Daniel Houstie."

58. Mask, ROM 23136
A thinly carved mask, rectangular in shape, with an open mouth and round eyes. The painted design, which does not follow the lines of the carving, is distinguished by three teardrop shapes that sweep across the forehead above the brows. Flaps, probably of leather, that could be moved up and down to cover the eyes were once sewn with sinew into thin grooves under the brows. The flaps were manipulated by strings that ran through four holes burned through the wood, one at each corner of a square area surrounding each eye. There are adze marks on the back of the mask and a stick, pegged horizontally above the mouth, which the wearer held in his teeth to keep the mask on.

Accessioned 1 January 1902 as NS 23136, "Stick, Sinash [Siwash] (or Interior Indian) mask, purchased from Solomon." Collected at Bella Bella.

28 cm high x 18.4 cm wide x 11 cm deep

Carved wood. Black design on a natural wood background, lips and brows painted red-brown. Holes along the top of the mask indicate that the mask once had hair. Remains of sinew that was sewn and pegged into the wood above the eyes. Horizontal mouthpiece pegged on back.

CONDITION
Appears to be old. The hair and the leather flaps are gone, the wood is worn around the edges, and the paint is peeling in spots.

COMMENTS
Because the eyes of this mask could be made to open and close, it may be associated with the Sleeping spirit dance (see No. 60). Large's note that it is a "Stick, Sinash [Siwash] (or Interior Indian) mask" is misleading because it is typically Heiltsuk in style. One explanation of this terminology may be that the mask represents a person from the Interior. One of the many kinds of ˇX̌íx̌ís Returned from Heaven (dhuẁláx̌a) spirits, according to Drucker (1940:215), was "a minor one . . . a Stick [Interior] Indian spirit (aLasiml) who dances with feathers, bows, and so on."

Associated Objects: No. 59, mask, also purchased from Solomon. Nos. 57, 60, other masks in the Large Collection. Another mask from Bella Bella with flaps over the eyes, NMAI 2182, was collected by Reverend Crosby in 1906, and a mask collected at Port Simpson (ROM HN.365), perhaps by Crosby, has moveable leather flaps over the eyes.

Published: Black 1989:279, pl. 20.

59. Mask, ROM 23137
(See also p. 13)
A thinly carved mask of a human face with a blue star pattern. The mask is predominantly natural wood, with black brows, moustache, and beard, and a small red mouth. Each rectangular ear has the remains of two wooden plugs about 3 cm apart.

Accessioned 1 January 1902 as NS 23137, "Stick Sinash [Siwash] (Interior Indian) mask, purchased from Solomon." Collected at Bella Bella.

26 cm high x 24.5 cm wide x 13.5 cm deep

Carved hardwood; light blue, black, and red paint.

CONDITION
Appears to be old. The right ear is black at the back, as if it has been charred. The wood is worn around the edge, and the blue paint looks faded.

COMMENTS
This is a typically Heiltsuk mask, resembling others (e.g., RBCM 10, collected by F. Jacobsen in 1893) that were used in dances of the Returned from Heaven (dhuẁláx̌a) series. Large's attribution to the Interior Indians may have been intended to convey the information that such masks were no longer used in his Methodist village.

Associated Objects: No. 58, mask, also collected from Solomon; Nos. 57, 60, other masks in the Large collection.

Published: Black 1989:277, pl. 19.

60. Mask, ROM 27875
(See also p. 40)
A mask with exaggerated features and moveable eyes. Heavy eyebrows, painted with bands of horizontal lines, extend over hollow eye sockets into which are set pivoting, egg-shaped orbs. The heavy cheek ridges, also decorated with parallel hatching, curve under the eyes and extend to the prominent, hooked nose. The wide mouth curves slightly upward and is defined by wide, flaring lips above a sharp, protruding chin. At one time the mask had hair, a moustache, and a goatee of fur. The rotating orbs of the eyes, which are fringed with long black lashes, are carved and painted on one side with a half circle (eyes closed) and on the other with a white circular pupil (eyes open). A tube of black rubber (?) is nailed to each orb and to the top of the inside of

the mask. Strings attached to metal loops on the back of each orb allowed the wearer to open and close the eyes. When the mask was "asleep," the orbs were pulled down, extending the rubber bands. When the strings were released, the rubber contracted and the eyes snapped open. Nails at the sides of the eye sockets controlled the extent of the pivot.

Accessioned 6 November 1906 as NS 27875, "dance mask." Sold to the OPM for $3.

28 cm high x 22.8 cm wide x 24 cm deep

Carved wood painted green and red on black. Remains of pale fur/hair attached with metal nails to head, upper lip, and chin; black bristles on eye orbs. String, metal eyelets, rubber (?) tubing, and metal nails attached to eyes at the back. A small block of wood is nailed to the back of the mask under the left eye. Remains of leather harness attached to side of mask.

CONDITION
Fur/hair and leather harness have worn away. Rubber tubes are dry, brittle, and broken.

COMMENTS
This mask resembles No. 57, a mask made by Daniel Houstie and may also be made by Houstie (see Appendix D). Rotating eyes may indicate an association with the Sleeping spirit (Kḷytlis'naulauks) dance which was performed by Chief Robert Bell at Chief Moody's father's wedding feast (Olson 1935, 1949:34). Boas (1897:655–66) describes the Tsimshian version of this dance as follows: the owner of the spirit of sleep wears a mask and appears to be sleeping; a chief tries to wake him by pulling the drowsiness from him by both hands; the eyes of the mask roll open and the dancer stands up; the chief opens his hands, releasing the spirit of sleep and causing all people to close their eyes and doze off; after some time the chief again gathers up the drowsiness and the people wake up and sing. Olson (1935, 1949:34) reports that at a Bella Bella wedding Robert Bell danced for a short time and fell asleep; then all of the audience, with the exception of two or three chiefs, slept.

Associated Objects: No. 57, grotesque mask made by Daniel Houstie; No. 56, mask with moveable eyes collected from Solomon. Another grotesque Heiltsuk mask with moveable eyes, NMAI 9751, was collected by George Emmons

in 1906. Similar Heiltsuk masks that do not have moveable eyes and are identified as Wild Man of the Woods or pḵvs: NMAI 5/9833, McM 1984.5 (Fig. 16), AMNH 16/4736 collected by George Hunt, NMNH 217408.

61. Cane or Talking Stick,
ROM 23143
(See also p. 33)

An elaborately carved, L-shaped stick made of hardwood with a warm patina. Although the design is dynamic and complex, the carving is shallow and the figures are contained within the cylinder of the cane. The top (handle) of the stick is the head of a wolflike being with a long snout and is reminiscent of the long-beaked Cannibal bird masks of the tánís ceremonial. The wolfish creature holds a small skeletal figure, the skull of which is carved from a natural burl in the wood, in its teeth. The wolflike creature has small ears and its hands are cupped, like the paws of a bear. Feathers are incised on its side; on its back is the indication of a backbone or perhaps a snake. It holds a skull with potlatch rings in its paws/hands and stands on the head of a human figure. The human figure has upraised arms and slightly bent knees, with feather designs incised on its wrists and feet. In the centre of its body is carved another small human figure.

Accessioned 1 January 1902 as

NS 23143, "carved walking stick, made by Daniel Houstie." Collected at Bella Bella.

105.6 cm long x diam. 8 cm; handle, 17.2 cm long

Carved hardwood with honey-coloured patina; abalone inlay in eyes.

CONDITION
Good; looks new. There are burn marks on the chin, shoulder, and nose of the wolflike creature.

Associated Objects: NMNH H89101 and PS E3660 are carved walking or talking sticks from Bella Bella with similar motifs. The top, or handle, of NMNH 89101 is a grotesque head with hooked nose and tubular nostrils that resembles central Northwest Coast Cannibal bird masks; the top of PS E3660 represents the head of a snake holding a frog in its teeth. PH 87183, a carved staff depicting a long-legged, ravenlike bird with a small grotesque creature on its body, is similar in style and materials to No. 61, and may also have been made by Houstie. Also probably made by Houstie is RBCM 2312, a carved yew staff depicting a human figure, a lizardlike creature, and a whale; it was made at Bella Bella but collected at Bella Coola by C. F. Newcombe in 1913. Nos. 66–67, whistles, were collected from Daniel Houstie. For a list of objects made by Houstie, see Appendix D.

Published: ROM 1976:11, "ceremonial staff."

62. Club or Talking Stick,
ROM 23144
(Colour photo, p. 108)
A heavy club or stick carved with three crest figures, from top to bottom: a wolf holding a small figure in its paws, a squatting bear with upraised paws, and a whale holding the handle of the stick in its mouth. The wolf has a black mask painted over the eye area; the bear's fur is indicated by irregular black hatching; the whale has bushy black eyebrows. Eyes are inlaid with abalone.

Accessioned 1 January 1902 as NS 23144, "war club, made by Chief Robt. Bell." Collected at Bella Bella.

82 cm long x 10.2 cm wide x 9 cm thick

Carved wood with black and brown paint, abalone inlay.

CONDITION
Good.

COMMENTS
The War dancer (UwinalaL), of the first-ranked dance of the Returned from Heaven (dhuẃláx̌a) series, carries a club carved with family crest figures. He runs through the village, entering houses and destroying property, and strikes those that do not perform properly during the dance (Olson 1954:248).

Associated Objects: No. 63, ceremonial club; for other objects made

by or collected from Chief Robert Bell, see No. 35.

63. Club, ROM 27866
(Colour photo, p. 64)
Club made from a tapered piece of wood, incised and painted to represent the profile head and body of a bird, probably Raven. The shaft is inset with a shaped grey stone that projects at right angles to the shaft and is painted to represent the bird's beak. Abalone is inlaid in the eyes and in ovoids at the wing tips. There is cedar-root wrapping on the end of the handle.

Accessioned 6 November 1906 as NS 27866, "painted war club." Sold to the OPM for $5.

56.2 cm long x 16 cm wide x 5.5 cm thick

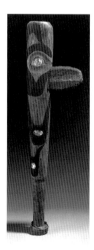

Carved cedar and grey, porous pecked stone; black and transparent reddish brown paint. Abalone

inlay in shaft of club; cedar-root wrapping on handle.

CONDITION
One side is blackened. Cedar wrapping is broken and loose.

COMMENTS
According to Drucker (1950:187), the Heiltsuk had plain wooden war clubs. This club was probably a ceremonial weapon such as that used by the Oweekeno War dancer whose club represented one of his crests (Drucker 1940:205; Olson 1954:248). Stylistic analysis suggests that it was made by Daniel Houstie (see Appendix D).

Associated Objects: No. 62, war club made by Chief Robert Bell, No. 65, war spear. See No. 50 for other black and brown painted ceremonial objects.

Published: Black 1989:285, pl. 28.

64. Talking Stick, ROM 27882
(Colour photo, p. 101)
A canelike stick with complex three-dimensional carving. At the top is a bird with flat ears and a long, hooked beak. The bird sits on the head of a wolflike animal, which holds a small human figure in its four paws. The little figure stands astride the neck of another wolflike animal which stands on all fours on the back of a third wolflike animal, which in turn is supported on the shoulders of three standing humans. The humans stand on the top and brim

of a large, ringed hat on which is carved a small killer whale. The hat sits on the head of a large standing figure that wears a short garment and holds a large digging stick. Below the figure is a short cylindrical handle.

Accessioned 6 November 1906 as NS 27882, "carved ceremonial wand." Sold to the OPM for $10. Identified in the price list (NS file) as "carved cane."

93.5 cm long x 5.5 cm wide x 16 cm thick

Hardwood with a honey-coloured patina; black, red-brown, rosy red, and blue paint.

CONDITION
Good; paint may have faded.

COMMENTS
A talking stick such as this was used by a chief or by an orator who spoke on a chief's behalf. The bird at the top of the stick is probably a Cannibal bird. The figures below it illustrate the Heiltsuk ('Uyalitx̌v) origin myth of the Dog's Wife, or Mother-of-Dogs (see pp. 97–98).

Associated Objects: No. 61, talking stick made by Daniel Houstie.

65. Spear,
ROM 27911/906.2.8/HN.1298
(Colour photo, p. 65)
A long, heavy, carved spear with an incised leaf-shaped blade. The spear is carved with the following images (end to point): a human-like figure, a wolf, a beaver, and a birdlike being that holds the blade in its long, spotted snout. At the blunt end of the spear is a row of feathers above a plain band. Below is the large head of the human figure with a wide nose and a large, toothy mouth. The figure sits with its elbows and knees bent, its hands under its chin, and the tail of the wolf between its legs. The wolf faces towards the point of the spear and holds a small figure with raised arms in front of its body, on the other side of the shaft. Below the wolf is a seated beaver. Below the beaver, rows of feathers indicate the neck of the birdlike creature holding the blade in its mouth. The blade extends into the shaft and forms the teeth of the birdlike creature.

Accessioned 6 November 1906 as NS 27911, "war spear, carved whale rib point." Sold to the OPM for $20.

219.9 cm long (includes blade, 44.9 cm long) x 6.6 cm wide x 5 cm thick

Carved hardwood, brown and black paint. Abalone inlay in eyes, bone (possibly whalebone) blade. Bone and shaft bound with leather and pitch. A metal staple on the underside of the shaft near the end holds the remains of a leather thong.

CONDITION
Looks new.

COMMENTS
This spear was probably associated with the Winter Ceremonies. Stylistic analysis indicates that it may have been made by Daniel Houstie (see Appendix D). Long, heavy lances were carried by the Kwakwaka'wakw Nulamal (fool) dancers, the ˇX̌íx̌ís Spearing-the-heavens dancer—the War dancer of the Returned from Heaven (dhuẁláx̌a) series—the ˇX̌íx̌ís Spearing-in-a-canoe dancer, and the Heiltsuk Finding-a-supernatural-treasure dancer—the first-ranked of the dhuẁláx̌a series (Boas 1897:469; Drucker 1940:211, 215). The lances used by these dancers had rows of carved heads or skulls suspended from them. The Kwakwaka'wakw of Kingcome Inlet had a similar lance in the form of a whale with a metal blade in its mouth (UBC-

MOA A3630). It was a ceremonial harpoon that played a role in the formal exchange of wealth, in the form of a Copper, as part of the marriage transaction (see No. 62). It was used "to spear copper like a whale at marriage transfer ceremony" (Hawthorn 1967:164).

Associated Objects: The cooking tongs (No. 109) have a similar spotted, birdlike head as a handle. See No. 50 for other black and brown painted ceremonial objects.

66. Whistle, ROM 23111
Lightweight, reedless whistle.

Accessioned 1 January 1902 as NS 23111, "dance whistle." Collected from Daniel Houstee (Houstie), Bella Bella.

27.6 cm long x 3.5 cm wide x 3.3 cm thick

Two pieces of cedar bound together with flattened cedar root.

CONDITION
Not discoloured; may have been new when collected.

COMMENTS
Whistles like this one were the voices of the spirits of the Winter Ceremonies (see No. 70).

Associated Objects: No. 70, six reedless whistles; No. 66 appears to be part of the same set. No. 67, another whistle collected from Houstie. For a list of objects made by Houstie, see Appendix D.

67. Whistle, ROM 23138
A long whistle incised with a simple design showing the eye and tail of an unidentified being.

Accessioned 1 January 1902 as NS 23138, "dance whistle." Collected from Daniel Houstie, Bella Bella.

50.1 cm long x 3.8 cm wide x 1.6 cm thick

Two pieces of thin cedar lashed together with flattened cedar root.

CONDITION
Damaged. The wood has been eaten away on one side.

Associated Objects: No. 66, cedar

No. 66 (top), No. 67

whistle collected from Houstie; No. 70, six whistles, possibly collected from Houstie. For a list of objects made by Houstie, see Appendix D. Other decorated whistles in the Large Collection: Nos. 68–69.

68. Whistle, ROM 23155
(See also p. 37)
Whistle in the shape of a tapered cylinder, widest towards the top, with a small projection at top to accommodate cedar wrapping. The whistle is engraved to represent a figure with a face and raised arms on one side, and with spine, ribs, and legs on the other. The figure's mouth is the hole through which the high-pitched whistle sounds. The whistle is blown through a slit at the base. The bottom of the cylinder is bound with cedar root.

Accessioned 1 January 1902 as NS 23l55, "Indian dance whistle." Collected from Chief Robt. Bell, Bella Bella.

29 cm long x diam. 5 cm

Wood (not cedar) crudely carved, bound with cedar root or withe. Engraved lines filled with black paint.

CONDITION
Looks new.

COMMENTS
The carving is rough; northern Northwest Coast formline conventions are not followed.

Associated Objects: Nos. 66–67, 69–70; NS 28221, whistles. See No. 35 for other objects made by or collected from Bell.

69. Bellows Whistle, ROM 27867/906.2.3
A large, cylindrical whistle carved and painted to represent a face, the mouth of which is the hole through which the whistle sounds. The sound was originally produced by a bellows tied onto the bottom. The back of the whistle is painted with simple ovoids and irregular vertical lines to indicate hair. When blown, the whistle makes a deep, hollow sound.

Accessioned 6 November 1906 as NS 27867, "large dance whistle." Sold to the OPM for $5.

Wooden section, 25.5 cm long x diam. 8 cm; remains of bellows skin, 6 cm long

Carved cedar, painted black and brown, with abalone ovals inlaid in eyes. String and cedar root or withe at the "neck" hold the remains of a skin bladder or bellow (probably fish or bird skin). A crown of skin was also bound to the top of the head with string.

CONDITION
The bellows and crown have worn away; the skin that remains is very brittle.

COMMENTS
This whistle was probably associated with the Olala' dancer. According to Boas (1897:653–54), the large whistles used to imitate the cries of the Olala' spirit had a deep, hollow sound and were carved or painted with the design of the head of a corpse. Some were attached to a bellows so that they

could be carried under the arm and blown without being seen. Stylistic analysis suggests that this whistle was made by Daniel Houstie (see Appendix D).

Associated Objects: See No. 50 for other black and brown painted ceremonial objects in the Large Collection. Other whistles: Nos. 66–68, 70.

70. Whistles, ROM 28215–28220
Six reedless whistles made of two pieces of thin cedar bound together with flattened cedar root. ROM 28215–28217 and 28219 are cylindrical whistles with binding at each end. ROM 28218 has one square end and is bound together at the narrow end and at the neck of the whistle below the squared end. ROM 28220 is a small, rectangular "invisible" whistle with a single row of binding.

Purchased October 1906 and catalogued 29 April 1907 as NS 28215–28220, "dance whistle[s]."

Measurements are length x width x thickness. ROM 28215, 31.5 x 4. x

3.4 cm; ROM 28216, 34.2 x 4.2 x 3 cm; ROM 28217, 32.5 x 3.3 x 3.2 cm; ROM 28218, 27.9 x 3.4 x 2.3 cm; ROM 28219, 20.5 x 2.5 x 2.3 cm; ROM 28220, 9.6 x 4.3 x 3.1 cm

Each whistle consists of two pieces of thin cedar bound with flattened cedar root.

CONDITION
Binding is loose.

COMMENTS
These six whistles are probably a set or part of a set. There was a great variety of whistles, each dance having "its own set, distinguished by tone or decoration" (Drucker 1950:268). An identical cylindrical whistle (No. 66) was collected from Daniel Houstie and may be part of this set. The whistles were the voices of the spirits that entered the villages during the sacred winter season and were heard during the Winter Dances. "Invisible" whistles such as ROM 28220 could be concealed by the dancer and blown without being seen by the audience. In 1893, F. Jacobsen collected a flat cedar whistle (RBCM 128) with wide

ends which he associated with a Bella Bella "summer dance" (a Returned from Heaven or dhuẁláx̌a ceremony). Tubular, reedless whistles are used in the Shaman's (čaíqa), rather than the dhuẁláx̌a, ceremonies (Drucker 1940:205; McIlwraith 1948, vol.2, pl. iii; Olson 1935, 1949:34, 43).

Associated Objects: NS 28221, whistle, exchanged with the National Museum of Australia in 1907; No. 66, whistle collected from Daniel Houstie; Nos. 67–69, whistles.

FISHING GEAR: HOOKS, SINKERS, AND OTHER GEAR

71. Fish Hook, ROM 23145

A V-shaped fish hook made from a single piece of bone. The blunt end of the hook is incised on one side only with the design of a profile face (facing left), and a circle of abalone is inlaid in the eye. A bone barb is attached to the lower shaft with a wrapping of split cedar root or withe. There is a wrapping of the same material on the upper shaft for attachment of a line.

Accessioned l January 1902 as NS 23145, "old time halibut hook and sinker, made by Daniel Houstie. (Hooks are made from scapula of mountain sheep)." Collected at Bella Bella.

19.2 cm long x 12.9 cm wide at top x 1.9 cm thick

Carved, incised bone (mountain-sheep scapula?), bone barb (deer bone?), abalone inlay, split cedar root or withe.

CONDITION
Good; appears new.

COMMENTS
This hook appears to be a bone version of the one-piece northern halibut hook, such as No. 73, which was traditionally made from a forked branch of wood. It was no doubt made to illustrate old-time fishing methods rather than for use. The face carved in the arm of the hook opposite the barb represents the spirit helper from whom the fisherman would seek supernatural power to assist him in catching the large, strong halibut. Such faces are found on many wooden one-piece halibut hooks (see Stewart 1977: 46–51). Their presence illustrates the unity of Northwest Coast native technology and spirituality.

Associated Objects: The original accession data lists a sinker with this hook, but I could not find a sinker with this number in ROM Ethnology; however, there is an identical hook in the collection (No. 77). For other objects made by Daniel Houstie, see Appendix D.

Published: ROM 1976:9, "bone fish hook."

72. Iron Fish Hook, ROM 23187

U-shaped iron fish hook wound at both ends with string over cedar root.

Accessioned 1 January 1902 as NS 23187, "modern harpoon hook." Collected at Bella Bella.

15.8 cm long x 8 cm wide at top x 0.4 cm thick

Iron hook with iron barb, bound with fine string wound over cedar root.

CONDITION
Good.

COMMENTS
The use of iron may have prompted the designation "modern." Niblack (1890, pl. xxxi, fig. 152) illustrates an iron fish hook that was modelled on the wooden prototype. As early as 1792, Moziño observed: "In former days [the Nuu-chah-nulth] had only fish hooks which they made from shell; but at present these have been abandoned because of the great collection they have made of iron ones" (1972:46).

Associated Objects: See Appendix G.

73. Fish Hooks, ROM 27850–27854 (Colour photo, p. 32)

Five V-shaped, one-piece halibut hooks with bone barbs and twisted cedar line attached. (NS 27853 was not available for study.)

Accessioned 6 November 1906 as NS 27850–27854, "five halibut fish hooks." Sold to the OPM for $2.50.

Measurements are length x width at top x thickness. ROM 27850, 27.4 x 15 x 1.9 cm ; ROM 27851, 28 x 13.4 x 3 cm; ROM 27852, 28.5 x 16.5 x 2.5 cm; ROM 27854, 25.5 x 13.2 x 2 cm

Carved from a single branched piece of wood with line made of two-stranded Z-twist cedar rope. Line is tied on. Bone (deer bone?) barb is lashed on with flattened cedar root over netting string.

CONDITION
Appear to be unused.
COMMENTS
These northern-style halibut hooks are found in other collections from Bella Bella (e.g., RBCM 715–719,

made from hemlock knots) and may have been typical of the area, despite Drucker's observation (1950:168) that the Bella Bella did not use V-shaped halibut hooks. For the method of attaching ropes and barbs, see Stewart (1977:46–47). For the method of making cedar rope, see Stewart (1984:148–53). Niblack (1890:299) describes the gear necessary for halibut fishing.

Associated Objects: Nos. 71, 77, bone fish hooks. See Appendix G for a list of all fishing gear sent by Large from Bella Bella to the OPM.

Published: Rogers 1970:9.

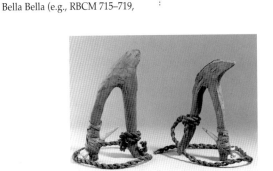

74. Fish Hook, ROM 28209
Two-part hook with upper arm carved in the shape of a halibut.

Purchased October 1906 and catalogued 29 April 1907 as NS 28209, "old time halibut hook."

33.8 cm long x 11.5 cm wide at top x 6.6 cm thick

Carved wood (cedar?), iron barb. Bound together and barb attached with root or withe.

CONDITION
Good.

COMMENTS
Two-part halibut hooks were typical of the northern Northwest Coast. For a discussion of their manufacture and use, see Stewart (1977:46–55). Drucker (1950:168) thought that this type of hook was used by the Haisla but not by the Heiltsuk.
Associated Objects: No. 73, one-piece halibut hooks; NS 28210, NS 28211, traded to the National Museum of Australia in 1907, were also catalogued as "old time hal-

ibut hook[s]" and are probably also two-part hooks.

75. Fish Hook, ROM 28212
Small U-shaped hook made of flexible wood with bark line attached. It was stored with the line wrapped around the hook to keep the ends of the hook together.

Purchased October 1906 and catalogued 29 April 1907 as NS 28212, "cod hook."

15.5 cm long x 4.8 wide at top x 1.6 cm thick. Line, 14 cm long

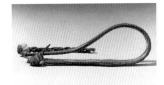

Carved and steam-bent flexible wood, hardwood hook, cedar-bark line attached to hook with string.

CONDITION
Good.

COMMENTS
This is a hook for black cod. Niblack (1890:238–39) illustrates such a hook, showing how the flexible arms are separated by a small stick when in use. When the fish takes the bait from the barb, the stick is knocked out and the hook closes on its mouth. When the hook is not in use the lashing is wound around the arms, draw-

ing the ends together to preserve the hook's tension; see also Stewart (1977:40).

Associated Objects: NS 28213, cod hook, exchanged with the National Museum of Australia in 1907. For other fishing gear in the Large collection, see Appendix G. NMAI 11/3863 is a similar bentwood hook from Bella Bella.

76. Fish Hook, ROM 28214
Square, U-shaped iron hook with length of leather attached.

Purchased October 1906 and catalogued 29 April 1907 as NS 28214, "iron hook."

13.5 cm long x 7.5 cm wide at top x 0.8 cm thick

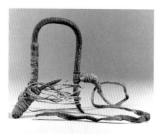

Iron, leather. The arm opposite the barb is bound with thin twine to which a long leather thong is attached and bound with thick string. The barb is bound on with heavy string. A thin string is attached behind the barb for securing the bait.

CONDITION
Good.

COMMENTS
This hook was probably for catching salmon (cf. square, U-shaped salmon gig illustrated by Niblack [1890:289]).

Associated Objects: No. 72, iron fish hook. For other fishing gear collected by Large, see Appendix G.

77. Fish Hook, ROM 956x16.1
Hook made from a natural V of bone, incised on one side with profile head (facing right) with abalone inlay in eyes.

There is no accession data for this object.

22.8 cm long x 11.6 cm wide at top x 1.7 cm thick

Incised bone (mountain sheep scapula?), abalone inlay. Bone barb (deer bone?) bound on with split cedar root or withe; opposite arm bound with cedar root or withe for attachment of line.

CONDITION
Good.

COMMENTS
See No. 71.

Associated Objects: This hook is identical to No. 71, bone fish hook made by Daniel Houstie, except that the head faces the other way. For other fishing gear collected by Large, see Appendix G.

78. Stone Sinker, Perforated, ROM 23129
A rounded, wedge-shaped stone, roughly carved on both sides to represent a creature whose fins, wide mouth, and round eyes indicate that it is a whale. A rope has been knotted through a hole in the broad end of the stone, just below the whale's eyes.

Accessioned 1 January 1902 as NS 23129, "stone halibut sinker." Collected from Old Sandy, Bella Bella.

19.5 cm long x 12 cm wide at top x 9.2 cm thick

Carved, pecked stone, rope. Stone has a pocked surface; it is white with flecks of darker colour and a

black deposit on one side. Rope is commercially made.

CONDITION
The edges of the carving have been rounded by wear or exposure.

COMMENTS
Sinkers like this one were used for weighing the wooden hooks used to catch the bottom-feeding halibut (Stewart 1977:30–31).

Associated Objects: NS 23128, stone axe, collected from Old Sandy. No. 79, halibut sinker.

Published: ROM 1976:9, "stone sinker for halibut line."

79. Sinker Stone, ROM 27923
Wedge-shaped stone carved in the shape of a whale with round eyes, wide mouth, a dorsal fin on the head, and a fin on each side. The whale's tail is tucked under its chin. Behind the whale is an uncarved cylinder, rounded at the end. On each side of the stone, approximately where the tail of the whale curves under the chin, a hole has been bored. There is also a hole in the cylindrical end of the stone on the left side only. The holes do not go all the way through the stone.

Accessioned 6 November 1906 as NS 27923, "carved stone halibut sinker." Sold to the OPM along with four stone war clubs (ROM 27922, NS 27919–27921) for $12.

19.7 cm long x 11 cm wide at top x 8 cm thick

Carved, pecked stone. Three holes bored into stone. Holes have traces of wood (cedar?) in them.

CONDITION
Worn; looks old.

COMMENTS
This sinker would have been tied to a halibut line to keep the wooden halibut hooks near the bottom where halibut feed. The shape of the sinker facilitated attachment with cedar-bark line.

Associated Objects: No. 78, pecked stone sinker, No. 119, mortar No. 122, pile driver, all of pecked stone.

80. Fish Club, ROM 23160
Club made from a piece of naturally curved hardwood, with shallow carving. The shaft is straight. The wood widens and bends at the end, forming the head of the club, which is carved to represent a bird's head with a curved beak. On the left side of the head is a raised arm and hand; on the right there are two rows of feathers at the neck.

Accessioned 1 January 1902 as NS 23160, "club, used to stun halibut with before hauling it into canoe." Collected at Bella Bella.

44.6 cm long x 11.5 cm wide x 7.2 cm thick

Carved wood.

CONDITION
Good.

COMMENTS
Drucker (1950:170) differentiates between the ball-ended halibut club and the straight salmon club. Large's identification of this club as a halibut club is probably correct. Its iconography suggests a transformation theme. Because the bird has both feathers and a human hand and arm, it may show Raven in human form.

Associated Objects: For a list of fishing gear in the Large Collection, see Appendix G.

81. Leister Spear, ROM 28200
Short, three-pronged harpoon head, triangular in shape, with handle made of a split stick. The head of the spear has two long prongs with single inward-facing barbs flanking a shorter straight point. On the handle are two flattened projecting knobs with a recessed area between them.

Purchased October 1906 and catalogued 29 April 1907 as NS 28200, "old time spear."

66.5 cm long x 13.2 cm wide at top x 8.5 cm thick

Wood, metal barbs, string, pitch. The barbs are attached to the shafts with pitch-covered string wrappings. All three prongs are joined to the short, divided handle with a heavy wrapping of pitch and string.

CONDITION
Old and worn. Appears to have been used.

COMMENTS
This is the detachable head of a long fishing spear. The split handle would have been fixed to the end of a long shaft and bound securely between the two raised knobs. According to Drucker (1950:168), the leister was used for fishing through the ice in winter. Olson (1935, 1949:8) recorded that spring salmon were speared with a two-pronged harpoon; see also Stewart (1977:74).

Associated Objects: For other fishing gear collected by Large, see Appendix G.

Published: Rogers 1970:8; ROM 1976:9, "leister (fish spear)."

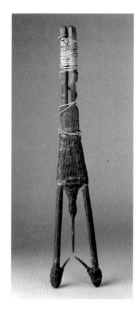

Gaming Paraphernalia: Gambling Sticks, Playing Discs

82. Four Wooden Sticks, ROM 27902–27905

Four polished sticks, each painted with a different pattern of red and black straight and diagonal stripes.

Accessioned 6 November 1906 as NS 27902–27905, "four gambling sticks, bone." Sold to the OPM for 50 cents (for four).

Each, 12.8 cm long x diam. 0.7 cm

Wood (yew?) with shiny, honey-coloured patina. Painted as follows: ROM 27902, three thin red bands with two thicker black bands between; ROM 27903, two thin black bands, one wide red band, two thin diagonal red bands with a thin black band between them; ROM 27904, one thin black band at one end, three thin red bands in the centre; ROM 27905, two thin red bands and two closely spaced thin red bands.

CONDITION
Good; part of a set of 40 to 50 sticks.

COMMENTS
The highly polished, smooth surfaces of these four wooden sticks led Large to believe that they were made of bone. They are part of a set of 40 to 50 sticks used in the gambling game of lípa, or Hat (Curtis 1915:47; Olson 1940:187). Drucker (1950:268-69) describes how the game is played.

Associated Objects: NS 27908–27909, sealbone gamblers; NS 27924–27930, 28230–28232, 28247, gambling discs; NS 27943–27965, 28225–28229, gambling stones.

83. Stone Disc, ROM 23123

A very light, porous stone disc with slightly raised sides and a hole in the centre.

Accessioned 1 January 1902 as NS 23123, "stone playing disc." Collected from Alfred Wilson, Bella Bella.

Diam. 8.5 cm; hole in centre, diam. 1.5 cm

Carved pumice stone. Traces of light ochre paint on one side.

CONDITION
Traces of paint and surface patina.

COMMENTS
A number of stone discs, some of them perforated and many made from vesicular lava, have been found in central Northwest Coast archaeological sites. Their purpose is not known, but they are thought to have been used for gaming or in ceremonies (Stewart 1973:85). A similar stone in the National Museum of Natural History (NMNH 20608) is called a "chunkee stone," probably referring to the game in which stone discs, 7.5 to 15 cm in diameter, were rolled at a series of goals formed by sticks placed about 15 cm apart. If the stone passed between the sticks the owner of the goal had to pay the other players (Olson 1935, 1949:28). In a similar game a target stone made from porous lava rock was rolled along the ground by one team while the opposing team

No. 82 (left), No. 83 (centre), No. 84

shot at it with arrows.

Associated Objects: No. 1, Haida basket, also obtained from Wilson; No. 84, NS 23122, playing discs.

84. Woven Cedar Disc, ROM 23124
A doughnut-shaped ring made of pounded cedar root in a checker-board weave.

Accessioned 1 January 1902 as NS 23124, "cedar playing disc." Collected from J. Quanootme, Bella Bella.

3.3 cm thick x diam. 9.3 cm

Woven cedar bark.

CONDITION
Good.

COMMENTS
Stewart (1984:156) illustrates a large (diam. 23 cm) cedar ring that was used in a ring-and-pin game. Drucker (1950:20) recorded that rings made of seal humerus, roots, or split sticks were used in such games but gives no specific data for the Heiltsuk region.

Associated Objects: No. 83, NS 23122, playing discs.

JEWELLERY: COPPER, SILVER

85. Bracelet, ROM 27914
Heavy tube of solid copper, slightly flattened on the sides and bent into an open oval shape.

Accessioned 6 November 1906 as NS 27914, "[one of] two copper bracelets, one of [them] native." Sold to the OPM for $8 (for both). The inventory of specimens (NS file) lists "two copper bracelets, one of them native copper."

9.8 cm long x 6.7 cm wide x 2.3 cm thick; outside circumference 24.8 cm

Hammered copper.

CONDITION
Dark patina, suggesting age.

COMMENTS
This is an old-style copper bracelet. In 1888, Niblack (1890:262) observed that native bracelets of copper (as well as bone, horn, shell, and iron) had been replaced by silver bracelets. James Swan collected a similar copper bracelet from Bella Bella in 1875 (NMNH 20625).

Associated Objects: NS 27913, copper bracelet.

86. Brooch, ROM 23116/902.2.2
(See also p. 84.)
A silver pin in the shape of two eagles with wings spread and profile heads flanking a Copper. The eagles have crest-shaped plaques on their chests. The Copper is engraved with eyes, mouth, and a T-shaped "body."

Accessioned 1 January 1902 as NS 23116, "silver brooch made by Oliver." Finding spot: Alert Bay.

5.7 cm long x 2.2 cm wide

Engraved silver. Crest-shaped plaques are gold in colour.

CONDITION
Good.

COMMENTS
The eagle is both a Northwest Coast crest and a national symbol of countries such as Russia and the United States whose citizens traded and lived on the Northwest Coast. It was not uncommon for native artists, particularly silver carvers, to incorporate non-native iconography in the eagle crests they depicted. Imagery taken from the American dollar, on which a Bald Eagle is pictured with head in profile, wings raised and outstretched, tail spread, chest covered by a plaque, and talons grasping an olive branch and a bundle of arrows, was popular on Northwest Coast silver jewellery of the nineteenth century. The maker of this pin has combined a simplified version of this

No. 86 (left), No. 88 (centre), No. 89

American symbol with a uniquely native symbol, the Copper. Although there were two silver carvers living in Bella Bella by 1907, all the silver jewellery in Large's 1901 collection is from Alert Bay, Fort Rupert, or the Fraser River.

Associated Objects: No. 87, bracelet, No. 88, brooch, both silver, made by Oliver.

87. Bracelet, ROM 23117
(Not available for photography)
Silver bracelet engraved with the image of an eagle surrounded with foliate scrolls. The depiction of the Bald Eagle, with head in profile, a crest-shaped plaque on its chest, an olive branch in one foot, and arrows in the other, derives from the national symbol of the United States (see No. 86).

Accessioned 1 January 1902 as NS 23117, "bracelet made by Oliver." Finding spot: Alert Bay.

3.8 cm high x diam. 5.7 cm; out-

side circumference 18.3 cm

Engraved silver. Crest-shaped plaque is gold in colour.

CONDITION
Good.

COMMENTS
Silver jewellery was sold to tourists who visited the coastal communities, and also through jewellers in Vancouver and Victoria. It was also commissioned and worn by First Nations people themselves. Seven hundred silver bracelets and a large quantity of rings and brooches were among the goods at a wedding feast that were "promised by the groom's brother-in-law, a worker in gold and silver" (Curtis 1915:131). Similar motifs are found on other Kwakwa̱ka̱'wakw bracelets (e.g., RBCM 5080) and on Haida bracelets (Holm 1983a:123).

Associated Objects: Nos. 86, 88, silver brooches made by Oliver. No. 92, NS 27884/906.2.2, bracelets.

88. Brooch, ROM 23118/902.2.1
(See also p. 84.)
Silver brooch in the shape of an eagle with profile head, outspread wings, and a crest-shaped plaque on its chest.

Accessioned 1 January 1902 as NS 23118, "eagle brooch made by Oliver." Finding spot: Alert Bay.

4 cm long x 2.9 cm wide

Engraved silver. Crest-shaped plaque is gold in colour.

CONDITION
Good.

COMMENTS
The iconography of this pin is based on the formalized representation of the Bald Eagle seen on the American dollar (see Nos. 86–87).

Associated Objects: No. 86, brooch, No. 87, bracelet, both silver, made by Oliver.

89. Brooch, ROM 23173/902.2.3
(See also p. 84.)
Thin silver brooch in the shape of a fish, engraved with fish design on one side only. A thin wire attached to a loop on the back fits under another loop to form the fastener.

Accessioned 1 January 1902 as NS 23173, "silver brooch (sockeye salmon)." Finding spot: Fraser River.

7.5 cm long x 2.2 cm wide

Engraved silver.

CONDITION
Good.

COMMENTS
This pin is probably a souvenir of Steveston, a large cannery complex on the Fraser River. Large was in charge of the Japanese hospital there in the summer of 1898 and visited Steveston again with his wife shortly after their marriage in Vancouver in May 1899.

Associated Objects: Silver jewellery: Nos. 86, 88 brooches, No. 87, bracelet, made by Oliver, Alert Bay; Nos. 90–91, earrings from Fort Rupert; No. 92, NS 27884, bracelets; No. 93, stick pin; NS 27885, brooch; NS 27887, earrings.

90. Pair of Earrings, ROM

23174/902.2.4 A&B

Engraved silver earrings, each a flat half-circle in the shape of an animal or fish with a large snout. A thin ear wire extends from each animal's tail to its mouth.

Accessioned 1 January 1902 as NS 23174, "silver earrings." Finding spot: Fort Rupert.

Each, 2.5 cm long x 1.9 cm wide

Engraved silver.

CONDITION
Good.

COMMENTS
This type of earring was common among the Tlingit. Niblack (1890, pl. iv, fig. 13) illustrates a similar pair (NMNH 19551), identified as Tlingit nose rings. Gunther illustrates a gold pair identified as ear

pendants worn by Gunyah, a Tlingit chief (PAM 48.3.757a–b). According to Gunther (1966:236), the animal represented is a fish.

Associated Objects: See No. 89. For a list of objects from Fort Rupert, see Appendix E.

91. Pair of Earrings, ROM

23175/902.2.5

Small engraved silver earrings, each a half-circle in the shape of an animal or fish with a large snout. A thin ear wire extends from each animal's tail to its mouth.

Accessioned 1 January 1902 as NS 23175, "silver earrings, childs." Finding spot: Fort Rupert.

Each, 2.2 cm long x 1.4 cm wide

Engraved silver.

CONDITION
Good.

COMMENTS
These earrings are smaller versions of No. 90, pair of earrings.

Associated Objects: See No. 89. For a list of objects from Fort Rupert, see Appendix E.

92. Bracelet, ROM 27883

Wide bracelet with shallow engraving. The formline design represents a large-faced animal with three potlatch rings (?) between the eyes, two wide U-forms under the mouth, claws and U-forms at the sides, and a tail motif at the back.

Accessioned 6 November 1906 as NS 27883, one of "two large silver bracelets." Sold to the OPM for $6.50 (for both).

4.7 cm high x diam. 6 cm; outside circumference 20 cm

Engraved silver.

CONDITION
Good.

COMMENTS
The design on this bracelet resembles Tschumos, a Haida crest animal. According to Large, there were two silver carvers living at Bella Bella in 1907, one of whom was Fred Anderson (he did not record the name of the other carver).

Associated Objects: See No. 89.

93. Brooch, ROM 27886

Thin brooch in the shape of a double fleur-de-lis on a twisted silver pin; spade shape in the centre.

Accessioned 6 November 1906 as NS 27886, "stick pin 'silver'." Sold to the OPM for $1.

5.7 cm long x 1.9 cm high

Engraved silver; spade shape is gold coloured.

CONDITION
Good.

COMMENTS
The design on this bracelet is copied from a European motif.

Associated Objects: Nos. 86, 88, brooches that also incorporate non-native iconography, made by Oliver, Alert Bay. See also No. 89.

PENDANTS

94. Animal Tooth, Perforated, ROM 23102

Tooth of an animal with a hole drilled in the top.

Accessioned l January 1902 as NS 23102, "bear's tooth pendant." Collected from Chas. Windsor, Bella Bella.

6.6 cm long x 2 cm wide

Bear's (?) tooth.

CONDITION
Worn, apparently old; broken at point.

COMMENTS
Pendants made from the teeth of wolf, bobcat or fox, seal, and young sea lion are illustrated in Stewart (1973:144): "The teeth of land and sea mammals were often decoratively used, and among the men of some tribes, they were worn as ear and nose pendants."

Associated Objects: NS 23103, small stone axe, NS 23105, playing disc, collected from Windsor. Other perforated ornaments collected by Large: No. 95, abalone shell pendant, No. 96, three small Coppers, No. 97, slate crow's head.

95. Shell Rectangle, Perforated, ROM 23120

A small rectangular piece of abalone with a hole in either end.

Accessioned 1 January 1902 as NS 23120, "shell pendant (abalone)." Collected from Bob Lawson, Bella Bella.

2.4 cm long x 3.1 cm wide x 0.2 cm thick

Abalone.

CONDITION
Good.

COMMENTS
Pierced abalone rectangles were used as ear pendants. Charles Nowell, a Kwakwaka'wakw chief, recalled hearing about how ear pendants were worn (see also Niblack [1890, p. vii, fig. 21]):

Before my time, I am told, they used to pierce the nose and wear a shell ring in it. I never saw anybody with these rings in their noses, but I have seen my mother's brother had three holes on the ear and three earrings made out of abalone shells. The lowest

was the biggest . . . . Some women were the same, and when they die, they take off the small ones and put a big abalone shell about four inches square in the ear when they are buried. These abalone shells is like gold to the Indians. A big shell about three or four inches across used to be like ten dollars. [Ford 1941:46]

Square pieces of abalone were also sewn onto blankets (Boas 1932:73). The more valuable shells were from southern waters (in 1840, George Hunt's grandfather sailed to Hawaii and brought back abalone shells to sell [Curtis 1915:6]). This pendant was cut from the smaller, less luminous, northern abalone.

Associated Objects: Other perforated ornaments collected by Large: No. 94, animal-tooth pendant, No. 96, three small Coppers, No. 97, slate crow's head.

96. Three Miniature Coppers, ROM 27894–27896

Small Coppers with rounded, convex tops and raised, T-shaped ridges.

Accessioned 6 November 1906 as NS 27894–27696, "three small coppers." Sold to the OPM for $1.50 (for the three).

Measurements are length x width at top. ROM 27894, 9.5 x 6.5 cm;

ROM 27895, 7.3 x 5.9 cm; ROM
27896, 7.7 x 5.9 cm

Cut and shaped sheet copper.
ROM 27894 is not pierced; ROM
27895 has a small hole at the centre top; ROM 27896 has a small
hole at the centre bottom.

CONDITION
Good.

COMMENTS
Miniature Coppers, which had
symbolic as well as real monetary
value, were worn on button blankets and hats and as ear ornaments. Among the Nuxalk, according to McIlwraith (1948, 1:457), "a
person mourning a consort must
wear a hat decorated with miniature coppers of which the bottoms
are bent upwards. Should this be
omitted, when the offender remar-
ries, the new husband or wife will
soon die." And according to Boas
(1906:243), hundreds of "small imitations of copper plates" were, like
sticks of bracelets and box covers,
given as part of a dowry; although
they had "only symbolic value"
they could be "used as coin in
exchange for . . . objects of value."

Associated Objects: For other perforated ornaments, see No. 95.

97. Slate Bird's Head, ROM 28233
Small piece of black slate carved
in the shape of a bird's head, with
two holes drilled at either side of
the flat end.

Purchased October 1906 and catalogued 29 April 1907 as NS 28233,
"slate crow ornament."

5.7 cm high x 2.9 cm wide x 0.6 cm
thick

Argillite or black slate.

CONDITION
Good.

COMMENTS
Large described this as a crow, but
it may represent Raven. It was
probably worn as a charm (cf.
NMAI 11/3885, a small ivory
charm in the shape of Raven's
head, collected at Bella Bella).

Associated Objects: For other perforated ornaments, see No. 95.

SPOONS: HORN,
WOOD

98. Spoon, ROM 23109
Horn spoon, bowl inlaid with two
small rectangles of abalone. The
handle is carved with four small
figures, the lower two perhaps
depicting a whale and rider whose
feet straddle the bowl of the
spoon. The back of the bowl is
incised with a formline design.

Accessioned 1 January 1902 as NS
23109, "Chief's horn spoon."
Collected from Herbert Humchil
(Humchit), Bella Bella (Bertie
Humchitt, 1881–1974?).

26.3 cm long; width of bowl, 7 cm

Carved and steam-bent mountain-
goat horn with abalone inlay.
Handle and bowl pegged together.

CONDITION
Back of bowl is worn. Right foot of
lower figure is broken off.

COMMENTS
The bowls of mountain-goat-horn
spoons were formed by splitting
the horn at the base, steaming it to

make it pliable, rolling it out flat, and then shaping it in a two-part carved wooden mould. Spoon handles were carved from another horn, with the natural curve of the horn incorporated into the design (see Niblack [1890:318] and Gunther [1966:24] for discussions of the process).

Associated Objects: Nos. 99–100, chiefs' spoons.

99. Spoon, ROM 23110
Horn spoon with abalone inlay in the handle. The handle is carved in the shape of an animal, which holds the bowl in its mouth. The animal is surmounted by a small crouching figure. Where handle and bowl join, the back of the bowl is incised with a formline design.

Accessioned 1 January 1902 as NS 23110, "Chief's horn spoon." Collected from Bob Lawson, Bella Bella.

28.1 cm long; width of bowl, 6.6 cm

Carved and steam-bent mountain-goat horn with abalone inlay. Handle and bowl are pegged together.

CONDITION
Piece of abalone is missing.

COMMENTS
The small crouching figure may represent an insect. It has a long tongue, which extends between the palms of its upraised hands, and it appears to have two pairs of legs (below the figure's raised palms, the soles of its feet are visible, and at each side of the spoon is a bent leg in profile). See No. 98 for a discussion of how horn spoons were made.

Associated Objects: Nos. 98, 100, chiefs' spoons.

100. Spoon, ROM 23176
Spoon with a plain, dark bowl and an ivory-coloured handle, simply carved to represent an upside-down creature, probably a land otter. The round head of the creature has two eyes. Just above its neck is the square peg that joins the two parts of the spoon. Its curved body is decorated with a chevron pattern that represents the creature's backbone. The handle tapers to a plain point.

Accessioned 1 January 1902 as NS 23176, "Chief's spoon, very old." Collected from Chief Nooneyuas (Núṅukvas), Bella Bella.

24.9 cm long; width of bowl, 6.1 cm

Carved and steam-bent mountain-sheep-horn bowl with carved bone or antler handle, pegged together with a horn peg.

CONDITION
Worn; warm patina suggests age. Bowl is chipped.

COMMENTS
Gunther (1966, cat. nos. 384, 402) illustrates two similar spoons, both collected from the Tsimshian. They have handles made from caribou antler carved to represent a land otter (a powerful spirit helper), with simple carving of head and backbone. Their documentation suggests that they belonged to a medicine man or shaman. Núṅukvas may have been a medicine man, for, according to Large, he treated Old Dick's swollen hand by cutting off the first joint of one of Dick's fingers, thereupon producing a piece of copper that was thought to have caused the swelling (*MB* 5, no. 4[1909]:699). Like mountain-goat horn, mountain-sheep horn was

fashioned into spoons by steaming and shaping in a wooden mould (Niblack 1890: 318).

Associated Objects: Nos. 98–99, chiefs' spoons.

101. Spoon, ROM 27890
Small, plain horn spoon with notched handle.

Accessioned 6 November 1906 as NS 27890, "[one of] six assorted horn spoons." Sold to the OPM for $5 (for six spoons).

16.5 cm long; width of bowl, 5.9 cm

Carved and steam-bent mountain-goat horn.

CONDITION
Good; horn is dry and dark; looks old.

COMMENTS
This is a common type of spoon.

Associated Objects: Nos. 98–103, NS 27888–27889, NS 27892, horn spoons.

102. Spoon, ROM 27891
Small spoon with short handle carved in the shape of a being with its arms raised under its chin. The bowl is engraved with two vertical bands of parallel hatching.

Accessioned 6 November 1906 as NS 27891, "[one of] six assorted horn spoons." Sold to the OPM for $5 (for six spoons).

16 cm long; width of bowl, 5 cm

Carved and steam-bent mountain-goat horn.

CONDITION
Good.

COMMENTS
The design of this spoon is typical of the central Northwest Coast.

Associated Objects: See No. 101.

103. Spoon, ROM 27893
Small undecorated spoon with short handle.

Accessioned 6 November 1906 as NS 27893, "[one of] six assorted horn spoons." Sold to the OPM for $5 (for six spoons).

14.1 cm long; width of bowl, 4.5 cm

Carved and steam-bent mountain-goat horn.

CONDITION
Good.

COMMENTS
This is a common type of spoon.

Associated Objects: See No. 101.

104. Spoon, ROM 23177
Wooden spoon painted with a crude formline design representing the head of an animal, probably a bird.

Accessioned 1 January 1902 as NS 23177, "common wooden spoon." Collected at Bella Bella.

26.5 cm long; width of bowl, 6.5 cm

Carved hardwood painted with black and brown (or perhaps faded red) design.

CONDITION
The paint is faded, but the spoon does not appear to have been used.

COMMENTS
This type of painted spoon was a common Bella Bella product made for the curio and tourist trades. Another spoon of the same type from Bella Bella (CMC VII-EE-39) is inscribed on the back: "Mulligan spoon Bella Bella Indians Expression of Eternal friendship." According to Holm (1983a:81), painted wooden spoons like these were made for sale as early as the mid-nineteenth century. The following stylistic characteristics of this particular spoon support an attribution to Captain Carpenter: swelling formlines, Z-hatching, long eye with open end, long ovoid pupil, eyelid line curving above pupil but relatively straight below.

Associated Objects: Nos. 98–103, NS 27888, NS 27892, spoons. Similar spoons in other collections: UBC-MOA A1656 collected by Reverend Raley at Kitamaat; NMAI 1/8037 collected by Reverend Crosby from Bella Bella in 1908; CMC VII-EE-39 collected at Bella Bella; RBCM 946 collected by C. F. Newcombe from Bella Bella.

105. Spoon, ROM 27857
Spoon with a large bowl and a slightly tapered rectangular handle. The handle has bevelled sides and a rounded back and is incised with a geometric pattern as follows: a row of X-pattern, a row of back-slanting hatching (\ \ \), a row of forward-slanting hatching (/ / /), and a row of cross-hatching.

Accessioned 6 November 1906 as NS 27857, "big spoon 'plain'." Sold to the OPM for 75 cents.

30.2 cm long; width of bowl, 11.2 cm

Carved and incised hardwood.

CONDITION
Wood is worn and has a dark, greasy patina.

COMMENTS
This is an old spoon.

Associated Objects: See No. 104.

106. Bark Beater, ROM 23108

Ridged beater of the type used to pound yellow cedar bark. The handle curves downward slightly; the top extends beyond the hammer in two earlike projections.

Accessioned l January 1902 as NS 23108, "whalebone hammer for beating cedar mats." Collected at Bella Bella.

27.5 cm long x 4.5 cm wide x 3.3 cm thick

Carved from a single piece of whalebone.

CONDITION
Appears to be old and weathered. Bone is dry and blackened. "Ears" and end of handle have crumbled away.

COMMENTS
Boas (1909:368–69) describes the method of preparing yellow cedar bark: the bark of yellow cedar was taken from the trees when the sap began to run, was dried in the sun for six to eight days, and was then soaked in sea water for twelve days. The treated bark was then laid on a flat stone, pounded with a beater to separate it into fibres, and left to dry for four days. It was folded and stored for future use. Stewart (1984:125–26) comments: "Because of the amount of

oil in fresh whalebone, a beater of this material gave the tool the necessary weight, and probably imparted some of the oil to the bark also." The grooves in the hammer prevented the beater from sticking to the bark.

Associated Objects: Nos. 108, 114, 116, bark beaters.

107. Shell, ROM 23112

Half of a mussel shell, used as a knife.

Accessioned 1 January 1902 as NS 23112, "mussel shell used as a knife in early days." Collected at Bella Bella.

21 cm long x 8 cm wide x 3.8 cm thick

Mussel shell, apparently unaltered.

CONDITION
Cracked.

COMMENTS
This shell does not appear to have been sharpened or modified and may not have been used as a knife. According to Drucker (1950:170), mussel-shell knives were used by all central

Northwest Coast groups except the Haisla for scaling and splitting fish and for scraping hemlock bast, cedar bark, and spruce roots. Larger sharpened mussel shells were used to engrave wood (Boas 1909:405; Curtis 1915:15–16, 26, 39). One text (Boas 1928:157) refers to the skinning of a bear with a mussel-shell knife.

Associated Objects: None.

108. Bark Beater, ROM 23159

Ridged beater of the type used to pound yellow cedar bark. The handle curves slightly upward and extends beyond the hammer in two earlike projections. The hammer, which flares out at the bottom, is pierced by a long, rectangular hole. The top is decorated with a circle-and-dot design.

Accessioned 1 January 1902 as NS 23159, "whalebone mat beater—used in early days to pound the cedar bark."

33 cm long x 4.8 cm wide x 4.2 cm thick

Carved from a single piece of whalebone. Engraved design.

CONDITION
Appears well used, smooth, shiny

patina. The underside of the hammer is dark and worn.

COMMENTS
See Comments for No. 106.

Associated Objects: Nos. 106, 114, 116, bark beaters.

Published: ROM 1976:7, "bark beater."

109. Tongs, ROM 27849
Wooden tongs with handle carved and painted to represent the head of a bird. Feather motifs are painted on the shaft.

Accessioned 6 November 1906 as NS 27849, "tongs for hot stones for cooking." Sold to the OPM with cedar cooking box (No. 37) for $3.

69.8 cm long x 3.7 cm wide x 3 cm thick

Made from a single piece of cedar, carved, and split below the handle but not reinforced. Design painted in black and brown. Abalone discs inlaid in eyes.

CONDITION
New and unused.

COMMENTS
These tongs are not functional and, like the associated cooking box (No. 37), must have been made to illustrate the "old time" cooking method of the Heiltsuk; see Stewart (1984:84) for a description of the process. They were probably made by Daniel Houstie (see Appendix D).

Associated Objects: See No. 37.

110. Scraper, ROM 27861
A knifelike bone implement with a rounded point.

Accessioned 6 November 1906 as NS 27861, "bone implement for removing bark from Hemlock." Sold to the OPM for $1.

29.5 cm long x 3.2 cm wide x 1.9 cm thick

Carved bone, probably whalebone.

CONDITION
Bone is dry and old. There is a notch about one quarter of the way down from the handle (i.e., the widest end) and the tip has crumbled away.

COMMENTS
Curtis (1915:39–40) describes how this implement was probably used: "A piece of whale-rib with sharpened end" was used to score and remove the bark of the hemlock. The bast (inner bark) was scraped from the outer bark with a mussel-shell knife. It was steamed, kneaded, made into loaves, and dried, to be eaten with oolichan oil throughout the winter. The bark was traditionally processed in mid-June at Rivers Inlet. Niblack (1890, pl. xx, fig. 79a) illustrates a scraper "for removing the inner integument or bark from trunk of pine tree for food."

Associated Objects: Possibly NS 27906 and NS 28248, which were accessioned as "bone chisels."

111. Maul Handle, ROM 27863
A handle of a hafted stone maul, made from a branching stick. It is roughly T-shaped, with a long shaft meeting the hammerlike end at an angle. The bulbous ends and the grooves in the cross-piece facilitated the secure attachment of a carved stone hammer (now missing) against the handle's flat top.

Accessioned 6 November 1906 as NS 27863, "maul handle." Sold to the OPM for 25 cents. Entered on the price list (NS file) as a "war club handle."

22 cm long x 14.8 cm wide x 6.7 cm thick

Carved wood.

CONDITION
No stone or bindings attached.

COMMENTS
A stone hammer would have been lashed to this handle with cedar root or withe. Stewart (1984:30) describes this kind of tool:

While the southern peoples used the hand maul (held directly in the hand), the northern nations, Tsimshian, Haida, and Tlingit, devised a heavy-

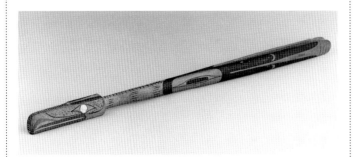

duty implement—the hafted maul, which was a heavy stone head lashed onto a long haft. Using a hafted maul, a man could deliver a blow with great force, much like a sledge hammer.

Associated Objects: No. 125, hafted maul; Nos. 118, 124, maul stones; possibly NS 27919–27920, and NS 27922, which were accessioned as "stone war clubs."

112. Bone Disc, ROM 27899
Disc with a small circular depression in the centre.

Accessioned 6 November 1906 as NS 27899, "[one of] two bone discs." Sold to the OPM for $2 (for the two).

1 cm thick x diam. 5.5 cm

Carved bone.

CONDITION
Good.

COMMENTS
Unlike No. 113, this disc is not pierced; its function is not known. It is included here because it was accessioned with No. 113 as one of

"two bone discs." Except that there is a shallow depression rather than a hole in this disc, it has the same form as No. 113. Since No. 113 is probably a spindle whorl, I suspect that this disc is an unfinished whorl.

Associated Objects: No. 113, pierced bone disc.

113. Bone Disc, ROM 27900
(Not available for photography)
Disc with a hole in the centre.

Accessioned 6 November 1906 as NS 27900, "[one of] two bone discs." Sold to the OPM for $2 (for the pair).

0.4 cm thick x diam. 5.7 cm

Carved bone.

CONDITION
Good.

COMMENTS
This artifact may be a spindle whorl. Larger spindle whorls (approximately 10 to 13 cm in diameter) were used to spin yellow cedar bark and goat wool for blankets (Drucker 1950:194–95, 262). Smaller spindle whorls were used to spin nettle fibre and light yarns (Stewart 1973:124). Boas (1909:373) describes the spinning of nettle fibre into thread for nets by means of a maple spindle and a small whalebone whorl, which was polished and rubbed with deer tallow. The whorls were 7 to

8 cm in diameter; the size depended on the type of thread being made.

Associated Objects: No. 112, bone disc.

114. Bark Beater, ROM 27907
Ridged beater of the type used to pound yellow cedar bark. The ends of the handle and the top are rounded and overhang the hammer.

Accessioned 6 November 1906 as NS 27907, "whalebone cedar bark beater." Sold to the OPM for $1.

19.4 cm long x 4 cm wide x 3 cm thick

Carved from a single piece of whalebone.

CONDITION
Looks old, bone is dry and worn.

COMMENTS
See Comments for No. 106.

Associated Objects: Nos. 106, 108, 116, bone bark beaters.

115. Drill, ROM 28224
A short, thin metal point set in a lightweight cedar shaft. Both point and shaft are cylindrical.

Purchased October 1906 and catalogued 29 April 1907 as NS 28224, "canoe awl."

Length of shaft, 22.8 cm; length of metal point, 2.9 cm

Carved cedar, metal.

CONDITION
Good.

COMMENTS
A note appended to the NS catalogue entry by "B. T." in 1964 suggests that this item might be a "drill of bow drill," and it was probably used, as the original accession note suggests, to drill very small holes into the sides of a canoe under construction. Holes were drilled into the outside of a canoe after it was shaped. The canoe was then turned over and the wood on the inside was carved away until the holes made by the drill were visible (Boas 1909:321; Stewart 1984:55).

Associated Objects: For other woodworking tools, see Appendix G.

116. Bark Beater, ROM 28246
Ridged beater of the type used to pound yellow cedar bark. The handle widens slightly at the end; the top extends beyond the ham-

mer in two earlike projections. There is an oval hole through the side of the hammer.

Purchased October 1906 and catalogued 29 April 1907 as NS 28246, "mat beater (bone of whale)."

23.1 cm long x 3.6 cm wide x 4 cm thick

Carved whalebone.

CONDITION
Looks old; appears to have been used; bone has smooth patina.

COMMENTS
See Comments for No. 106.

Associated Objects: Nos. 106, 108, 114.

117. Stick, ROM 28307
An implement with a wide, flat top (or base) and a long curved shaft, made from a naturally T-shaped piece of wood.

Purchased October 1906 and catalogued in 1907 as NS 28307, implement "for drying nets, etc."

95 cm long x 38 cm wide at top x 7.5 cm thick at top

Carved wood.

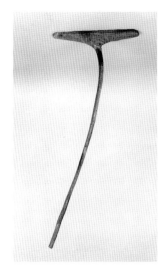

CONDITION
Blackened areas. Flat surface has honey-coloured patina.

COMMENTS
Large's description of this stick as an implement for drying nets is probably correct, but I was unable to discover how it may have been used. It was entered in the NS catalogue some time after the other objects in the 1906 collection and may originally have been NS 23107.

Associated Objects: None.

118. Maul, ROM 23133
A shaped hammer or maul, made from heavy grey-brown stone. The back of the maul is flat and there are wide grooves in the stone to allow for the attachment of a long wooden handle, now missing.

Accessioned 1 January 1902 as NS 23133, "stone hammer (Hous-'te)."

Collected from Fireman, Bella Bella. 16 cm long x 9.8 cm wide x 11 cm thick at bottom

Carved, pecked stone.

CONDITION
Worn and chipped.

COMMENTS
From the accession data it would appear that Large heard the Heiltsuk name for stone maul and transliterated it as " Hous-'te."

Associated Objects: No. 124, maul; No. 111, maul handle; No. 125, NS 23131, NS 23132, hammers.

119. Mortar, ROM 23172
A mortar in the shape of a frog with a shallow depression in its back. The frog has a large head, round raised eyes, a wide mouth, and small limbs carved in relief at the sides and back.

Accessioned 1 January 1902 as NS 23172, "mortar, representing a frog." Collected at Bella Bella.

8.5 cm high x 15 cm long x 14 cm wide

Carved, pecked brownish stone.

CONDITION
Scraped along the bottom of the stone. Black and brown patina. Material makes it hard to judge the age of this artifact.

COMMENTS
Mortars of this type were used on the Northwest Coast from prehistoric times. This one was probably used to grind tobacco; in early times, native tobacco was chewed rather than smoked (Niblack 1890, pl. lxiii, figs. 337–39). The frog was a common motif for such mortars (Duff 1975:186–88). A frog bowl made from vesicular basalt excavated at Kwatna (a site on Kwatna Inlet, Burke Channel) has been dated to 1500–1850 (Carlson 1976a:129).

Associated Objects: This is the only stone mortar in the Large Collection.

120. Chisel, ROM 23186
Green stone chisel with a tapered handle of light wood. The stone is a tapered wedge with a flattened edge.

Accessioned 1 January 1902 as NS 23186, "stone axe (Klah-qua-bah-la)." Collected at Bella Bella.

No. 121 (left), No. 120

35.1 cm long x 4 cm wide at top of blade x 3 cm thick at binding

Carved green stone bound to a thin cedar handle with split cedar root or withe. In a 1974 notation in the NS catalogue list, Fred Wick of the ROM Department of Mineralogy identified the stone as "a dirty quartz."

CONDITION
No signs of wear.

COMMENTS
Large's documentation implies that the Heiltsuk word for stone axe is Klah-qua-bah-la. In Heiltsuk, qéncabálá means adze (Rath 1981). Boas (1909:319–20) illustrates a similar tool.

Associated Objects: No. 121, chisel.

Published: Rogers 1970:11.

121. Chisel, ROM 27859
Small, sharpened wedge of green stone bound to a long, thin handle. The handle, a stick of wood with the bark left on it, is wrapped at the end with a grommet of twisted cedar root or withe.

Accessioned 6 November 1906 as NS 27859, "[one of] two stone axes, with handles, as used in getting cedar boards from tree." Sold to the OPM for $1 (for the two).

Handle, 34.3 cm long x diam. 4.2 cm; blade, 2.3 cm long x 2.3 cm wide x 0.6 cm thick

Jadeite, wooden stick with dark red bark covered with white spots, leather, cedar root or withe. The chisel head is set into the handle and lashed to it with leather.

CONDITION
Good.

COMMENTS
Used in conjunction with a stone hand maul, a chisel such as this removed chips of wood and roughly shaped the surface of a plank or a carving. The twisted cedar root or withe grommet at its end prevented the wood from splitting when hit with the maul (Boas 1909:380; Curtis 1915:15; Niblack 1890:282; Stewart 1984:34–35).

Associated Objects: No. 120, chisel. NMNH 20604 is a similar implement.

122. Pile Driver, ROM 27915
Carved stone with flat bottom and rounded top. There are two long oval depressions in the bottom and two deep ridges in the sides of the stone. The stone is roughly oval in shape, with flat sides and carved, rounded ends. A face with large round eyes, a round nose, and a wide mouth has been pecked into one end.

Accessioned 6 November 1906 as NS 27915, "[one of] four carved stone hammers, 'flat', for driving stakes in river." Sold to the OPM for $12 (for the four).

32 cm long x 19 cm wide x 9 cm thick

Carved, pecked stone.

CONDITION
Brown patina on top.

COMMENTS
This is a pile driver for pounding stakes for fishing weirs into a river bed, carved to represent a whale or frog. The stone was held with the fingers in the depressions on the bottom and the thumbs in the ridges in the top. The flattened end was held towards the body; the rounded end pointed away from the user. Boas (1909:318) identified this type of pile driver as Bella Coola (Nuxalk), and it may be typical of the Bella Coola/Bella Bella area, where weir fishing was a major industry.

Associated Objects: No. 123, NS 27916, NS 27918, pile drivers.

123. Pile Driver, ROM 27917
Carved rectangular stone with flat bottom and rounded top. There are two deep oval depressions in the bottom, and two long, slanting ridges in the sides of the top. The edges are rounded. One end is almost straight.

Accessioned 6 November 1906 as NS 27917, "[one of] four carved stone hammers, 'flat,' for driving

stakes in river." Sold to the OPM for $12 (for the four).

32.5 cm long x 22.4 cm wide x 8.5 cm thick

Carved, pecked stone.

CONDITION
Dark patina. Traces of brown ochre colour in pits on the bottom (flat) side.

COMMENTS
See No. 122.

Associated Objects: No. 122, NS 27916, NS 27918, pile drivers.

124. Maul, ROM 27921
Carved stone hammer with one flat side and a deep groove in the centre. The hammer end is blunt, the other end rounded.

Accessioned 6 November 1906 as NS 27921, "[one of] four stone war clubs, one on handle." Sold to the OPM along with halibut sinker (No. 79) for $12.

12.4 cm long x 7.5 cm wide x 8 cm thick

Carved, pecked stone, possibly brown granite.

CONDITION
Large chip in square (hammer) end.

COMMENTS
The flat side would have been tied against a wooden haft with cedar withes, which would be held in the groove. See also Stewart (1984:30) quoted in catalogue entry for No. 111.

Associated Objects: See No. 111.

125. Hafted Maul, ROM 28206
Stone maul with long, curved wooden haft made from naturally T-shaped stick.

Purchased October 1906 and catalogued 29 April 1907 as NS 28206, "stone hammer."

Maul stone, 11.3 cm high x 12.8 cm wide x 9 cm thick; handle, 67.4 cm long x diam. 3 cm; top of handle, 11.8 cm long x 5.7 cm wide

Stone, wood, string. The flat side of the maul is tied to the haft with string. The string passes over a groove in the stone and around

both arms of the T, which swell slightly at the ends to keep the string from slipping off.

CONDITION
Wooden handle appears charred.

COMMENTS
An undated notation in the NS catalogue reads: "Haft probably authentic (Leechman)." The string is not original; the hammer and handle would have been joined with root, withe, or rawhide binding (see ROM HN.130 for authentic binding). Boas (1909:314) indicated that this type of hafted stone sledge hammer is apparently typical of the Bella Bella region:

The Kwakiutl claim that grooved and perforated stone hammers with long handles (dexuma'no) like those of the Bella Bella and other northern tribes, were not made. It is said about 1840 a hammer of this type was intraded through the intermarriage of a Kwakiutl and a Bella Bella.

Associated Objects: Collected by Large: No. 118, NS 23101, NS 23106, NS 23131–23132, NS

23179–23181, stone hammers; No. 124, NS 27919–27920, NS 27922, NS 23178, stone war clubs; No. 111, maul handle. Similar stone mauls from Bella Bella: NMNH 20596, UBCMOA A1104.

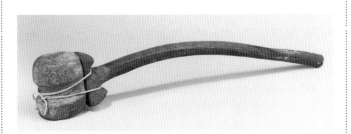

Miscellaneous

126. Canoe Bailer, ROM 23158
A traditional Kwakwaka'wakw bailer made from a single sheet of bark, the ends bent up, pleated together, and lashed to a straight transverse handle, notched where the bark is wrapped around it.

Accessioned 1 January 1902 as NS 23158, "cedar bark canoe baler [bailer]." Finding spot: Fort Rupert.

17 cm high x 35 cm long x 23 cm wide

Cedar bark with cedar handle, bound together with cedar root or withe.

CONDITION
Looks new.

COMMENTS
A note written in the NS catalogue list in 1975 reads: "totally unsuitable shape for canoe bailer—also leaks"; this is, however, the typical canoe bailer of the southern Northwest Coast. Boas (1909:447) and Stewart (1984:120, 164) describe and illustrate identical bailers made by the Kwakwaka'wakw and Coast

Salish, respectively. Drucker (1950:182) says that the Bella Bella, Nuxalk, and Haisla did not use this kind of bailer, but that the Oweekeno and ˇXíx̌ís did. The more northerly tribes used a wooden bailer shaped like a scoop. A bailer of the northern type, NMNH 20629, was collected at Bella Bella.

Associated Objects: For a list of objects from Fort Rupert see Appendix E. FMNH 19179 is a similar Kwakwaka'wakw bailer.

127. Tooth, Perforated, ROM 23165
A hollow animal's tooth with a small hole in the side.

Accessioned 1 January 1902 as NS 23165, "bear tooth tobacco pipe." Collected at Bella Bella.

6 cm high x 2 cm wide x 2.5 cm thick

Tooth, possibly bear's, perforated.

CONDITION
Probably old; blackened inside; appears to have been used. Chipped at end.

COMMENTS
This tooth was used to smoke tobacco, although Drucker (1950:203) asserted that tobacco was not smoked by the Heiltsuk. Tobacco was available through trade from the time of earliest contact with Russians and Europeans, and a native form of tobacco for chewing was grown on the Queen Charlotte Islands (Niblack 1890, pl. lxiii, figs. 337–39).

Associated Objects: This is the only pipe from the Northwest Coast in the Large Collection. (A "small pipe" was received, apparently from Large, in 1904 and entered into the OPM catalogue as NS 28249 on 29 April 1907. It was labelled as coming from "Bexley Tp." and "Innisfil Tp.," both in Ontario, and is therefore not included in this study.)

128. Painted Shell, ROM 27872
Clam shell with a loosely painted formline design of an animal. The back of the creature follows the

perimeter of the shell and a clawed forelimb curves inward from the juncture of the body and head ovoids. At the end of the U-form tail a flipper is indicated by an ovoid and a U-shape. A small hooked shape hangs below the creature's mouth.

Accessioned 6 November 1906 as NS 27872, "painted clam shell." Sold to the OPM for 50 cents.

4.5 cm high x 17 cm long x 13.9 cm wide

Clam shell with green and red painted design on the inside.

CONDITION
Good.

COMMENTS
This is probably a trinket, made for sale. The meaning of the design is not clear, but similar energetic, freehand drawing is found on many Bella Bella pieces in museum collections (e.g., paddle AMNH 16/697 and bowl UBCMOA A403).

Associated Objects: None.

REFERENCES

Abbreviations used in the references are listed on p. viii. Both published and unpublished references are included here. Unpublished material is not grouped by depository, but it should be noted that information concerning Methodist missions on the Northwest Coast was found in the United Church of Canada archives in Toronto and Vancouver, and in the Heiltsuk Cultural Education Centre, Waglisla. The importance of the HCEC as a resource for all aspects of this study is reflected in this list.

AMNH
    1900   Correspondence file, 1900. AMNH.

Barbeau, Marius
    1950   *Totem Poles.* 2 vols. Bulletin No. 119, Anthropological Series No. 30. Ottawa: NMC.
    1953   *Haida Myths Illustrated in Argillite Carvings.* Bulletin No. 127, Anthropological Series No. 32. Ottawa: NMC.

Barner, Arthur
    n.d.   "Bella Bella Mission Manuscript Journal." Manuscript. United Church of Canada, B.C. Conference Archives, Vancouver. Copy on file at HCEC.

Barraclough, W. H.
    1902   "Home Mission Problems—Salaries." *Western Methodist Recorder* 4(10):5–6.

Beavis, R. B.
    n.d.   Manuscript. United Church of Canada, B.C. Conference Archives, Vancouver. Copy on file at HCEC.

Black, Martha
    1988   "The R. W. Large Collection: A Bella Bella Document." Master's thesis, York University, Toronto.
    1989   "Looking for Bella Bella: The R. W. Large Collection and Heiltsuk Art History." *The Canadian Journal of Native Studies* 9(2):273–92.
    1992   Black, Martha. "Displays and Captures: Some Historic Photographs from the Northwest Coast." *American Indian Art Magazine* 18(1):68–75.

Boas, Franz
    1897   "The Social Organization and the Secret Societies of the Kwakiutl Indians." *Report of the United States National Museum, 1895,* pp. 311–738. Washington, D.C.: Smithsonian Institution Press.
    1906   "Tribes of the North Pacific Coast." *Annual Archaeological Report Ontario, 1905,* pp. 235–49.
    1909   *The Kwakiutl of Vancouver Island.* American Museum of Natural History Memoir 8. New York: AMNH.
    1916   *Tsimshian Mythology.* Thirty-First Annual Report of the Bureau of American Ethnology, 1909–10. Washington, D.C.: Smithsonian Institution Press.
    1923   *Bella Bella Notes.* American Philosophical Society Microfilms 372, roll 1, PABC, reel A-236.
    1924   "The Social Organization of the Tribes of the North Pacific Coast." *American Anthropologist* 26:323–32. Reprinted *in* Franz Boas, *Race, Language and Culture,* pp. 370–78. New York: The Free Press, 1940.
    1928   *Bella Bella Texts.* Columbia University Contributions to Anthropology 5. Reprint. New York: AMS Press, 1969.
    1930   *The Religion of the Kwakiutl Indians.* Columbia University Contributions to Anthropology 10. Reprint. New York: AMS Press, 1969.
    1932   *Bella Bella Tales.* Memoirs of the American Folk-Lore Society 25. New York: American Folk-Lore Society.
    1969   *The Ethnography of Franz Boas: Letters and Diaries Written on the Northwest Coast from 1886 to 1931,* ed. Ronald P. Rohner. Translated by Hedy Parker. Chicago: The University of Chicago Press.
    1974   *The Shaping of American Anthropology 1883–1911: A Franz Boas Reader,* ed. George W. Stocking, Jr. New York: Basic Books.

Borden, Charles E.
    1979   *Origins and Development of Early Northwest Coast Culture to About 3000 B.C.* Archaeological Survey of Canada. National Museum of Man Mercury Series. Ottawa: NMC.

Brown, Pam
    n.d.   "Reasons for the Lack of Discourse about the Society and Art of Heiltsuk People." Typescript. Private collection (M. Black).

Canada Census
    1881   Dominion of Canada Census, 1881. On file at HCEC.

Carlson, Roy L.
    1976a   "Prehistoric Art of the Central Coast of British Columbia." *In* Roy L. Carlson, ed., *Indian Art Traditions of the Northwest Coast,* pp. 122–29. Burnaby: Archaeology Press, Simon Fraser University.
    1976b   "Prehistory of the Northwest Coast." *In* Roy L. Carlson, ed., *Indian Art Traditions of the Northwest Coast,* pp. 13–32. Burnaby: Archaeology Press, Simon Fraser University.

Carpenter, Jennifer
    1984   "Origin of the Word 'Bella Bella': Research Report to Heiltsuk Band Council." Typescript. On file at HCEC.

Coe, Ralph T.
    1976   *Sacred Circles: Two Thousand Years of North American Indian Art.* Exhibition catalogue. London: Arts Council of Great Britain.

Cole, Douglas
    1985   *Captured Heritage: The Scramble for Northwest Coast Artifacts.* Vancouver: Douglas and McIntyre.

Cole, Douglas, and Ira Chaikin
1990   *An Iron Hand Upon the People: The Law Against the Potlatch on the Northwest Coast.* Vancouver/Seattle: Douglas and McIntyre/University of Washington Press.

Crosby, Thomas
1914   *Up and Down the North Pacific Coast by Canoe and Mission Ship.* Toronto: The Missionary Society of the Methodist Church, The Young Peoples' Forward Movement Department.

Curtis, Edward S.
1915   *The Kwakiutl.* The North American Indian 10. Reprint. New York: Johnson Reprint, 1970.

DIA
—   Department of Indian Affairs, Canada. *Annual Reports.* Ottawa: Dominion of Canada Sessional Papers.

Drucker, Philip
1940   "Kwakiutl Dancing Societies." *Anthropological Records* 2(6):201–30.
1950   "Culture Element Distributions: 24, Northwest Coast." *Anthropological Records* 9(3):157–294.
1955   *Indians of the Northwest Coast.* American Museum of Natural History, Anthropological Handbook No. 10, New York. Reprint. Garden City, N.Y.: The Natural History Press, 1963.
1965   *Cultures of the North Pacific Coast.* New York: Harper and Row.

Drucker Papers
—   Philip Drucker Papers. National Anthropology Archives, SI, Bureau of American Ethnology ms. 4516, 1938. Copy on file at HCEC.

Duff, Wilson
1964   *The Indian History of British Columbia, Volume 1: The Impact of the White Man.* Anthropology in British Columbia Memoir No. 5. Victoria: British Columbia Provincial Museum.
1975   *Images: Stone: B.C.: Thirty Centuries of Northwest Coast Indian Sculpture.* Exhibition catalogue. Toronto/Seattle: Oxford University Press/University of Washington Press.

Dunn, John
1844   *History of the Oregon Territory and British North American Fur Trade; with an Account of the Habits and Customs of the Principal Native Tribes on the Northern Continent.* London: Edwards and Hughes. Copy on file in the Baldwin Room, Metropolitan Toronto Reference Library, Toronto.

Emmons, George T.
1921   *Slate Mirrors of the Tsimshian.* Indian Notes and Monographs. New York: Museum of the American Indian.

Fisher, Robin
1977   "Missions to the Indians of British Columbia." *In* John Veillette and Gary White, *Early Indian Village Churches,* pp. 1–11. Vancouver: University of British Columbia Press.

Ford, Clellan S.
1941   *Smoke from Their Fires: The Life of a Kwakiutl Chief.* New Haven: Yale University Press.

Freeman, B. C.
n.d.   B. C. Freeman file. United Church of Canada, B.C. Conference Archives, Vancouver.

Garfield, Viola
1949   "Native Americans of the Pacific Northwest." Viola Garfield Collection, University of Washington Libraries, Seattle. Microfilm.

Garrad, Charles
1987   *The Annual Archaeological Reports of Ontario 1887–1928: A Research Guide.* Toronto: Ontario Archaeological Society.

Gladstone, Willie
n.d.   "The move to 'Qélc as told to David Gladstone in the Heiltsuk by Willie Gladstone." Transcribed and translated by Lillian Gladstone. Typescript. On file at HCEC.

Gough, Barry M.
1984   *Gunboat Frontier: British Maritime Authority and Northwest Coast Indians, 1846–1890.* Vancouver: University of British Columbia Press.

Gunther, Erna
1966   *Art in the Life of the Northwest Coast Indians.* Portland: PAM.

Haberland, Wolfgang
1975   *Donnervogel und Raubwal: Die Indianische Kunst der Nordwestküste Nordamerikas.* Exhibition catalogue. Hamburg: Hamburg Museum für Völkerkunde und Christians Verlag.

Hall, Judy
1983   "Canadian Ethnology Service, National Museum of Man, National Museums of Canada." *American Indian Art Magazine* 9(1):50–59.

Halpin, Marjorie M.
1986   *Jack Shadbolt and the Coast Indian Image.* University of British Columbia Museum of Anthropology Museum Note No. 18. Exhibition catalogue. Vancouver: University of British Columbia Press.

Harkin, Michael
1988   "Dialogues of History: Transformations and Change in Heiltsuk Culture, 1790–1920." Ph.D. diss. University of Chicago.

Hawthorn, Audrey
1967   *Art of the Kwakiutl Indians and Other Northwest Coast Tribes.* Vancouver: University of British Columbia Press.

HCEC
n.d.   "Provision of Protection, Shelter from the Elements." HCEC ms. CB 2a. HCEC.

Henderson

1892–1905   *Henderson's British Columbia Gazetteer and Directory of Mining Companies.* Victoria, Vancouver: Henderson Publishing Co. Copy on file at HCEC.

Hilton, Susanne F.

1990   "Haishais, Bella Bella, and Oowekeeno." *In* Wayne Suttles, ed., *The Northwest Coast*, pp. 312–22. *Handbook of the American Indian,* vol. 7. Washington, D.C.: Smithsonian Institution Press.

Hinsley, Curtis M., Jr.

1981   *Savages and Scientists: The Smithsonian Institution and the Development of American Anthropology 1846–1910.* Washington, D.C.: Smithsonian Institution Press.

Hobler, Philip M.

1970   "Archaeological Survey and Excavations in the Vicinity of Bella Coola." *B.C. Studies* 6–7:77–94.

Hodge, Frederick Webb, ed.

1910   *Handbook of American Indians North of Mexico.* Bureau of American Ethnology Bulletin No. 30. Washington, D.C.: Smithsonian Institution Press.

Holm, Bill

1965   *Northwest Coast Indian Art: An Analysis of Form.* Thomas Burke Memorial Washington State Museum Monograph No. 1. Seattle: University of Washington Press.

1972   "Heraldic Carving Styles of the Northwest Coast." In *American Indian Art: Form and Tradition*, pp. 76–83. Minneapolis: Walker Art Center and the Minneapolis Institute of Art.

1976   "Form in Northwest Coast Art." *In* Roy L. Carlson, ed., *Indian Art Traditions of the Northwest Coast*, pp. 33–45. Burnaby: Archaeology Press, Simon Fraser University.

1981   "Will the Real Charles Edensaw Please Stand Up?: The Problem of Attribution in Northwest Coast Indian Art." *In* Donald N. Abbott, ed., *The World Is As Sharp As a Knife: An Anthology in Honour of Wilson Duff*, pp. 175–200. Victoria: British Columbia Provincial Museum.

1983a   *The Box of Daylight: Northwest Coast Indian Art.* Exhibition catalogue. Seattle: Seattle Art Museum and the University of Washington Press.

1983b   *Smoky-Top: The Art and Times of Willie Seaweed.* Thomas Burke Memorial Washington State Museum Monograph No. 3. Exhibition catalogue. Seattle: University of Washington Press.

1987   *Spirit and Ancestor: A Century of Northwest Coast Indian Art at the Burke Museum.* Thomas Burke Memorial Washington State Museum Monograph No. 4. Seattle/Vancouver: University of Washington Press and the Thomas Burke Memorial Washington State Museum/Douglas and McIntyre.

Holm, Bill, and William Reid

1975   *Form and Freedom: A Dialogue on Northwest Coast Indian Art.* Exhibition catalogue. Houston: Rice University Institute for the Arts.

Hopkins, Joann, Jennifer Carpenter, and Clarence Martin

1990   "Threatened Legacy: Heiltsuk Heritage Properties, 1986." Typescript. On file at HCEC.

Jacknis, Ira S.

1974   "Functions of the Containers." *In* William C. Sturtevant et al., *Boxes and Bowls: Decorated Containers by Nineteenth-Century Haida, Tlingit, Bella Bella and Tsimshian Indian Artists*, pp. 16–19. Exhibition catalogue. Washington, D.C.: Smithsonian Institution Press.

1991   "The Northwest Coast." *In* Diana Fane, Ira Jacknis, and Lise M. Breen, *Objects of Myth and Memory: American Indian Art at the Brooklyn Museum*, pp. 233–79. Exhibition catalogue. New York/Seattle: The Brooklyn Museum/University of Washington Press.

Jacobsen, Johan Adrian

1977   *Alaskan Voyage 1881–1883: An Expedition to the Northwest Coast of America.* Translated by Erna Gunther. Chicago: University of Chicago Press.

Jonaitis, Aldona

1988   *From the Land of the Totem Poles: The Northwest Coast Indian Art Collection at the American Museum of Natural History.* New York/Vancouver: AMNH/Douglas and McIntyre.

Jonaitis, Aldona, ed.

1991   *Chiefly Feasts: The Enduring Kwakiutl Potlatch.* Exhibition catalogue. Vancouver/New York: Douglas and McIntyre/AMNH.

Killan, Gerald

1983   *David Boyle: From Artisan to Archaeologist.* Toronto: University of Toronto Press.

Knight, Rolf

1978   *Indians at Work: An Informal History of Native Indian Labour in British Columbia 1858–1930.* Vancouver: New Star Books.

Kolstee, Anton Frederik

1988   "To Impersonate the Supernatural: Music and Ceremony of the Bella Bella/Heiltsuk Indians of British Columbia." Ph.D. diss. University of Illinois at Urbana-Champaign.

Large, Richard Geddes

1951   *Soogwilis: A Collection of Kwakiutl Designs and Legends.* Toronto: The Ryerson Press.

1968   *Drums and Scalpel: From Native Healers to Physicians on the Northwest Coast.* Vancouver: Mitchell Press.

Large, R. W.
1905   "Mortuary Customs in British Columbia." *Annual Archaeological Report Ontario, 1904*, pp. 100–l01.
n.d.   *Souvenir of Bella Bella, B.C.* Prince Rupert Presbytery Bella Bella file. United Church of Canada, B.C. Conference Archives, Vancouver. Copy on file at HCEC.

Large Biographical file
—   R. W. Large Biographical file. Archives of the United Church of Canada, Victoria University, Toronto.

LaViolette, F. E.
1973   *The Struggle for Survival: Indian Cultures and the Protestant Ethic in British Columbia.* 2nd. ed. Toronto: University of Toronto Press.

Lillard, Charles, ed.
1984   *Warriors of the North Pacific: Missionary Accounts of the Northwest Coast, the Skeena and Stikine Rivers and the Klondike.* Victoria: Sono Nis Press.

Lincoln, Neville J., and John C. Rath
1980   *North Wakashan Comparative Root List.* Canadian Ethnology Service Paper No. 68, National Museum of Man Mercury Series. Ottawa: NMC.

Low, Jean
1982   "Dr. Charles Frederick Newcombe: The Alienist Who Became Collector of the Native Art Treasures of the Pacific Northwest." *The Beaver* (Spring), pp. 32–39.

M'Closkey, Kathy
1985   "The Art/Craft Distinction in Relation to the Bifurcation of Mental and Manual Labour Implicit in Kantian Aesthetics." Paper presented at the Fifth National Native Art Studies Association Conference, Ann Arbor/Detroit, 19 October.

McIlwraith, T. F.
1948   *The Bella Coola Indians.* 2 vols. Toronto: University of Toronto Press.

Mackenzie, Alexander
1962   *First Man West: Alexander Mackenzie's Journal of His Voyage to the Pacific Coast of Canada in 1793,* ed. Walter Sheppe. Montreal: McGill University Press.

McKervill, Hugh W.
1964   *Darby of Bella Bella.* Toronto: Ryerson Press.

Macnair, Peter L., Alan L. Hoover, and Kevin Neary
1980   *The Legacy: Continuing Traditions of Canadian Northwest Coast Art.* Exhibition catalogue. Victoria: British Columbia Provincial Museum.

Matthews, J. S., ed.
1934   "Catalogue of Indian Relics collected by Dr. G. H. Raley while serving over fifty years as Missionary to the Indians of British Columbia." Typescript. Private collection (M. Black).

Maud, Ralph
1983   *A Guide to B.C. Indian Myth and Legend: A Short History of Myth-Collecting and a Survey of Published Texts.* Vancouver: Talonbooks.

MB
1903–1913 *Missionary Bulletin.* Toronto: The Methodist Young People's Forward Movement for Missions, Methodist Church (Canada, Newfoundland, Bermuda).

Mitchell, Donald H.
1981   "Sebassa's Men." *In* Donald N. Abbott, ed., *The World Is As Sharp As a Knife: An Anthology in Honour of Wilson Duff,* pp. 79–86. Victoria: British Columbia Provincial Museum.

MO
1888–1909 *Missionary Outlook.* Toronto: Methodist Church (Canada, Newfoundland, Bermuda).

Moziño, Jose Mariano
1792   *Noticias de Nutka: An Account of Nootka Sound in 1792.* Translated and edited by Iris Higbie Wilson. Seattle: University of Washington Press, 1970.

Needham, Harold G.
1970   "The Origins of the Royal Ontario Museum." Master's thesis, University of Toronto.

Neilson, Nora
1981   "Ministry in Bella Bella," *Mandate* (January–February), pp. 7–11. Prince Rupert Presbytery Bella Bella file. United Church of Canada, B.C. Conference Archives, Vancouver.

Newcombe, C. F.
n.d.   Newcombe Family Correspondence, Series B. ADD MSS 1077, vol. 7, folder 12. PABC

Niblack, Albert P.
1890   *The Coast Indians of Southern Alaska and Northern British Columbia.* Report of the United States National Museum 1888. Reprint. New York: Johnson Reprint, 1970.

NMAI
1922   NMAI collection record, 1922. Copy on file at HCEC.

NS file
—   Normal School file, Ethnology collections, Department of Anthropology, Royal Ontario Museum, Toronto.

Olson, Ronald L.
1935, 1949 Bella Bella Fieldnotes. University of California Microfilm cu-23.1, No. 66. The Bancroft Library, University of California Archives, Berkeley.
1940   "The Social Organization of the Haisla of British Columbia." *Anthropological Records* 2(5):169–200.
1954   "Social Life of the Owikeno Kwakiutl." *Anthropological Records* 14(3):213–59.

1955   "Notes on the Bella Bella Kwakiutl." *Anthropological Records* 14(5):319–48.

Osterhout, S. S.

n.d.   S. S. Osterhout file. United Church of Canada, B.C. Conference Archives, Vancouver.

Phillips, Ruth B.

1989   "What is 'Huron Art'?: Native American Art and the New Art History," *The Canadian Journal of Native Studies* 9(2):161–86.

Pomeroy, John Anthony

1980   "Bella Bella Settlement and Subsistence." Ph.D. diss. Simon Fraser University, Burnaby.

Poutlass, Mrs.

1908   "Slaughter Illahee." PABC add. mss. 199.

Raley, George H.

1902a   "Charlie Amos 'Wahuksqumalayou'." *Na-Na-Kwa; or, Dawn on the Northwest Coast* 17. On file at PABC.

1902b   "Dance Masks." *Na-Na-Kwa; or, Dawn on the Northwest Coast* 20. On file at PABC.

1904a   "Fall Exhibition." *Na-Na-Kwa; or, Dawn on the Northwest Coast* 26. On file at PABC.

1904b   "Bella Bella Notes." *Na-Na-Kwa; or, Dawn on the Northwest Coast* 27/28. On file at PABC.

1917   "Some Phases of the Native Problem in B. C." *Western Methodist Recorder* 16(11):4–7. PABC.

Rath, John C.

1981   *A Practical Heiltsuk-English Dictionary with a Grammatical Introduction.* 2 vols. Canadian Ethnology Service Paper No. 75, National Museum of Man Mercury Series. Ottawa: NMC.

Reid, Martine J.

1987   "Silent Speakers: Arts of the Northwest Coast." *In* Julia Harrison, ed., *The Spirit Sings: Artistic Traditions of Canada's First Peoples,* pp. 201–36. Toronto/Calgary: McClelland and Stewart/Glenbow Museum.

Rogers, Edward S.

1970   *Indians of the North Pacific Coast.* Toronto: ROM.

ROM

1959   Royal Ontario Museum Division of Art and Archaeology. *Masks: The Many Faces of Man.* Toronto: ROM.

1976   Royal Ontario Museum Department of Ethnology. *Northwest Coast Gallery.* Toronto: ROM.

Sawyer, Alan R.

1983   "Toward More Precise Northwest Coast Attributions: Two Substyles of Haisla Masks." *In* Bill Holm, *The Box of Daylight: Northwest Coast Indian Art,* pp. 143–47. Exhibition catalogue. Seattle: Seattle Art Museum and the University of Washington Press.

Sewid-Smith, Daisy (My-yah-nelth)

1979   *Prosecution or Persecution.* Cape Mudge, British Columbia: Nu-Yum-Baleess Society.

Shore Papers

—   T. E. Egerton Shore Papers. Archives of the United Church of Canada, Victoria University, Toronto.

SI 4686

—   Accession file 4686, Smithsonian Institution. Copy on file at HCEC.

Simonsen, Bjorn O.

1973   *Archaeological Investigations in the Hecate Strait-Milbanke Sound Area of British Columbia.* Archaeological Survey of Canada Paper No. 13, National Museum of Man Mercury Series. Ottawa: NMC.

Stevenson, David

n.d.   "A History of the Oowekeeno People of Rivers Inlet." Typescript. On file at HCEC.

Stewart, Hilary

1973   *Artifacts of the Northwest Coast Indians.* Toronto: General Publishing.

1977   *Indian Fishing: Early Methods on the Northwest Coast.* Seattle/Vancouver: University of Washington Press/Douglas and McIntyre.

1984   *Cedar: Tree of Life to the Northwest Coast Indians.* Vancouver: Douglas and McIntyre.

Stocking, George W., Jr.

1985   *Objects and Others: Essays on Museums and Material Culture.* History of Anthropology 3. Madison: University of Wisconsin Press.

Streich, Anja P.

1983   "The Bella Bella Gravesites Project." Typescript. On file at HCEC.

Swanton, John R.

1905   *Contributions to the Ethnology of the Haida. Jesup North Pacific Expedition,* ed. Franz Boas, vol. 5, part 1. American Museum of Natural History Memoir 8(1), pp. 1–300. Reprint. New York: AMS Press, 1975.

Tate, C. M.

1909   "Church Opening at Bella Bella." *Western Methodist Recorder* 11(9):11–12. PABC.

1916   "How Bella-Bella Jack Spent Christmas and What it Meant to His Tribe." *Western Methodist Recorder* 16(6):4. PABC.

1917   "Bella-Bella Jack as a Missionary to his Tribe." *Western Methodist Recorder* 16(10):10. PABC.

n.d.   Manuscript. United Church of Canada, B.C. Conference Archives, Vancouver. Copy on file at HCEC.

Tolmie, William Fraser
1963 *Physician and Fur Trader: The Journals of William Fraser Tolmie.* Foreword by Richard Geddes Large. Vancouver: Mitchell Press.

Townsend-Gault, Charlotte
1988 "Kwakiutl Ready-Mades?" *Vanguard* (November), pp. 28–33.

UBCMOA
1975 *Northwest Coast Indian Artifacts from the H. R. MacMillan Collections in the Museum of Anthropology.* Vancouver: University of British Columbia Press.

Usher, Jean
1981 "William Duncan of Metlakatla: The Victorian Origins of a Model Indian Community." *In* W. Peter Ward and Robert A. J. McDonald, eds., *British Columbia: Historical Readings,* pp. 126–53. Vancouver: Douglas and McIntyre.

Vancouver, George
1798 *Voyage of Discovery to the North Pacific Ocean and Around the World.* Vol. 2. Bibliotheca Australiana No. 36. Reprint. Amsterdam/New York: N. Israel/Da Capo Press, 1967.

Vastokas, Joan M.
1986/87 "Native Art as Art History: Meaning and Time from Unwritten Sources." *Journal of Canadian Studies* 21(4):7–36.
1987 "The Individual Artist in Traditional Native Society." Paper presented at the Second Annual Native Art Studies Association of Canada Conference, Halifax, 13 November.

Vickers, Mary
1985 Taped interview, August 1985. HCEC II 26.

Walbran, John T.
1909 *British Columbia Coast Names 1592–1906: Their Origin and History.* Reprint. Vancouver: J.J. Douglas, 1971.

Walker Art Center
1972 *American Indian Art: Form and Tradition.* Exhibition catalogue. Minneapolis: Walker Art Center and the Minneapolis Institute of Art.

Williams, R. J.
1900–1901 *Williams' British Columbia Directory, Containing General Information and Directories of the Various Cities and Settlements in the Province: With a Classified Business Directory.* Victoria: R. J. Williams. Copy on file at HCEC.

Work, John
1945 The Journal of John Work, 1835, ed. Henry Drummond Lee. Archives of British Columbia Memoir 10. Victoria: Charles F. Banfield.

Wrinch, H. C.
n.d. H. C. Wrinch file. United Church of Canada, B.C. Conference Archives, Vancouver.

Wyatt, Victoria
1989 *Images from the Inside Passage: An Alaskan Portrait by Winter and Pond.* Seattle/Juneau: University of Washington Press/Alaska State Library.